Development Economics

Development Economics

By
Madhusudana H.S.
Associate Professor,
Department of Economics,
Government First Grade College, Vemagal, Kolar, Karnataka

New Century Publications
New Delhi, India

NEW CENTURY PUBLICATIONS
4852 / 24, 1st Floor,
Ansari Road, Daryaganj,
New Delhi – 110 002 (India)

Tel.: 011-4101 7798; 4358 7398; 98117 88655
E-mail: info@newcenturypublications.com
www.newcenturypublications.com

Editorial office:
4800 / 24, Bharat Ram Road,
Ansari Road, Daryaganj,
New Delhi – 110 002

First Published: **2022**

ISBN: **978-81-7708-533-4**

Published by New Century Publications and printed at Milan Enterprises, New Delhi

Designs: Patch Creative Unit, New Delhi

PRINTED IN INDIA

About the Book

Development economics is a branch of economics which deals with economic aspects of the development process in less developed countries (LDCs). Its focus is not only on methods of promoting economic growth but also on improving the general well-being of common people through health, education, workplace conditions, and other aspects of human development. Development economics involves the creation of theories and methods that aid in the determination of policies and practices for economic and social security of the population at large.

The purpose of economic activities going around is to produce goods and services to satisfy the wants of people. How well and to what extent these wants are satisfied is the basic issue in development economics. Traditionally, economic growth is defined as sustained increase in per capita real income of a country. However, economic growth in numbers alone, without improvement in living standards and overall quality of life, is not enough. Hence, economists insist on economic development which is a much wider term as compared to economic growth. Economic development emphasizes that everyone should enjoy a minimum level of economic security. The ultimate objective of all economic efforts is human development which encompasses quality of life, the level of well-being and access to basic social services. Thus, development today is no longer confined to growth in national income alone.

Inclusive growth is the new paradigm that is related essentially to equality and opportunity for all and sundry for productive and meaningful life with freedom and equality. In other words, it means inter-group, inter-sector as well as inter-regional equity. Growth is inclusive when it creates economic opportunities along with ensuring equal access to them.

The concept of development is inextricably linked with environment protection. Sustainable development is a strategy for improving the quality of human life, while living within the carrying capacity of supporting eco-system. Sustainable development is that which meets the needs of the present without compromising on the ability of future generations.

The study of development economics raises awareness regarding economic policies and practices being followed in a country. It also helps in gaining a better understanding of the dynamics of development process, both at the international and domestic levels.

This book explains various aspects of development economics. It would help teachers and students of the subject to understand the basic concepts, components and processes of development economics.

The book contains 30 chapters which have been organized into 2 parts.

Part I (chapters 1 to 15) is titled Underdeveloped Countries and Growth Models. It explains and examines the following models of economic growth propounded by economists from time to time: W.W. Rostow's stages of economic growth, economic growth model of Robert Solow, Harrod-Domar growth model, big push model of Paul Rosenstein-Rodan, critical minimum effort theory of Harvey Leibenstein, Ragnar Nurkse's balanced growth theory, Albert Hirschman's theory of unbalanced growth, and Simon Kuznets inverted U hypothesis. Other topics included in this part, among others, are location of industry, infrastructure and logistics, agriculture and economic development, and public goods and the problem of free-riding.

Part II (chapters 16 to 30) is titled Aspects and Approaches to Economic Development. It includes, among others, the following topics: Demographic transition theory and demographic dividend hypothesis, Harris-Todaro model of rural-urban migration, dualism and economic development, entrepreneurship and start-ups, financial inclusion and financial literacy, urbanization policies and issues, foreign trade and economic development, sustainable economic development, and globalization.

About the Author

Dr. Madhusudana H.S. is presently Associate Professor, Department of Economics, Government First Grade College, Vemagal, Kolar District, Karnataka. He obtained his M.A. (Economics) and M.Phil. degrees from Bangalore University, Bangalore in 1993 and 1996 respectively. He received his Ph.D. degree from Sri Krishnadevaraya University, Ananthapuramu, Andhra Pradesh in 2005. He has participated and presented research papers at various national and international conferences. He has visited University of Malaysia and University of Singapore as a resource person. He has to his credit more than 25 publications in national and 20 publications in international peer-reviewed journals of repute.

He has also published 7 books on various aspects of the Indian economy, namely *Rural Development and Poverty Alleviation in India* (2012), *Indian Economy towards Inclusive Growth* (2013), *Infrastructure Development and the Role of Public-Private-Partnership (PPP)* (2017), *Agricultural Crisis and Farmers-friendly Reforms in India* (2018), *Foreign Direct Investment (FDI) and Ease of Doing Business in India* (2019), *Foreign Trade and Export-Import Policy of India* (2020), and *Disinvestment and Privatization of Public Sector Enterprises (PSEs) in India* (2021).

Contents

Preface

Development economics is a branch of economics which deals with economic aspects of the development process in less developed countries (LDCs). Its focus is not only on methods of promoting economic growth but also on improving the general well-being of common people through health, education, workplace conditions, and other aspects of human development. Development economics involves the creation of theories and methods that aid in the determination of policies and practices for economic and social security of the population at large.

The purpose of economic activities going around is to produce goods and services to satisfy the wants of the people. How well and to what extent these wants are satisfied forms the core of the study of development economics. Two concepts, viz. economic growth and economic development become relevant in this context.

Economic growth is defined as sustained increase in per capita real income of a country. Two conditions need to be satisfied for this to happen: (a) there is increase in real national income, and (b) the rate of increase in real national income is more than the rate of increase in population.

However, economic growth in numbers alone, without improvement in living standards and overall quality of life, is not enough. Hence, economists insist on economic development which is a much wider term as compared to economic growth. Economic development emphasizes that everyone should enjoy a minimum level of economic security. The ultimate objective of all economic efforts is human development which encompasses quality of life, the level of well-being and access to basic social services. Thus, development today is no longer confined to growth in national income alone.

Economic development is a multi-dimensional term. It is interlinked with the entire economic, social, and cultural fabric of society. It aims at bringing about qualitative changes leading to an upward movement of the entire social system. This approach to development is markedly different from the earlier approaches that regarded expansion of economic opportunities as a necessary precondition for development. Over concentration on single dimension of income alone is at best an oversimplification and at worst a gross distortion of reality because high growth rates do no automatically translate into higher levels of human development.

Economic development is a journey, not a destination. It encompasses all aspects and facets of human life from birth to death. It includes basic material needs like food, clothing and shelter to higher ones such as social, mental, intellectual, emotional and spiritual aspirations. Economic development is a process. It is not an event or a happening. As a long drawn process, it may stretch over days, months, years, decades and even centuries. However, the success of a developmental initiative largely depends on the will of the nation and sincerity of its political leadership to see it through amidst all adversity.

Economic development is holistic. It is comprehensive and multifaceted in approach. Real development gives precedence to enhancing human well-being over material opulence, to expanding capabilities over maximizing incomes and to enlarging freedoms over optimizing growth. All this is done by the people themselves through active participation in various processes meant to improve and enrich their lives.

Inclusive growth is the new paradigm that is related essentially to equality and opportunity to all and sundry for productive and meaningful life with freedom and equality. Inclusive growth may be defined as growth that promotes equal opportunities and increases access to these opportunities, i.e. growth that allows all members of society to participate in and contribute equally to development efforts, regardless of individual circumstances. Thus, inclusive growth means inter-group, inter-sector as well as inter-regional equity. Growth is inclusive when it creates economic opportunities along with ensuring equal access to them.

The vicious nexus between poverty and uncontrolled population is a huge obstacle in the way of achieving development objectives. Unchecked population not only slows down the pace of development but also accentuates the ecological crisis thereby preventing the benefits of development from reaching one and all.

Productivity of an economic system depends, to a large extent, on the supply and quality of its natural resources. In fact, natural and environmental resources are the basis of all economic activities. Soil, forests, mines, water, air and other natural resources are productive assets of an economy. Since the beginning of Industrial Revolution in Britain in the middle of the 18th century, economic growth has required the burning of coal and oil as fuel for production in the economy. Burning coal contributes to the greenhouse effect, which it is hypothesized will raise the temperature of the earth, causing severe global climate problems. The degradation of the atmosphere is, to a certain extent, an unavoidable consequence of economic growth. However, if this growth is not carefully monitored, environmental problems will arise.

Thus, the concept of development is inextricably linked with environment protection. Sustainable development is a strategy for improving the quality of human life while living within the carrying capacity of supporting eco system. Sustainable development entails commitment, protection and preservation. Sustainable development is that which meets the needs of the present without compromising the ability of future generations.

The study of development economics raises awareness regarding economic policies and practices being followed in a country. It also helps in gaining a better understanding of the dynamics of development process, both at the international and domestic levels.

Kolar
July 2022

Madhusudana H.S.

Explanation of Select Terms Related to Development Economics

Agro Forestry: Agro forestry means practice of agriculture and forestry on the same piece of land. It has been defined as a sustainable management system for land that increases overall production, combines agricultural crops and animals simultaneously. It also connotes a land use system that integrates trees, crops and animals in a way that is scientifically sound, ecologically desirable, practically feasible and socially acceptable to the farmers.

Alfred Weber's Theory of Industrial Location: Alfred Weber, a German economist, enunciated a systematic theory of industrial location in 1909. Weber's theory of location is purely deductive in its approach. He formulated a theory of industrial location in which an industry is located where the transportation costs of raw materials and final product is a minimum.

Backward and Forward Linkages: A backward linkage is created when a project encourages investment in facilities that enable the project to succeed. A forward linkage is created when investment in a particular project encourages investment in subsequent stages of production. Normally, projects create both backward and forward linkages. Investment should be made in those projects that have the greatest total number of linkages. Projects with many linkages will vary from country to country. Knowledge about project linkages can be obtained through input and output studies. Example of an industry that has excellent backward and forward linkages is the steel industry. Backward linkages include coal and iron ore mining. Forward linkages include items such as steel utensils.

Balanced Growth Theory: Balanced growth theory is an economic theory pioneered by the economist Ragnar Nurkse (1907-1959). The theory hypothesises that the government of any underdeveloped country needs to make large investments in a number of industries simultaneously. This will enlarge the market size, increase productivity, and provide an incentive for the private sector to invest. Nurkse was in favour of attaining balanced growth in both the industrial and agricultural sectors of the economy. He recognised that the expansion and inter-sectoral balance between agriculture and manufacturing is necessary so that each of these sectors provides a market for the products of the other and, in turn, supplies the necessary raw materials for the development and growth of the other.

Big Push Model of Growth: Paul Rosenstein-Rodan propounded this model of growth in 1943. Analysis of this economic model ordinarily involves using game theory. This model emphasizes that underdeveloped countries require large amounts of investments to embark on the path of economic development from their present state of backwardness. This theory proposes that a 'bit by bit' investment programme will not impact the process of growth as much as is required for developing countries. In fact, injections of small quantities of investments will merely lead to wastage of resources. There is a minimum level of resources that must be devoted to a development programme if it is to have any chance of success. Launching a country into self-sustaining growth is a little like getting an airplane off the ground. There is a critical ground speed which must be passed before the craft can become airborne.

Capitalist Economy: It is a form of economic organization characterized by private ownership of the means of production. A capitalist society like US exhibits the following features: (a) right to private property prevails (b) law of inheritance operates (c) means of production are owned by private individuals, (d) means of production are used for maximising profits for their owners, (e) right of free enterprise is guaranteed, (f) there is competition among firms, and (g) price mechanism allocates resources.

Cobb-Douglas Production Function: Named after its authors, Paul H. Douglas and Charles Cobb, it is a linear and homogeneous production function yielding constant returns to a proportionate increase in the use of all inputs. It takes the following form: $Y = kL^{a}C^{(1-a)}$ where Y represents income (output), L is the quantity of labour input, C is the capital employed and k and a are positive constants (and $a < 1$).

Constant Returns to Scale: It refers to that situation where if factors are increased in a given proportion, the output also increases in the same proportion. For example, if capital and labour are doubled, the output is also doubled. We may come across such a production situation in real life. If one worker working on a machine produces 5 units of a commodity, it can be expected that two workers working on two identical machines will produce 10 units of the commodity.

Critical Minimum Effort Model: The critical minimum effort theory was propounded by Harvey Leibenstein (1922-1994) in his book *Economic Backwardness and Economic Growth*. He was a Ukrainian-born American economist. One of his most important contributions to economics was the critical minimum effort thesis in development economics. He also introduced the concept of X-inefficiency. He maintains that underdeveloped countries are characterized by vicious circle of poverty which keeps them around a low income per capita equilibrium state. This circle is believed to be so vicious and deep rooted that no small effort can be expected to break it up. The only way out to develop these countries is to make minimum amount of investments (critical minimum effort) based on relationships between factors, per capita income, population growth, and investment, which would raise the per capita to a level at which sustained development could be maintained.

Demographic Dividend Hypothesis: Population growth and its relation to economic growth has been a matter of debate for a long time. The earlier view was that population growth impedes economic growth because it puts pressure on the available resources, resulting in reduction in per capita income and resources. This, in turn, results in deterioration in quality of life. Contrary to this view, several of the East Asian countries have been able to achieve economic prosperity and improvement in quality of life in spite of population growth. This has been attributed to the increase in productivity due to development and utilization of innovative technologies by the young educated population who formed the majority of the growing population. Developing countries can reap this demographic dividend only if there is massive investment in human resources development in terms of healthcare, higher education and skill formation.

Demographic Transition Theory: According to the theory of demographic transition, propounded by A.J. Coale and E.M. Hoover, every country passes through the following three stages of demographic transition. During the first stage, the economy is rural and agriculture is the main occupation of the people. Techniques of production are primitive and per capita income is low. This type of economy is characterised by high birth rate and high death rate. The second stage is marked by the beginning of the process of economic development. Living standard of the people starts improving. In this stage, death rate declines sharply owing to improved medical facilities, particularly eradication of mass-killing diseases like smallpox, cholera and plague. However, birth rate continues to remain at high levels because social and religious beliefs about marriage and family size take much longer time to change. In the third stage, the economy moves from an agrarian to an industrial society. There is an increasing trend toward urbanisation and small families for achieving a higher standard of living. The economy is characterised by low birth rate and low death rate, resulting in stable or marginally increasing population.

Density of Population: Density of population means the average number of persons living per squire kilometre of area. Geographical area remaining the same, an increase in population means increase in the density of population.

Digital Financial Inclusion: It refers broadly to the use of digital financial services to advance financial inclusion. These include payments, transfers, savings, credit, insurance, securities, financial planning and account statements. They are delivered via digital/electronic technology such as e-money (initiated either online or on a mobile phone), payment cards and regular bank accounts. Beyond the income dimension, digital financial inclusion includes users who are shut out of the financial system based on gender, language spoken, disabilities, and even lack of a mobile phone.

Direct versus Portfolio Investment: There are two main types of foreign investments: direct investments and portfolio investments. Direct investments are real investments in factories, capital goods, land, and inventories where both capital and management are involved and the investor retains control over use of the invested capital. Direct investment usually takes the form of a firm starting a subsidiary or taking control of another firm (for example, by purchasing a majority of the stock). In the international context, direct investments are usually undertaken by multinational corporations engaged in manufacturing, resource extraction, or services. Portfolio investments, on the other hand, are purely financial assets, such as bonds, denominated in a national currency. With bonds, the investor simply lends capital to get fixed payouts or a return at regular intervals and then receives the face value of the bond at a pre-specified date. Portfolio or financial investments take place primarily through financial institutions such as banks and investment funds.

Dual Economy: It refers to the existence of two separate economic sectors within one country, divided by different levels of development, technology, and different patterns of demand. The concept was originally created by Julius Herman Boeke to describe the coexistence of modern and traditional economic sectors in a colonial economy. Dual economies are common in less developed countries, where one sector is geared to local needs and another to the global export market. Dual economies may exist within the same sector, for example a modern plantation or other commercial agricultural entity operating in the midst of traditional cropping systems.

Eco-Industrial Park: An eco-industrial park (EIP) or estate is a community of manufacturing and service businesses located together on a common property. Member businesses seek enhanced environmental, economic and social performance through collaboration in managing environmental and resource issues. By working together, the community of businesses seeks a collective benefit that is greater than the sum of individual benefits each company would realise by only optimizing its individual performance. The goal of an EIP is to improve the economic performance of the participating companies while minimizing their environmental impacts. Components of this approach include green design of the park infrastructure (new or retrofitted); cleaner production; prevention of pollution; energy efficiency and inter-company partnering. An EIP also seeks benefits for neighbouring communities to assure the net impact of its development is positive.

Economic Growth and Economic Development: Economic growth means sustained increase in per capita real income of a country. Two conditions need to be satisfied for this to happen: (a) there is increase in real national income, and (b) the rate of increase in real national income is more than the rate of increase in population. Strictly speaking, economic growth and economic development are not interchangeable terms. Economic development is a much wider term. It includes economic growth and at the same time encompasses questions regarding pattern of production, distribution of income and consumption behaviour of the people. In other words, economic development is economic growth plus qualitative changes in productivity, socio-economic institutions and distribution pattern. Economic development looks at a wider range of statistics than just increase in real per capita income. Development is concerned with how people are actually affected. It looks at their actual living standards and the freedom they have to enjoy a good standard of living.

Economic Model: An economic model is a statement of relationship among economic variables. It is used to explain the cause and effect relationship among variables. Economic models are helpful in explaining and predicting economic phenomena like rate of growth of an economy. Aggregate models deal with the economy as a whole. Sectoral models examine particular sectors of the economy like industry or agriculture. Inter-industry models explain relationship among various sectors of the economy, using the popular technique of input-output matrices.

Economic System: An economic system is a man-made device designed to facilitate the use of resources and the distribution of output. It consists of a complex set of institutions, laws and objectives. Every economy has to accomplish certain basic tasks. These are: (a) allocation of resources among competing uses, (b) choice of technology, and (c) distribution of output.

Entrepreneur: An entrepreneur is an individual who organizes and operates a business or businesses, taking on financial risk to do so. The entrepreneur is commonly seen as an innovator of new ideas, and business processes. Management skill and strong team building abilities are often perceived as essential leadership attributes for successful entrepreneurs. Leadership, management ability, and team-building are considered to be the essential qualities of an entrepreneur.

Entrepreneurship: Entrepreneurship is the quality of being an entrepreneur, i.e. one who *undertakes an enterprise*. The term puts emphasis on the risk and effort taken by individuals who both own and manage a business, and on the innovations resulting from their pursuit of economic success.

Environmental Economics: Environmental economics is a branch of economics which deals with the inter-relationships between environment and development. Environmental economics examines the interface between economic agents and environment. Economic activities of human beings have a profound impact on natural environment. Hence, use/abuse of natural resources has raised many moral, legal and practical questions for present and future generations. There has been a gradual shift in many developed countries from command and control type of policy approach to environmental policy goals. Presently, many governments require cost-benefit analysis of policy options with regard to changes in environmental legislations by resetting environmental standards and introducing new policy instruments for environmental protection. Environmental economics has also made significant contributions to valuation techniques and design of new policy instruments for pollution control and management.

Environmental Pollution: Demographic expansion, over exploitation of natural resources, mega development projects—with least concern for sustainability and conservation—have greatly affected the environment. The magnitude and alterations that humanity can make to environment, threaten to undermine the basic natural process that sustains biosphere. The process of economic development necessarily entails exploitations of natural resources. However, when such exploitation becomes indiscriminate and is undertaken without adequate environmental safeguards, the consequences can be disastrous. Pollution can be defined as an undesirable change in the physical, chemical, or biological characteristics of the air, water or land that can harmfully affect health, survival or activities of human beings or other living organisms. Pollution refers essentially to a process by which a resource is rendered unfit for some beneficial use. Of the various kinds of pollution (air, water, land, noise, radiation and odour) that affect the quality of life in India, water pollution is by far the most serious in its implications for the health and well-being of the people.

Environmental Taxes: An environment or green tax is imposed on a product that damages the environment, in an attempt to reduce its production or consumption. Well-designed environmental taxes and other economic instruments can play an important role in ensuring that prices reflect environmental costs, in line with the *polluter pays principle*. Environmental taxes can be simple and efficient financial instruments for improving the productivity of natural resources. Environmental taxes on water and fossil fuels need not be part of the general revenues of a government. Rather they should be directly ploughed back into environmentally sustainable action on these fronts. Coal cess is a good example of environment tax imposed by Government of India in recent times, whose proceeds are channelled to the National Clean Energy Fund.

Financial Exclusion: Financial exclusion is the inability of individuals, households or groups to access financial services in an appropriate form. Financial exclusion is either a cause or a consequence of social exclusion, or both. Access to financial services is essential for citizens to be economically and socially integrated in today's society. It is also a requirement for employment, economic growth, poverty reduction and social inclusion. In most developing countries, a large segment of society, particularly low-income people, has very little access to financial services, both formal and semi-formal. As a consequence, many of them have to necessarily depend either on their own or high cost informal sources of finance such as moneylenders. This is particularly true for the sporadic financing requirements of low income households for non-productive consumption purposes and other emergency requirements such as medical expenditure. Benefits of growth, therefore, tend to concentrate in the hands of those already served by the formal financial system.

Financial Inclusion: Financial inclusion may be defined as the process of ensuring access to financial services and timely and adequate credit where needed by vulnerable groups such as weaker sections and low income groups at an affordable cost. The essence of financial inclusion is in trying to ensure that a range of appropriate financial services is available to every individual and enabling them to understand and access those services. Apart from the regular form of financial intermediation, it may include a basic no-frills banking account for making and receiving payments, a savings product suited to the pattern of cash flows of a poor household, money transfer facilities, small loans and overdrafts for productive, personal and other purposes, insurance (life and non-life) etc. While financial inclusion, in the narrow sense, may be achieved to some extent by offering any one of these services, the objective of *comprehensive financial inclusion* would be to provide a holistic set of services encompassing all of the above.

Financial Literacy: It is the possession of a set of skills and knowledge which allow an individual to make informed and effective decisions with all of his financial resources. Understanding basic financial concepts allows people to know how to navigate in the financial system. Lack of awareness of digital financial literacy, especially among the rural population, is a major challenge in developing countries. There is an urgent need to create awareness among the citizens, especially in rural and semi-urban areas regarding digital finance services and also enable/support in access to digital finance services options.

Gender Equality: Gender equality is a constituent of development as well as an instrument of development. No country can be deemed developed if half of its population is severely disadvantaged in terms of basic needs, livelihood options, access to knowledge, and political voice. It is an instrument of development because without gender equality other goals of development will also be difficult to achieve, namely the goals of poverty alleviation, economic growth, environmental sustainability etc. A natural corollary of ensuring gender equality is the elimination of gender discrimination. Inequalities between girls and boys in access to schooling or adequate healthcare prove a very serious disadvantage to women and girls and limit their capacity to participate in the benefits of development.

Globalization: Globalization implies widening and deepening integration with the *globe*, i.e. with people and processes abroad. The 1990s witnessed a paradigm shift towards market-oriented economic policies and a careful dismantling of obstacles in its wake. Globalization has resulted in the creation of a new business framework. The trend towards the evolution of a global society is generally thought of in economic terms and in terms of the consequences of the revolution in communication technologies. There is undoubtedly much greater economic integration among the nations of the world today.

Green Growth: Green growth involves rethinking growth strategies with regard to their impact on environmental sustainability and the environmental resources available to poor and vulnerable groups. It is significant to note that many stimulus packages announced globally to combat recession incorporated a green component. International experience is that green growth promotes inclusivity. Further, the renewable energy sector is relatively labour-intensive, with the potential for generating more jobs than the oil and gas industries.

Harris-Todaro Model: Named after John R. Harris and Michael Todaro, it is an economic model used in development economics and welfare economics to explain some of the issues concerning rural-urban migration. It is considered one of the starting points of the classic rural-urban migration theory. The hypothesis and predictions of Harris-Todaro model have been subjected to econometric evaluation and have been corroborated by several studies. The key hypothesis of Harris-Todaro model is that migrants react mainly to economic incentives, earnings differentials, and the probability of getting a job at the destination. The rural-urban migration will occur when the urban expected wage exceeds the rural wage.

Harrod-Domar Growth Model: It is a synthesis of the results of two consecutive independent studies by British economist Roy Harrod's *Theory of Dynamic Theory* (1939) and the American economist Evsey Domar's *Capital Expansion, Growth and Jobs* (1946). Harrod-Domar model is used in development economics to explain an economy's growth rate in terms of the level of savings and capital-output ratio.

Human Development Index (HDI): HDI is estimated in terms of a long and healthy life, education and knowledge, and enjoyment of a decent standard of living. The development of human capabilities must be the first priority, for three reasons. First, these capabilities are actually ends in themselves. Second, they are also important instrumentalities which interact positively with others to raise the productive capacity of an economy and therefore its ability to satisfy the material needs of its population. Third, proper development of human capabilities will also ensure that growth is more inclusive in the sense that the marginalised and disadvantaged sections of society will be more able to access the opportunities thrown up by the growth process.

Inclusive Growth: Inclusive growth is the new paradigm that is related essentially to equality and opportunity to all and sundry for productive and meaningful life with freedom and equality. Inclusive growth may be defined as growth that promotes equal opportunities and increases access to these opportunities, i.e. growth that allows all members of society to participate in and contribute equally to development efforts, regardless of individual circumstances.

Infrastructure: Infrastructure is generally defined as the physical framework of facilities through which goods and services are provided to the public. Its linkages to the economy are multiple and complex, because it affects production and consumption directly, creates positive and negative spill over effects (externalities), and involves large flows of expenditure. In economic literature, infrastructure is popular by the name *overhead capital* which represents basic services without which primary, secondary and tertiary productive activities cannot function. Generically, infrastructure has the following distinct components: (a) energy, (b) transport, (c) telecommunications, and (d) special economic zones (SEZs).

Innovation: Innovation is a process whereby people or groups of people with an entrepreneurial mindset (organizations, enterprises) develop new ideas or absorb and adapt existing ones. Joseph Schumpeter (1883-1950), an American economist, was one of the first academicians to study the idea of innovation. He developed a theory of economic and social change which focused on the importance of innovation and the factors influencing it. He suggested an important distinction between invention and innovation. According to him, invention is the first occurrence of the idea for a new product or process while innovation occurs when the idea is put into practice. Thus, refrigerator was an invention; but double-door refrigerator was an innovation.

Kuznets Inverted U Hypothesis: This hypothesis was advanced by economist Simon Kuznets in the 1950s and 1960s. According to this hypothesis, as an economy develops, market forces first increase and then decrease economic inequality. The relationship between income inequality and economic development has popularly been characterized by the Kuznets' inverted U curve, which shows that income inequality tends to increase at the initial stage of development and then decrease as the economy develops.

Law of Diminishing Returns: Historically, the law of diminishing returns is associated with agricultural operations, with land being the fixed factor and labour being the variable factor. However, this law holds good for all those productive activities where increasing quantities of a variable factor are applied to a given quantity of a fixed factor. Modern economists regard labour (L) and capital (K) to be the most significant factors of production, considering land as either unimportant or a part of capital. The law of diminishing returns states that if increasing quantities of a variable factor (labour) are applied to a given quantity of fixed factor (land), the marginal product of the variable factor will eventually decline.

Location of Industry: It refers to establishment of an industry or cluster of industries in a particular location or region due to availability of cheap factors of production, transport and infrastructural facilities, demand incentives, raw materials etc. These are some of the factors which attract entrepreneurs to set up their plants in a particular area. Once the process starts, it has a tendency to accelerate.

Logistics: Logistics refers to a series of services and activities, such as transportation, warehousing, and brokerage that help to move goods and establish supply chains across and within borders. Although these services and activities are carried out by private firms for the benefit of private firms, service delivery and the efficiency of supply chains depend on public sector provisions and interventions in a number of domains. Logistics uses publicly funded or regulated infrastructure.

Lorenz Curve: Lorenz curve is a graphical representation of the distribution of income developed by Max Lorenz in 1905. The graph plots percentiles of the population on the horizontal axis (or x-axis) according to income and plots cumulative income on the vertical axis (or y-axis). The Lorenz curve is accompanied by a straight diagonal line with a slope of 1, which represents perfect equality in income distribution. A perfectly equal income distribution would be one in which every person has the same income. This can be depicted by the straight line, called the *line of perfect equality*. The Lorenz curve lies beneath it, showing the observed or estimated distribution of income. The area between the straight line and the curved line, expressed as a ratio of the area under the straight line, is called the Gini coefficient, a scalar measurement of inequality. The farther the curve moves from the baseline, represented by the straight diagonal line, the higher the level of inequality.

Micro Finance: Micro finance is the provision of a diverse range of financial services and products including small loans (micro credit), savings accounts, insurance, pensions and money transfers. These are designed to assist people living in poverty who are not able to access financial services in the mainstream banking sector because they have no collateral, formal identification or steady income.

Mixed Economy: A mixed economy is one where capitalism and socialism coexist. In the real world, there are no purely capitalist or socialist economies. Even in US, some buildings, equipment and machines are owned by the government. Contrarily, in a socialist state some small farms or shops are owned by private individuals. Strictly speaking, every economy of the world is a mixed economy. The important thing is the degree by which an economic system is diluted by a different form of economic organization. In US, the dilution of capitalism is very less while it is quite significant in Russia. A good example of a mixed economy is provided by India where government owns a substantial part of the resources, particularly in the industrial and financial sectors.

Pareto Optimality Criterion: This famous criterion of social welfare was suggested by the Italian economist Vilfredo Pareto (1848-1923). It refers to economic efficiency which can be objectively measured. The Pareto optimality (or Pareto efficiency) criterion may be defined in the following different ways. Any change which makes at least one individual better-off and no one worse-off is an improvement in social welfare. Conversely, any change which makes no one better-off and at least one worse-off is a decrease in social welfare. To put it differently, a situation in which it is impossible to make anyone better-off without making someone worse-off is said to be Pareto-optimal or Pareto-efficient.

Production Function: It explains the technological relationship between inputs and output. $P = f(F_1, F_2, ...F_n)$. In this equation, P is the quantity of production and $F_1, F_2, ...F_n$ are the quantities of different factors of production. Modern economists emphasise the importance of labour (L) and capital (K) in the production process. Land as a factor of production is considered unimportant or as a part of capital and thus ignored. Therefore, the simplified production function becomes: $P = f(L, K)$.

Public Goods: Public goods include roads, public parks, and street lights etc. Public goods may give rise to the *free rider problem*. A free-rider is a person who receives the benefit of a good without paying for it. The free rider problem is an economic concept of a market failure that occurs when people are benefiting from resources, goods, or services that they do not pay for.

Sargent Florence's Theory of Industrial Location: According to Sargent Florence, geographical location of an industry is not as important as the distribution of occupied population. His main consideration is that occupational distribution of population should be the main and primary factor for taking into consideration the location of an industry.

Self-help Group (SHG): A SHG is a small voluntary association of 10-20 poor people from the same socio-economic background who come together for the purpose of addressing their common socio-economic problems through self-help and mutual-help. They collect small savings (thrift) on regular basis. Out of the pooled money, small interest bearing loans are given to the members and some amount is deposited with a bank regularly. The bank lends money for economic activities of the group without collateral security and at market rates.

Socialist Economy: It is an economic system under which means of production are owned by the state. A socialist or a centrally planned economy is totally different from a capitalist economy. It has the following features: (a) means of production are owned by the state, i.e. all land, buildings, factories, machines and equipments are the property of the government, (b) private property is prohibited barring the holding of small pieces of land for personal cultivation, petty trade transactions etc., (c) means of production are used by the state for the general welfare of society, (d) government enjoys monopoly in the production and distribution of goods and services, and (e) prices of commodities and factors of production are fixed by the government and therefore, price mechanism has limited role to play.

Solow Growth Model: It is a model of economic growth which analyzes changes in the level of output in an economy over time as a result of changes in population, savings rate, and the rate of technological progress. The Solow model is the basis for the modern theory of economic growth.

Stages of Economic Growth: These were advocated by American economist Walt Whitman Rostow in 1960. His model postulates that economic growth occurs in five basic stages of varying length: (a) traditional society, (b) transitional stage (or pre-conditions for take-off), (c) take-off, (d) drive to maturity, and (e) age of high mass consumption.

Start-up: A start-up company (or simply a start-up) is an entrepreneurial venture which is typically a newly emerged, fast-growing business that aims to meet a marketplace need by developing a viable business model around an innovative product, service, process or a platform. A start-up is usually a company designed to effectively develop and validate a scalable business model. Start-ups have high rates of failure, but the minority of successes includes companies that have become large and influential.

Sustainable Development: The concept of sustainable development is inextricably linked with environment protection. It is a strategy for improving the quality of human life while living within the carrying capacity of supporting eco system. It is clear from the above definition that sustainable development entails commitment, protection and preservation. Sustainable development advocates economic progress in an environmentally responsible manner. Sustainable development attempts to strike a balance between the requirements of economic development and the need for protection of the environment. It seeks to combine the elements of economic efficiency, inter-generational equity, social concerns and environmental protection. Although, the term sustainable development has many interpretations, it generally refers to non-declining human well-being over time.

Tax Holidays: Tax holidays have been the most popular form of tax incentives used by countries, especially developing economies. With a tax holiday, firms are allowed a period of time free from the burden of income taxation. Further, this initial period is sometimes extended to a subsequent period of taxation at a reduced rate of tax.

Unbalanced Growth Theory: The theory of unbalanced growth is associated with Albert O. Hirschman who propounded it in his book *The Strategy of Economic Development,* published in 1958. Hirschman maintains that it is not possible to always have broad growth across different sectors. He argues that as long as there is growth in some sector, it will create a dynamic pressure to grow other sectors at a later stage. Hirschman even argues that unbalanced growth and the dynamic tensions it creates helps to speed up economic development.

Unemployment: It is a situation when willing workers fail to get jobs at the prevailing wage rates. In other words, unemployment means involuntary idleness. From social point of view, unemployment means wastage of the precious labour resources of the country. For an individual, unemployment is a painful and demoralising experience. Employment to be gainful and sustainable has to be productive in character.

Unicorn Start-up: In business, a unicorn is a privately-held start-up company valued at over US$ 1 billion. The term was coined in 2013 by venture capitalist Aileen Lee, choosing the mythical animal to represent such successful ventures which are limited in number.

Vicious Circle of Poverty: There are circular relationships known as the *vicious circles of poverty* that tend to perpetuate the low level of development in less developed countries (LDCs). Ragnar Nurkse explains the idea in these words: "It implies a circular constellation of forces tending to act and react upon one another in such a way as to keep a poor country in a state of poverty. For example, a poor man may not have enough to eat; being underfed, his health may be weak; being physically weak, his working capacity is low, which means that he is poor, which in turn means that he will not have enough to eat and so on. A situation of this sort relating to a country as a whole can be summed up in the proposition: A county is poor because it is poor.

William Launhardt's Location Triangle Model: The analysis of William Launhardt provided the basis for the theory of industrial location. It was his contention that the decision to locate in a particular place would be based on transport costs of raw materials, inputs, finished goods etc. Using a simple model called the *location triangle* and the concept of ton-mileage, Launhardt suggested that as bulky products incur high transportation costs, the profits of finished goods should make these costs worthwhile. If not, a rational manufacturer would opt to relocate, always seeking the point of least transportation costs.

X-efficiency: In economics, X-efficiency is the effectiveness with which a given set of inputs are used to produce outputs. If a firm is producing the maximum output it can, given the resources it employs, such as men and machinery, and the best technology available, it is said to be technical-efficient. X-inefficiency occurs when technical-efficiency is not achieved.

Abbreviations/Acronyms

ADB	Asian Development Bank
ATMs	Automated Teller Machines
BoP	Balance of Payments
BOT	Build-Operate-Transfer
CGD	Centre for Global Development
EAM	East Asian Miracle
ECBs	External Commercial Borrowings
ECBs	External Commercial Borrowings
EIA	Environmental Impact Assessments
EIP	Eco-industrial Park
EMS	Environment Management Systems
FDI	Foreign Direct Investment
FDI	Foreign Direct Investment
GAF	Governance Analytical Framework
GDP	Gross Domestic Product
GIC	General Insurance Corporation of India
HDI	Human Development Index
HDR	Human Development Report
HYV	High Yielding Varieties
IBRD	International Bank for Reconstruction and Development
ICRAF	International Centre for Research in Agro-forestry
IDA	International Development Association
IFC	International Financial Corporation
IMF	International Monetary Fund
IPO	Initial Public Offer
IT	Information Technology
LDC	Less Developed Country
LIC	Life Insurance Corporation of India
MDGs	Millennium Development Goals
MFIs	Micro Finance Institutions
MIT	Massachusetts Institute of Technology
MVP	Minimum Viable Product
NABARD	National Bank for Agriculture and Rural Development
NGOs	Non-governmental Organizations
PPP	Public-Private-Partnership
R&D	Research and Development
S&T	Science and Technology
SDGs	Sustainable Development Goals
SEZs	Special Economic Zones
SHA	Shareholders' Agreement

SHG	Self-help Group
SHPIs	Self-help Promoting Institutions
SWD	Solid Waste Disposal
TQM	Total Quality Management
TRIPS	Trade-related Aspects of Intellectual Property Rights
UNCDF	United Nations Capital Development Fund
UNDP	United Nations Development Programme
UNDP	United Nation Development Programme
VAT	Value Added Tax
WGI	Worldwide Governance Index
WHO	World Health Organization
WTO	World Trade Organization

Part I
Underdeveloped Countries and Growth Models

1

Economic Growth and Economic Development

The purpose of economic activities going around is to produce goods and services to satisfy the wants of the people. How well and to what extent these wants are satisfied can be known by measuring the total output of goods and services in a country during a specified period (usually one year). This is the subject-matter of the study of economic growth and economic development.

1.1 Economic Growth and Economic Development Distinguished

1.1.1 Economic Growth: Economic growth means sustained increase in per capita real income of a country. Two conditions need to be satisfied for this to happen.

Firstly, there should be an increase in real national income of a country. National income is defined as the money value of goods and services produced in an economy during a year. The purpose of measuring national income is to know how the economy is performing over time. This is done by comparing national income in subsequent years to some year that is chosen as the *base year*.

National income is a macroeconomic variable. It is a flow concept measured over a period of time. Production flow in a country during a specified period consists of a number of heterogeneous commodities and services. These include motor cars, wheat, sugar, tea, services of doctors and teachers and thousands of such other items. These diverse items having their own distinct physical features and units of measurement cannot be added together. If we wish to total them up in a meaningful manner, it is necessary to give them a common expression, i.e. to use some kind of common unit. Money is the unit used for this purpose. Every product and service has a money value in the market (price) and by adding up money values of different goods and services we get a total called national income.

National income may be measured both at current and constant prices. At current prices it shows the total income during a year in terms of the prices prevailing in that particular year. For purposes of comparison over years it is not a true measure of real income because a part of the increase may be due to rising prices. When national income of a particular year is measured in terms of the price level of some base year, it is measured at constant prices or in real terms. The national income in real terms provides a measure of economic growth of an economy. The formula for converting national income at current prices to income at constant prices is as follows:

National income at current prices x 100/index of current prices = National income at constant prices or in real terms.

Secondly, even if national income increases in real terms it cannot be said to lead to economic growth necessarily. A better index of economic growth is increase in per capita real income. For this purpose, we have to consider the population variable. Clearly, if real national income and population increase at the same rate, the per capita real income will remain the same. For the per capita real income to increase, it is necessary that the rate of increase in real national income is more than proportionate to the rate of increase in population.

Since economic growth means increase in real per capita income, it can happen when the following two conditions are satisfied: (a) there is increase in real national income and (b) the rate of increase in real national income is more than the rate of increase in population.

1.1.2 Economic Development: Strictly speaking, economic growth and economic development are not interchangeable terms. Economic development is a much wider term. It includes economic growth and at the same time encompasses questions regarding pattern of production, distribution of income and consumption behaviour of the people. In other words, economic development is economic growth plus qualitative changes in productivity, socio-economic institutions and distribution pattern. Economic development looks at a wider range of statistics than just increase in real per capita income. Development is concerned with how people are actually affected. It looks at their actual living standards and the freedom they have to enjoy a good standard of living.

The ultimate objective of all economic efforts is human development which encompasses quality of life, the level of well-being and access to basic social services. Economic development insists that everyone should enjoy a minimum level of security. In fact, a system should be built in which the state bears the responsibility for providing and ensuring an elementary or basic level of security, and leaves room for partly or wholly contributory schemes. This will mean that the responsibility to provide a floor will be primarily that of the state, and it will be left to individual citizens to acquire higher levels of security through assumption of responsibility and contributory participation.

The notion of human well-being itself is more broadly conceived to include not only consumption of goods and services in general but more specifically to ensure that the basic material requirements of all sections of the population, especially those below the poverty line, are met and that they have access to basic social services such as health and education. Specific focus on these dimensions of social development is necessary because experience shows that economic prosperity, measured in terms of per capita income, alone does not always ensure enrichment in quality of life, as reflected, for instance, in the social indicators on health, longevity, literacy and environmental sustainability.

Economic growth in numbers alone without improvement in living standards and overall quality of life is meaningless. Health, education, a good physical environment and socio-economic-political freedom to lead a free and independent life—to name a few components of well-being—may be just as important. Income is just one aspect of the choices—and an extremely important one—but it is not the sum total of human existence. The Human Development Index (HDI) combines national income with two social indicators—adult literacy and life expectancy—to give a composite measure of human progress. The HDI fully recognizes that the concept of human development is much broader than its measurement. Thus, development today is no longer confined to growth in national income alone.

1.2 Dimensions of Economic Development

Economic development is the key to progress. It is measured in terms of improvement in the lives of the people and strengthening of the individual's and thereby a nation's capacity to deal with the rest of the world. Development is, therefore, interlinked with the entire social, political and cultural fabric of society. It aims at bringing about qualitative changes leading to an upward movement of the entire social system.

Economic development is a chain process. If one region develops, the adjoining region also develops. It gives impetus to development in all the regions that are economically connected with the adjoining region. Similarly, lack of development in one region promotes underdevelopment or slows down the pace of development in the adjoining region as well. This should be kept in mind during developmental planning.

Economic development is a journey, not a destination. It encompasses all aspects and facets of human life from birth to death. It includes basic material needs like food, clothing and shelter to higher ones such as social, mental, intellectual, emotional and spiritual aspirations.

Economic development is a process. It is not an event or a happening. As a long drawn process, it may stretch over days, months, years, decades and even centuries. However, the success of a developmental initiative largely depends on the will of the nation and sincerity of its political leadership to see it through amidst all adversity. The real objective of development, according to the United Nations Development Programme (UNDP), is to increase people's developmental choices to make development more democratic and participatory. These choices should include access to income and employment opportunities, education and health, and a clean and safe physical environment. However, enhancing the choices of one individual, or one section of society, should not restrict the choices of another. This calls for equity in human relationships.

Economic development is democratic. It provides equal opportunity to each and every individual to participate freely and fearlessly in all community decisions and to enjoy social, economic and political freedoms responsibly.

Economic development is participatory. It allows for private initiative and broad-based people's involvement at all levels— individual, local, national, international—and distributed well and benefiting all people. Development should be people-centric as it is the right of all people to individually and collectively speak their word. It is not the privilege of some few men, but the right of every man and woman. Since participation is crucial to sharing information, knowledge, trust, commitment and right attitudes for decision-making, the development edifice needs to be woven around people, not people around development. All men, women and children must be at the centre of its attention. At the same time, development should be sustainable as raising future production may involve sacrifices made in the present. Participation is closely linked to decentralization. It largely depends upon empowering the poor. Decentralisation or the devolution of power from higher level to the ground level is the essence of democracy. Its success depends on education, accountability and designing appropriate structures and sequences of decision-making.

Economic development is holistic. It is comprehensive and multifaceted in approach. Real development gives precedence to enhancing human well-being over material opulence, to expanding capabilities over maximizing incomes and to enlarging freedoms over optimizing growth. All this is done by the people themselves through active participation in various processes meant to improve and enrich their lives.

Thus, economic development is multi-dimensional. This approach to development is markedly different from the earlier approaches that regarded expansion of economic opportunities as a necessary precondition for development. Over concentration on single dimension of income alone is at best an oversimplification and at worst a gross distortion of reality because high growth rates do no automatically translate into higher levels of human development.

1.3 Determinants of Economic Development

Measuring economic development is not as precise as measuring national income because it depends on what factors are included in the measure. There are several different measures of economic development, some of which are described below.

1.3.1 Composition of National Income: It is the first determinant of economic development. If a great deal of production consists of war goods or other injurious items like cigarettes and liquor, the national income figures will not truly reflect economic development. However, instead of tanks and missiles if a greater part of national income is composed of textiles, sugar, milk and other wage goods, it will indicate enhanced economic well-being of the people.

1.3.2 Distribution of National Income: Economic development also depends on the manner in which national income is distributed among the people. Highly unequal distribution may increase the welfare of a small section of the population while the majority of the people remain deprived. It is therefore necessary to find out the degree of inequality in income distribution before drawing conclusion from national income figures.

Do people have sufficient resources to maintain a healthy diet and basics of life such as shelter? Economic growth may be essential to enable higher incomes for people to be able to buy more food. However, economic growth does not necessarily improve everyone's living standards. Economic growth could bypass the poorest sections of society because they do not have the ability to take part. A key issue is whether the benefits of economic growth are equitably distributed amongst different groups of society.

Economic growth may only benefit a small percentage of the population. For example, if a country produces more crude oil, it will see an increase in national income. However, it is possible, that this oil is owned by some families and the citizen does not really benefit from it.

1.3.3 Human Development Index (HDI): Human Development Report (HDR) published by the United Nations Development Programme (UNDP) estimates HDI) in terms of a long and healthy life, education and knowledge, and enjoyment of a decent standard of living. The development of human capabilities must be the first priority, for three reasons. First, these capabilities are actually ends in themselves. Second, they are also important instrumentalities which interact positively with others to raise the productive capacity of an economy and therefore its ability to satisfy the material needs of its population. Third, proper development of human capabilities will also ensure that growth is more inclusive in the sense that the marginalised and disadvantaged sections of society will be more able to access the opportunities thrown up by the growth process.

1.3.4 Inclusive Growth: Inclusive growth is the new paradigm that is related essentially to equality and opportunity to all and sundry for productive and meaningful life with freedom and equality. There is a lot of talk on growth and equity but there is no operational plan. An immediate plan for achieving equitable development is urgently needed. The challenge before the governments is to evolve a system in which reforms and globalization can proceed on one track, and the poor can be protected from the ill effects of it, on the other.

Inclusive growth may be defined as growth that promotes equal opportunities and increases access to these opportunities, i.e. growth that allows all members of society to participate in and contribute equally to development efforts, regardless of individual circumstances. This concept appears in Asian Development Bank's (ADB) *Strategy 2020* that examines the extent of inequality of opportunities and to what extent it can be overcome by different types of growth process. The main idea in the ADB's approach is to focus on productive employment as an important element of inclusive growth.

Inclusive growth, defined in a broader sense has three dimensions:

1. Equity among all sections of the society.
2. Equity among all sectors of the economy.
3. Equity among all regions in the country.

Thus, inclusive growth means inter-group, inter-sector as well as inter-regional equity. Growth is inclusive when it creates economic opportunities along with ensuring equal access to them.

Inclusive growth is the new mantra of national and international agencies like United Nation Development Programme (UNDP) and the World Bank. UNDP defines inclusive growth—by laying emphasis on the production and income side of the GDP—as "the process and the outcome where all group of people have participated in the organization of growth and have benefited equitably from it. Thus, inclusive growth represents an equation with organization on the left hand side and benefits on the right hand side".

1.3.5 Gender Equality: Gender equality is a constituent of development as well as an instrument of development. No country can be deemed developed if half of its population is severely disadvantaged in terms of basic needs, livelihood options, access to knowledge, and political voice. It is an instrument of development because without gender equality other goals of development will also be difficult to achieve, namely the goals of poverty alleviation, economic growth, environmental sustainability etc. A natural corollary of ensuring gender equality is the elimination of gender discrimination.

Inequalities between girls and boys in access to schooling or adequate health care prove a very serious disadvantage to women and girls and limit their capacity to participate in the benefits of development.

The socio-economic development of a country cannot be fully realized so long as its women are confined to subordinate position and their talents remain unexplored. Women entrepreneurship is becoming a reality now-a-days due to pull and push factors. Between the pull and push factors, the women take it as a real challenge with an urge to do something new and take up an independent occupation. In order to achieve the objective of social justice, it is necessary to harness the latent skills and potential of women, especially the rural women. They play a key role in the rapid and sustained economic development in rural areas and the ultimate prosperity and development of the nation.

Women's lack of economic empowerment not only impedes development and poverty reduction, but also has a host of other negative impacts including less favourable education and health outcomes for children. Thus, it is extremely important to ensure that women are economically, socially and politically empowered.

Empowerment of women through gainful employment is a constituent—as well as instrument—of economic development in any country. Effective and coordinated plans and programmes for the full implementation of women-oriented policies require a clear research-based knowledge of ground realities of the socio-economic status of women, particularly rural women. The realization of the goals of women empowerment needs to be supported by the allocation of necessary human and financial resources for specific and targeted activities to ensure gender equality at the local, regional, national, and international levels as well as by enhanced and increased international cooperation.

1.3.6 Levels of Environmental Standards: Productivity of an economic system depends, to a large extent, on the supply and quality of its natural resources. In fact, natural and environmental resources are the basis of all economic activities. Soil, forests, mines, water, air and other natural resources are productive assets of an economy. Since the beginning of Industrial Revolution in Britain in the middle of the 18th century, economic growth has required the burning of coal and oil as fuel for production in the economy. Burning coal contributes to the greenhouse effect, which it is hypothesized will raise the temperature of the earth, causing severe global climate problems. The degradation of the atmosphere is, to a certain extent, an unavoidable consequence of economic growth. However, if this growth is not carefully monitored, environmental problems will be incurred.

Increase in economic activities—due to growing population and/or enhanced consumption levels—often impacts environment negatively. Degradation of natural resources and losses in environmental quality adversely affect people at large. As a consequence of high level of economic activities, emissions, effluents and waste discharges exceed the carrying capacity of different resources. Economic growth without environmental considerations can cause serious damage to the quality of life of the present and future generations. It is in this context that economists distinguish between economic growth and economic development.

Economic progress improves our standard of living and makes our life more comfortable. On the other hand, it is this very progress that can lead to degradation of the environment. Any increase in national income would arise only from increased production of goods and services involving greater consumption of resources such as land, forest, fuels etc. whose supply is, essentially, limited. While some of these resources may be renewable, others get depleted and, ultimately, exhausted with continuous use. Any attempt to preserve the non-renewable resources might require compromising on the growth rates. As countries become more industrialized, augment their agricultural production, and expend greater amounts of fossil fuels, the environment often suffers. The challenge facing policymakers worldwide is to manage economic growth in a way that maximizes its benefits and reduces its costs, in terms of damage to both the environment and to the free market system.

The conflict between economic development and environment is, essentially, a conflict between short- and long-run priorities, between the interests of current and future generations. Large exploitation of natural resources today, while increasing the economic growth for the current generations, would lead to gradual exhaustion and degradation of these resources, thereby reducing their availability to future generations and adversely affecting their output, income and living standards.

1.3.7 Sustainable Development: The concept of sustainable development is inextricably linked with environment protection. It is a strategy for improving the quality of human life while living within the carrying capacity of supporting eco system. Sustainable development entails commitment, protection and preservation. Sustainable development is that which meets the needs of the present without compromising the ability of future generations. The heaviest burden in international economic adjustment has been carried by the world's poorest population. The consequence has been the considerable increase in human distress and over exploitation of land and water resources to ensure survival in the short term. Further, the desire to solve all social and human problems at one stroke has influenced the pace of development. Its reaction is visible in the atmosphere and in natural, physical and social environment. Awareness regarding the consequences of this event has developed into a consensus referred to as ecological concern.

Sustainable development advocates economic growth in an environmentally responsible manner. Sustainable development attempts to strike a balance between the requirements of economic growth and the need for protection of the environment. It seeks to combine the elements of economic efficiency, inter-generational equity, social concerns and environmental protection. Although, the term sustainable development has many interpretations, it generally refers to non-declining human well-being over time.

Economic growth and development have to be guided by the compulsion of sustainability, because no country can afford to ignore the economic as well as the environmental threat that a fast-deteriorating ecosystem poses to its economy. No country is immune to the reality of climate change, ecological degradation, depletion of the ozone layer and contamination of freshwater.

Sustainable development is a difficult balancing act in countries with low incomes.

Society has to simultaneously accomplish three things with trade-offs: improve economic well-being with social justice for the present generation, yet manage with more restrained use of land, air, forest, energy, and water resources, and protect future generations. The choices are more difficult in developing countries because they affect people's livelihoods. Such a 'stewardship' to succeed therefore needs to respond to people's needs, share information on choices and costs, and ensure participation and ownership.

Environment must not be considered as just another sector of national development. It should form a crucial guiding dimension for plans and programmes in each sector. This becomes clear only if the concern for environmental protection is understood in its proper context. Ecological degradation compromises the quality of life in the long-run.

To sum up, national income in its usual meaning is not necessarily an index of economic development of a country. The estimates of national income ought to be modified in terms of foregoing adjustments in order to be reflective of economic well-being. Population explosion poses a serious threat to development. The vicious nexus between poverty and uncontrolled population is a huge obstacle in the way of achieving development objectives. Unchecked population not only slows down the pace of development but also accentuates the ecological crisis thereby preventing the benefits of development from reaching one and all.

Economic development should be sustainable. It should meet the needs of the present without compromising the ability of the future generations to meet their own needs. This kind of development has to be seen and felt in terms of improved living conditions, better infrastructure, safety and security of citizens and above all, less polluted greener environment.

2

Characteristics of Underdeveloped Countries and the Vicious Circle of Poverty

2.1 Characteristics of Underdeveloped Countries

A typical underdeveloped country [or more appropriately a less developed country (LDC)] exhibits the following features:

2.1.1 Low Per Capita Real Income: Per capita income is a simple but very useful concept in economics. It is calculated by dividing national income by total population of a country. Per capita income = National income/Population.

Increase in real per capita income is the definition of a progressive economy. It is an index of the living standard of the people in a country. Increase in real per capita income can happen when the following two conditions are satisfied: (a) there is increase in real national income and (b) the rate of increase in real national income is more than the rate of increase in population.

Judging developing nations by this criterion one finds them in an extremely unsatisfactory position. The per capita income in underdeveloped economy is low and therefore majority of the population lives below the poverty line. It is one of the major characteristics of an underdeveloped economy.

2.1.2 Widespread Poverty: The final objective of all economic efforts is human development which encompasses quality of life, the level of well being and access to basic social services. Unfortunately, poverty is a widespread social evil in underdeveloped countries of the world, particularly in Asia and Africa.

There is no standard definition of poverty for all the countries of the world. Being a relative concept, the meaning of poverty differs from country to country. In India, poverty is defined in terms of a minimum (subsistence) level of living rather than a reasonable level of living. Thus, minimum physical quantities of cereals, pulses, clothing etc. are determined for a subsistence level. These physical quantities are multiplied by their prices and converted into monetary terms, determining the per capita consumption/income for subsistence level. Persons whose income/consumption is below this determined figure are considered to be below the poverty line.

The root cause of social insecurity is poverty and that is largely due to lack of adequate or productive employment opportunities. It is described as chronic or structural social insecurity, arising from insufficient degree of overall economic development. It is associated with other insecurities emanating from conventional contingencies such as the loss of employment, disability, old age, death etc. which are called the *second-order* type of insecurities or conventional social insecurity.

Widespread poverty in LDCs is attributable to a host of factors, viz. population explosion, lack of industrialisation, failure of land reforms and failure of fiscal policy to narrow the gap between the rich and the poor.

Poverty is a chronic and multi-dimensional phenomenon. There is geography of poverty, with poverty being concentrated in the rural areas of certain regions. There is sociology of poverty, with certain social groups suffering the most. There are identifiable occupational features of the poor. They are mostly agricultural labourers and artisans in rural areas, and casual workers in urban areas. Casual labourers in urban areas are essentially distress migrants from rural areas where agricultural land-man ratio is very adverse, and where agricultural incomes have not been growing

2.1.3 Unbalanced Occupational Structure: Occupational classification refers to the distribution of available occupations in a country into meaningful categories. In general, all occupations are broadly divided into three categories:

1. Primary sector (agriculture and allied activities).
2. Secondary sector (industrial activities).
3. Tertiary sector (services sector).

Occupational structure refers to the distribution of working persons across primary sector, secondary sector and tertiary sector.

There is a close relationship between economic development and occupational structure of a country. A higher per capita income country is always associated with a higher proportion of the working population employed in tertiary sector. Contrarily, a low per capita income country is always associated with a higher proportion of working population engaged in agriculture. It is in this sense that occupational structure in LDCs is unbalanced.

In the preliminary stage of economic growth, the proportion of the work force engaged in the agricultural and allied occupations is high. As the economy grows, the share of working population in primary sector declines and that of secondary and tertiary sectors increases. At high levels of economic development, the share of tertiary sector is more than that in secondary sector.

2.1.4 Heavy Population Pressure and Dependency Burden: In most of the underdeveloped economies, the population growth rate is very high as compared to developed economies. Population has been rising in most developing countries at rates varying between 2.0 and 3.5 percent per annum for the past few decades. Due to increased medical facilities there has been a gradual decline in the death rates in these countries. However, birth rates remain still high. Birth-rate is determined by factors like social and religious beliefs about marriage, family size, male children, and family planning methods. Clearly, it requires a much longer time to change the social attitudes of the people. In other words, birth-rate tends to fall after a time lag. The high birth rates and the declining death rates have caused population in LDCs to grow at an accelerated rate. These countries are in the *second stage* of demographic transition which is marked by population explosion. [1]

Population explosion in LDCs has nullified, to a large extent, the gains of developmental efforts. Unabated growth of population in has offset to a significant extent the fruits of economic growth and used up part of the potential savings which could have been utilized to raise capital per head and the productivity of the labour force at a faster pace. The pressure of population is felt in a variety of ways, particularly in terms of low per capita income, reduced availability of food, and unemployment.

2.1.5 Chronic Unemployment and Underemployment: Unemployment is a situation when willing workers fail to get jobs at the prevailing wage rates. In other words, unemployment means involuntary idleness. From social point of view, unemployment means wastage of the precious labour resources of the country. For an individual, unemployment is a painful and demoralising experience. Employment to be gainful and sustainable has to be productive in character.

Unemployment is a serious problem of LDCs. The poverty of the masses in these countries is closely related to the problem of unemployment. Economic security is one of the main components of human security. It constitutes the crux of social security in the conventional sense. Economic security requires employment and an assured source of income adequate for meeting one's basic needs.

In underdeveloped countries, production is carried on with insufficient amount of real capital per head of population. In almost all processes of production and distribution, the techniques are relatively backward leading to various forms of unemployment—seasonal unemployment in agriculture, and disguised or even manifest unemployment in certain industries and services.

Urban unemployment is classified into two categories: (a) industrial unemployment and, (b) educated unemployment. Industrial unemployment is the result of slow growth of industrial development vis-à-vis growth of labour force. Unemployment among the educated is mainly due to over emphasis on theoretical aspects of various subjects. The education system is cut-off from ground realities of the economy.

Rural unemployment in the agricultural sector is the most serious aspect of unemployment in LDCs. First of all, there is open unemployment among the landless agricultural workers. With the decline of cottage industries and handicrafts, the rural population has no alternative means of livelihood. They have to fall back on the agricultural sector which is already overcrowded. There is also considerable disguised unemployment in the agricultural sector. It means more people are engaged in agricultural operations than required. In technical language, the marginal productivity of many hands in the agricultural sector is zero. Yet another dimension of rural unemployment is the problem of seasonal unemployment. Agriculture by its very nature is a seasonal activity. For a significant part of the year, farmers are out of work. In the absence of supplementary sources of employment, they have to remain unemployed during slack agricultural season.

2.1.6 Low Rate of Capital Formation: The excess of production over consumption in a year is called capital formation. It is also called accumulation. The entire production of a year is not consumed. Production is normally higher than consumption. The surplus of production over consumption in a year is defined as capital formation. Capital formation consists broadly of the following:

1. Construction of new assets like buildings, roads and bridges.
2. Production of machinery and equipment.
3. Increase in the stocks of raw materials, semi-finished goods and finished goods in a year.

Deficiency of capital is an important feature of developing countries. Therefore, they are often called capital poor economies. The shortage of capital is reflected in the low capital-labour ratio in these countries. It is also reflected in the low rate of investment. Total investment is the sum of public investment and private investment (household investment and investment by the private corporate sector). Investment, especially private investment, is the key driver that drives demand, creates capacity, increases labour productivity, introduces new technology, allows creative destruction and generates jobs.

2.1.7 Poor Quality of Human Capital: The quality of human resources in terms of health and education is generally poor in LDCs. Human beings are the heartbeat of a country. Intangible assets, like human capital, decide the use of tangible and material resources to fulfil the objectives of any society. Since people constitute the most significant resource of any country, human development becomes critical for its socio-economic progress. Human resources in terms of demographic trends are important, as also the development of human resources through programmes in education, health, social welfare and science and technology.

Human resources are of critical importance for the growth of knowledge and technology, value addition and improvement of competitiveness in manufacturing through processes of continuous improvement. In fact, the human resources are the only *appreciating resources* in a manufacturing system. They are the only resources that have the motivation and ability to increase their value if suitable conditions are provided, whereas all other resources—machines, building, materials and so on—depreciate in value with time. The best enterprises view their people as their prime asset and the source of their competitive advantage. Nations that have achieved sustainable competitiveness in manufacturing even when they do not have required raw materials, such as Japan and South Korea, have created systems for the continuous improvement of the capabilities of their human resources.

2.1.8 Technological Backwardness: In developing countries, production techniques are inefficient over a wide range of industrial activity. This sorry state of affairs cannot be explained in terms of one or two factors. Lack of research and development (R&D), weak communication system between the research institutes and industries, abundance of labour and capital scarcity are some obvious reasons for the use of techniques which have otherwise become obsolete. Developing countries generally do not have large effective institutions working for discovering appropriate technology. Under the circumstances, an attempt is made to import technology from developed countries which often fails to adapt to local conditions. Moreover, whatever limited research is undertaken in industrial technology; its results fail to reach producers due to weak communication system. However, these factors do not explain wholly the continuance of outmoded techniques.

2.2 Vicious Circle of Poverty

Vicious circle of poverty implies a circular constellation of forces tending to act and react upon one another in such a way as to keep a poor country in a state of poverty. This situation can be summed up in the proposition: A country is poor because it is poor.

There are circular relationships known as the *vicious circles of poverty* that tend to perpetuate the low level of development in less developed countries (LDCs). Ragnar Nurkse explains the idea in these words: "It implies a circular constellation of forces tending to act and react upon one another in such a way as to keep a poor country in a state of poverty. For example, a poor man may not have enough to eat; being underfed, his health may be weak; being physically weak, his working capacity is low, which means that he is poor, which in turn means that he will not have enough to eat and so on. A situation of this sort relating to a country as a whole can be summed up in the proposition: A county is poor because it is poor.

The vicious circle of poverty operates both on the demand side and the supply side.

2.2.1 Demand Side: The demand side of the vicious circle is that the low level of real income leads to a low level of demand which, in turn, leads to a low rate of investment and hence back to deficiency of capital, low productivity and low income.

According to Nurkse, "On the demand side, the inducement of invest may he low because of the small purchasing power of the people, which is due to the small real income, which is again due to loco productivity. The level of productivity however, is the result of the small amount of capital used in production which in turn may be caused or at least partly caused by small inducement to invest.

Low Income → Low Demand → Low Investment → Low Productivity → Low Income

The vicious circle of poverty on demand side is shown in Figure 2.1.

Figure 2.1: Vicious Circle of Poverty on Demand Side

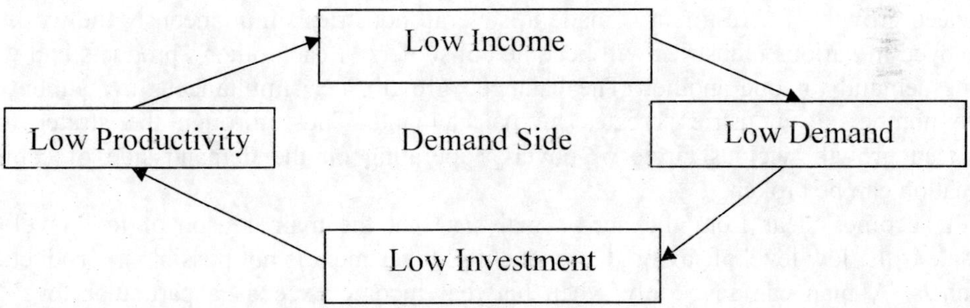

2.2.2 Supply Side: On the supply side, the low level of real income means low savings. The low level of saving leads to low investment and to deficiency of capital. The deficiency of capital, in turn, leads to low levels of productivity and back to low income. Thus the vicious circle is complete from the supply side.

Supply side of vicious circle indicates that in underdeveloped countries, productivity is so low that it is not enough for capital formation. According to Paul Samuelson, "The backward nations cannot get their heads above water because their production is so low that they can spare nothing for capital formation by which their standard of living could be raised". On the supply side there is small capacity to save resulting from low level of national income. The low real income is a reflection of low productivity, which, in turn, is due largely to the lack of capital. The lack of capital is a result of the small capacity to save and so the circle is complete.

Low Income → Low Saving → Low Investment → Low Production → Low Income

The vicious circle of poverty on supply side is shown in Figure 2.2.

Figure 2.2: Vicious Circle of Poverty on Supply Side

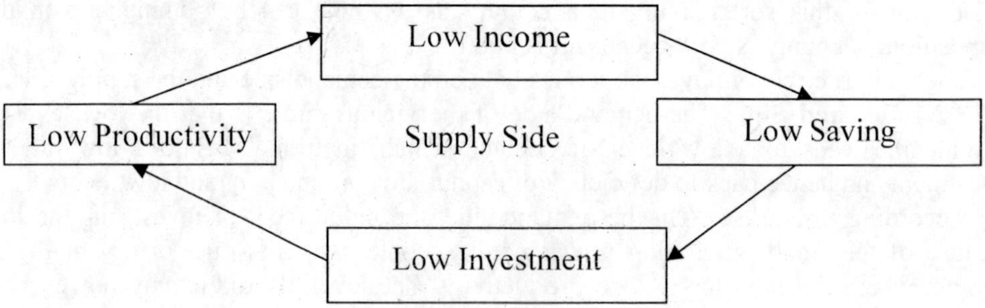

2.2.3 Breaking the Vicious Circle of Poverty: The vicious circle of poverty is associated with low rate of saving and investment on the supply side. In LDCs, the rate of investment and capital formation can be stepped up without reduction in consumption. For this, the marginal rate of savings is to be greater than average rate of savings.

To break the vicious circle on the demand side, Nurkse suggested the strategy of balanced growth. If investment is made in several industries simultaneously the workers employed in various industries will become consumers of each other's products and will create demand for one another. The balanced growth, i.e. simultaneous investment in large number of industries creates mutual demand. Thus, through the strategy of balanced growth, vicious circle of poverty operating on the demand side of capital formation can be broken.

It becomes clear from the above analysis, that the main reason of low level of income is the low level of saving. Consequently, investment is not possible in production channels. A man can save only when his real income exceeds a particular level of consumption. Generally, in LDCs, the society is divided into two groups, viz. rich and poor. Although, the rich group of the society is in a position to save, but they spend their savings on luxurious goods instead of investing it in productive channels.

Endnote

1. For the theory of demographic transition, see chapter 16 of this book.

3

Factors and Issues in Economic Development

Economic development implies an improvement in economic welfare through higher real incomes and other welfare indices such as improved literacy, better infrastructure, reduced poverty and better healthcare.

3.1 Factors in Economic Development

Following are the determinants of economic development in a country:

3.1.1 Human Resources: The resource base of a country consists of the following:

1. Human resources, i.e. size and quality of population.
2. Non-renewable resources like iron ore, petroleum and coal which are an endowment of nature and whose total size gets depleted with time.
3. Renewable resources such as wind and solar energy which can be continuously created and whose base can be expanded through human efforts.

Human beings are the heartbeat of a country. Human capital, an intangible asset, decides the use of tangible and material resources to fulfil the objectives of any society. Since people constitute the most significant resources of any country, human development becomes critical for its socio-economic progress. Human resources in terms of demographic trends are important, as also the development of human resources through programmes in health, education, social welfare and science and technology.

The skills, education and training of the labour force have a direct effect on the growth of an economy. A skilled, well-trained workforce is more productive and will produce a high-quality output that adds efficiency to an economy. A shortage of skilled labour can be a deterrent to economic growth.

Skill development is important because of its contribution to enhancing productivity at the individual, industry and also national levels because of the complementarities that exist between physical capital and human capital on the one hand and between technology and human capital on the other. Fast changing knowledge economies call for new core competencies among all learners in the society. Skill development is needed for more jobs and higher productivity. Creating jobs and increasing productivity are at the top of agenda for policymakers across the world. For developing countries that are seeking to grow in an inclusive way and reduce poverty, the challenge of expanding employment and productivity is a *sine qua non*.

The foundations of industrial and agricultural advance lie ultimately in the availability and effective use of human skills. Human skills are a formidable asset since they last not merely during one working life but because they are transmitted for generations. If these assets are used effectively, they may well turn out to be one of the most fruitful results of planning.

3.1.2 Natural Resources: Most natural resources, such as coal and petroleum, were formed millions of years ago. Other resources, such as sunlight, were present even before the earth was formed. Regardless, we all are dependent on these resources in some way or the other. These resources are termed as natural resources and are very important for life on earth. Natural resources are classified into: (a) renewable resources, and (b) non-renewable resources.

The resources which cannot be exhausted even after continuous utilization are termed as renewable resources. Examples of renewable resources are the sun, wind, and tidal energy. The resources which cannot be immediately replaced once they are depleted are called non-renewable resources. Examples of non-renewable resources include fossil fuels, such as coal, petroleum and natural gas and rare minerals typically found in meteorites.

The quantity and availability of natural resources affect the rate of economic growth. The discovery of more natural resources, such as oil or mineral deposits, will give a boost to the economy by increasing a country's production capacity. The effectiveness of a county at utilizing and exploiting its natural resources is a function of the skills of the labour force, type of technology and the availability of capital. Skilled and educated workers are able to use these natural resources to spur the growth of the economy. Natural resources cover a most extensive field and it is not possible to do more than touch upon a few broad features of the subject.

The most important natural resource is land which is the base for agricultural production. While population grows, the land surface is fixed and only a certain proportion of it is available for cultivation. The non-expandable land resources have to accommodate the competing demands for production of food, fodder, fibre and fuel, minerals, urbanisation, non-agricultural land use etc. for the increasing human and animal population.

Water is a prime natural resource, a basic human need and a precious national asset. Water has defined life in the world for thousands of years. Water is used for drinking, domestic and municipal uses, agricultural irrigation, industries, navigation, recreation etc. Access to adequate water is one of the leading factors in economic development of any country. Agricultural, industrial and domestic uses are competing more and more for a limited supply.

Forests play a vital role in social, cultural, historical, economic and industrial development of any country and in maintaining its ecological balance. They are the resource base for sustenance of its population and a storehouse of biodiversity. Other vocations of land use, such as agriculture and animal husbandry, are dependent on forests and forestlands. Forests not only maintain and improve the moisture regime and provide clean air but also produce humus and maintain soil fertility.

The metallurgical and mineral industries constitute the bedrock of industrial sector as they provide the basic raw materials for most of the industries. Amongst natural resources, minerals form a special category as they are wasting assets. Once they are taken out of the ground and utilised, they are lost for ever. They should, therefore, be treated on a different footing from replenishable natural resources. The development and management of mineral resources plays a major role in the industrial growth of a nation and its people at large. As minerals form the basis of modern industry in peace and in war, it is necessary to have a rational policy as regards their working and utilisation. The keynote of this policy should be conservation and economic working.

Expanded demand for natural resources and materials has led to technological developments which have in part overcome limitations and thus increased the supply of resources. The dynamic forces at work in creating shifts in the demand for and supply of natural resources necessitate their continuous study as well as reformulation of policies relating to them. Natural resources must be looked at in a coordinated manner and their investigation and utilisation planned for long-term needs. The extent to which resources have been studied and possibilities established ahead of needs is an important factor determining the rate at which the economy can grow. There is growing recognition of the need for conservation of natural resources in all fields.

3.1.3 Savings and Investment: In growth models, such as Harrod-Domar model, levels of savings and investment are seen as a key factor in determining economic growth. Higher savings enables a virtuous circle of increased investment, higher growth, and therefore, higher savings. Importance of domestic savings in developing economies is well-known. Gross domestic saving is composed of saving by household sector + private corporate sector + public sector. Savings by household sector account for a major share of total savings. Total investment is the sum of public investment and private investment (household investment and investment by the private corporate sector). Investment, especially private investment, is the key driver that drives demand, creates capacity, increases labour productivity, introduces new technology, allows creative destruction and generates jobs.

The balanced growth theory pioneered by the economist Ragnar Nurkse (1907-1959) hypothesis that the government of any underdeveloped country needs to make large investments in a number of industries simultaneously. This will enlarge the market size, increase productivity, and provide an incentive for the private sector to invest.

Improvements and increased investment in physical capital–such as roadways, machinery and factories–will reduce the cost and increase the efficiency of economic output. Factories and equipment that are modern and well-maintained are more productive than physical labour. Higher productivity leads to increased output. Labour becomes more productive as the ratio of capital expenditures per worker increases. An improvement in labour productivity increases the growth rate of the economy.

3.1.4 Level of Infrastructure and Logistics: In economic literature, infrastructure is popular by the name *overhead capital* which represents basic services without which primary, secondary and tertiary productive activities cannot function. The very success of social and economic transformation of an economy lies in providing inclusive and sustainable infrastructure amenities to the people and the pace of economic growth depends on how competently and judiciously an economy is able to address its infrastructure bottlenecks.

The infrastructure sector covers a wide spectrum of services. Some of these services have a direct impact on the working of business enterprises, while others are more important from a societal point of view. Each sub-sector of an infrastructural service is inherently unique in terms of its administration and operational structure, the regulatory framework governing its operations, the level of technology and the degree of commercialisation. In addition, while some services such as telecommunications can be provided on a strictly commercial basis, others like roads are expected to be fully provided by the state or at least part-subsidised.

Most directly, productive activities in industry, agriculture and services use electricity, telecommunications, water and transport as intermediate inputs. Even in the informal sector, infrastructure can be a major share of business expenses. A measurable benefit of investment in infrastructure is the reduced cost to users of each service unit consumed. This benefit is greater, the more the service is characterised by economies of scale.

If enterprises are unable to realise the benefit of efficient generation of infrastructure services, they are forced to seek higher-cost alternatives that may have unfavourable impacts on profits and production levels.

Logistics refers to a series of services and activities, such as transportation, warehousing, and brokerage, which help to move goods and establish supply chains across and within borders. Although these services and activities are carried out by private firms for the benefit of private firms, service delivery and the efficiency of supply chains depend on public sector provisions and interventions in a number of domains. Logistics uses publicly funded or regulated infrastructure. International trade is processed by border agencies. Services and logistics activities are regulated with fiscal, environmental, safety, land use, and competition objectives.

Logistics organizes the movement of goods through a network of activities and services operating at global, regional, and local scale. Logistics encompasses more than freight transportation. Traders delegate increasingly sophisticated tasks to networks of specialized service providers. Efficient logistics connects people and firms to markets and opportunities and helps achieve higher levels of productivity and welfare. Crucially, logistics is not only a private endeavour, but also a public policy concern. The performance and reliability of supply chains depend on an array of interventions, ranging from trade facilitation at the border to infrastructure and regulations and to urban planning and skills. Empirical evidence confirms that logistics and connectivity-related interventions have the highest potential to reduce the cost of trade and to boost integration in global value chains. Policy makers know that logistics matters and that they can improve the efficiency of the supply chains connecting their countries internally and externally.

3.1.5 Technological Progress: Improvements in technology have a high impact on economic growth. As the scientific community makes more discoveries, managers find ways to apply these innovations as more sophisticated production techniques. The application of better technology means the same amount of labour will be more productive, and economic growth will advance at a lower cost. Technological innovation and more education for workers will improve economic output which leads to a better living environment for everyone. Increases in labour productivity are much easier to achieve when investments are made on better equipment that require less physical work from the labour force. The per capita income and quality of life that a nation enjoys is, in the final analysis, dependent largely on the technology it adopts, and which in turn has to be appropriate to its endowments, resources and skills.

The foundations of industrial and agricultural advance lie ultimately in the availability and effective use of human skills. Human skills are a formidable asset since they last not merely during one working life but because they are transmitted for generations. If these assets are used effectively, they may well turn out to be one of the most fruitful results of planning.

The pace of economic development depends on a variety of factors which constitute the psychological and sociological setting within which the economy operates. A major element in this setting is the community's will to progress and its readiness to develop and adopt new and more efficient methods and processes of production. Basically, development involves securing higher productivity all round and this is a function of the degree of technological advance the community is able to make. The problem is not one merely of adopting and applying the processes and techniques developed elsewhere, but of developing new techniques specially suited to local conditions.

Modern technology is changing rapidly and no country can hope to maintain a steady pace of advance unless it keeps abreast of current developments. Techniques in turn affect and are affected by economic and social organisation. Certain forms of economic and social organisation are unsuited to or incapable of absorbing new techniques and utilising them to the best advantage. To some extent techniques must of course be adapted to economic and social organisation, but the latter has also to change in order to accommodate new techniques which need to be applied not merely in one or two isolated lines but in several lines of economic activity.

The vital role of science in modern life is now generally recognised. Apart from the vast changes it has brought about, the development of a scientific temper in the people is considered important. Improvements in techniques evolved as a result of scientific research bring about great increases in production in the different sectors of the economy. National resources are augmented by the substitution of cheap and abundant materials for those in scarce supply and by finding uses for materials which have remained unutilised. A balanced programme of research covering every sector of the economy is essential therefore for the development of a country.

High standards of living in the more advanced countries are the direct result of progress in science and technology and the rapid pace of development associated with it. The flow of new scientific knowledge is continuous and ever expanding and covers both pure and applied research. Pure research leads to new knowledge and understanding of nature and its laws, and creates the scientific capital from which practical applications of knowledge are drawn. New products and processes are based on new principles and concepts. The advance of technology presents new problems to science and also provides new tools with which to resolve them.

3.1.6 Foreign Investment: Since early 1980s, the world economy has witnessed a dramatic flow of foreign investment into developing economies, indicating that encouragement of foreign investment has become an integral part of the economic reforms process of these economies. Foreign investment is seen as an instrument of technology transfer, managerial skills, augmentation of foreign exchange reserves, export competitiveness and globalisation of the economy.

As against a highly suspicious attitude of these countries towards foreign investment in the past, most countries now regard foreign investment as beneficial for their development efforts and compete with each other to attract it. The explanation for this shift in attitude lies in the changes in political and economic systems that have occurred during the closing years of the last century. Many countries, particularly in Eastern Europe, have abandoned socialism in its various forms and embraced the market economy. In many of these countries, mass privatisation has taken place mainly with funds from abroad. The success of Southeast and East Asian economies is attributable, to a large extent, to a high level of foreign investment and export promotion.

Foreign direct investment (FDI) flows are usually preferred over other forms of external finance because they are non-debt creating, non-volatile and their returns depend on the performance of the projects financed by the investors. FDI also facilitates international trade and transfer of knowledge, skills and technology. In a world of increased competition and rapid technological change, their complimentary and catalytic role can be very valuable.

3.1.7 Entrepreneurship and Innovations: The growth and prosperity of all economies remains highly dependent on entrepreneurial activity. Entrepreneurs are the essence of economic growth as they provide a source of income and employment for themselves, create employment for others, produce new and innovative products or services, and drive greater upstream and downstream value-chain activities. Supportive environments are increasingly essential to successful entrepreneurship and these are evolving across the world. Developed economies generate entrepreneurial opportunities as a result of their wealth and innovation capacity, yet they also offer more wage employment options to attract those that might otherwise become independent entrepreneurs. If these opportunities for entrepreneurship and innovation are to be captured, it is essential to create an enabling eco-system for entrepreneurship to thrive and instil a mind-set and culture of opportunity and innovation-based motives and entrepreneurial incentives.

Innovation is a process whereby people or groups of people with an entrepreneurial mindset (organizations, enterprises) develop new ideas or absorb and adapt existing ones. Together with institutions and policies that affect their behaviour and performance, they create new products, processes, and forms of organization. Innovation is not only about scientists in laboratories, theoretical science, or new discoveries. It is about building the capacity to find solutions to practical everyday development problems. So, an innovative economy is marked by ideas for new products or new ways of doing things and transforming them into profitable products or activities Innovation can play a very important role in the development discourse, because it can offer a new approach to a system that is currently over-burdened by the multiple demands and has limited resources at its disposal. Enhanced focus on innovation can have an impact in diverse areas such as health and education delivery, governance, enterprise development and much more. Collectively, this can herald a generational change in the country and can lay out a chart for a more sustainable and inclusive growth paradigm.

3.1.8 Political Stability: Economic development requires a degree of political stability. Political stability of a country is an important driver of technological advancement. Availability of foreign funds and venture capital to finance technological development is relatively easy for politically stable economies. In contrast, in economies that are high in political instability, financing is more challenging. Political stability and the protection of private property are ranked as the most important factors for encouraging firms to invest in developing economies. Any sign of instability increases the economic and personal risk of investing in developing countries.

3.2 Issues in Economic Development

There are various issues in framing a suitable economic policy for the country. These, *inter alia*, include the following.

3.2.1 Determination of the Relative Roles of Public and Private Sectors: Industrial policy should clearly mention the responsibility of the government in the matter of promoting, assisting and regulating the development of industry in the national interest. In other words, the fields for the public and private sectors need to be demarcated. For example, in India, the Industrial Policy Resolution of 1948 envisaged a mixed economy for the country. It declared that public sector would play an effective and dominant role in the future economic development of India. This role was to be particularly significant in the establishment and development of heavy and basic industries. Certain crucial sectors for industrial development were reserved for Government initiative.

3.2.2 Relative Emphasis on Consumer Goods and Capital Goods Industries: Consumer goods (or consumption goods) are purchased and used by households. They have no future productive use. Contrarily, capital goods include machines, tools and implements which are purchased by manufacturers for producing other goods. The relative emphasis on the production of these two categories of goods has implications for the rate of growth of the economy.

3.2.3 Relative Roles of Large and Small-scale Industries: Apart from large-scale industries, micro, small and medium enterprises (MSMEs) also play an important role in the economic and social development of a country. MSMEs are the nursery for entrepreneurship, often driven by the individual creativity and innovation, with a significant contribution in the country's gross domestic product (GDP), manufacturing output, exports and employment generation.

3.2.4 Location Policy for Industries: There are various economic and social criteria to determine location of industries. Economic criteria include availability of raw materials, nearness to market and infrastructural facilities. These may be available in already developed areas. Social criteria include employment opportunities and laying of social and economic overheads in backward areas.

3.2.5 Concentrated versus Broad-based Entrepreneurship: Industrial policy must ensure the dispersal of ownership and avoid the growth of economic concentration and of monopolies.

3.2.6 Licensing Policy, Procedures, Rules and Regulations to Control Industrial Activities: Government has to put in place a variety of legislations and rules which are aimed at controlling and regulating the industrial activities in the economy. Necessary legislative framework is necessary for implementing the industrial policy and to enable the government to direct investment into desired channels of industrial activity through the mechanism of licensing keeping with national development objectives.

3.2.7 Role of Foreign Investment in Domestic Industrialization: Foreign investment is a subject of topical interest. Countries of the world, particularly developing economies, are vying with each other to attract foreign capital to boost their domestic rates of investment and also to acquire new technology and managerial skills. Intense competition is taking place among the fund-starved less developed countries to lure foreign investors by offering repatriation facilities, tax concessions and other incentives. However, foreign investment is not an unmixed blessing. Governments in developing countries have to be very careful while deciding the magnitude, pattern and conditions of private foreign investment.

4

Basic Problems of an Economy and Their Solution

Economics is a social science concerned with administration of scarce resources. Resources are of two types: (a) economic resources, and (b) non-economic resources. Economic resources like labour, capital equipment, and land are limited or scarce. They command a price. Contrarily, non-economic resources such as sunshine and air are unlimited in supply and, therefore, available free of cost. Economics deals with scarce resources.

4.1 What is an Economic System?

An economic system is a man-made device designed to facilitate the use of resources and the distribution of output. It consists of a complex set of institutions, laws and objectives. Every economy has to accomplish certain basic tasks. These are: (a) allocation of resources among competing uses, (b) choice of technology and (c) distribution of output.

Which is the best economic system? It is difficult to answer this question because it involves subjective preferences about welfare, progress, freedom and security. Still, attempts can be made to evaluate economic systems on certain rational criteria.

The first thing one would like to know about economies with different economic systems is how much they produce. The measure of production can be national income disaggregated into industrial and agricultural output, or into private goods and collective goods. Per capita real income would still be a better index. However, there are limitations of this criterion. Lower per capita income of a country does not necessarily mean that its economic system is inferior. In fact, a country's per capita income depends not only on its economic institutions but also on historical, political, cultural, geographical and social circumstances as well.

Rate of growth is an important criterion of successful economic performance. In most underdeveloped countries economic growth constitutes the major national objective and the success of the government is largely measured in terms of the rate of growth in national income. However, it would be wrong to assume that growth alone can solve social and economic problems. It is well-known that economic growth has contributed to the deterioration of the environment, as most industrialised societies have discovered to their sorrow. Some other criteria to judge the performance of different economic systems include: (a) economic stability, (b) individual's economic security, (c) equity and justice and (d) economic freedom.

4.2 Capitalist Economy

It is a form of economic organisation characterised by private ownership of the means of production. A capitalist society like the USA exhibits the following features:

1. Right to private property prevails.
2. Law of inheritance operates.
3. Means of production are owned by private individuals or groups of individuals (companies and partnership firms).
4. These means of production are used for maximising profits for their owners.
5. Right of free enterprise is guaranteed.
6. There is competition among firms.
7. Price mechanism allocates resources.

The chief advantages of capitalism include efficiency in production, competition, hard work, risk taking, research and development and innovations. Initiative and efficiency are inherent in the capitalistic form of economic organisation.

Recurrent business depressions are a great defect of capitalism. During a depression, the automatic controls of the price system fail, the industrial production is below installed capacity and there is widespread unemployment. Another disadvantage of capitalism is the presence of extreme economic inequalities. Capitalism also suffers from excessive emphasis on materialism, consumerism, selfishness and cut-throat competition.

4.3 Socialist Economy

It is an economic system under which means of production are owned by the state. A socialist or a centrally planned economy is totally different from a capitalist economy. It has the following features.

1. Means of production are owned by the state, i.e. all land, buildings, factories, machines and equipments are the property of the government.
2. Private property is prohibited barring the holding of small pieces of land for personal cultivation, petty trade transactions etc.
3. Means of production are used by the state for the general welfare of society.
4. Government enjoys monopoly in the production and distribution of goods and services.
5. Prices of commodities and factors of production are fixed by the government and therefore, price mechanism has limited role to play.

Advantages of a socialist society include: (a) equitable distribution of national output, (b) no exploitation of man by man, (c) employment guaranteed to every person and (d) high regard for social values.

Disadvantages of a socialist society include: (a) lack of incentives to work hard and take risks, (b) rigidity in the economy, (c) excessive bureaucratisation, and (d) loss of economic and political freedom.

4.4 Mixed Economy

A mixed economy is one where capitalism and socialism coexist. In the real world, there are no purely capitalist or socialist economies. Even in US, some buildings, equipment and machines are owned by the government. Contrarily, in a socialist state some small farms or shops are owned by private individuals. Strictly speaking, every economy of the world is a mixed economy. The important thing is the degree by which an economic system is diluted by a different form of economic organisation. In US, the dilution of capitalism is very less while it is quite significant in Russia. A good example of a mixed economy is provided by India where government owns a substantial part of the resources, particularly in the industrial and financial sectors.

4.5 Basic Features of an Economy

All economics of the world are characterised by three basic features which are the source of all economic problems.

1. **Resources are Limited:** Resources like land, minerals, and skilled workers are limited in every country. It is true that some economics have more resources than others but there is always a limit to the availability of resources everywhere. Since the resources are limited, the capacity of every economy to produce goods and services is also limited.
2. **Wants are Unlimited:** Human wants everywhere are unlimited or insatiable. Even in rich countries of the world, there is no end to the demand for goods and services. Human wants arise again and again and multiply with the advancement of society.
3. **Resources Have Alternative Uses:** Most economic resources can be put to various uses. For example, a hectare of land can be used for growing wheat or as a playground or as a garden and so on. However, it cannot be used for all these purpose simultaneously. Most economic problems arise because of this feature of resources.

4.6 Basic Problems of an Economy

Every country is faced with a host of economic problems. Some of these problems are specific to the country concerned. However, there are three economic problems which are common to all economies of the world. These three problems arise due to the foregoing characteristics of an economy. Since every country has to face these problems they are called central (or basic or fundamental) problems of an economy. These problems were there in olden days, are present in modern times and will be faced in future. These problems which arise in a given sequence are the following.

4.6.1 What to Produce? Since resources are scarce, it is not possible for a country to produce as much of every commodity as desired by its citizens. For example, if more land is devoted to the cultivation of wheat, less would be available for growing sugarcane. Similarly, if more steel is used for construction of buildings, less would be available for railways. In short, more of one commodity usually means less of others. Therefore, every economy must decide which goods to produce and in what quantity. This is precisely the problem of allocation of resources.

4.6.2 How to Produce? The second problem pertains to choosing an appropriate technology for the production of various goods and services. It is well-known that most commodities can be produced using different combinations of factors of production. For example, we can produce cloth using a modern automatic textile machine or with the help of handlooms. Apparently, some techniques use more capital as compared to labour and are, therefore, called capital-intensive or labour-saving techniques of production. Conversely, certain other methods of production use more of labour than capital and, therefore, are called labour-intensive or capital-saving techniques of production. Every society must decide which type of technique it has to adopt in the production process. In other words, this problem relates to the ratio in which factors of production (land, labour and capital) are to be used in the production process.

4.6.3 For Whom to Produce? Since resources are scarce, the production of goods and services is limited. It is not possible to satisfy all the wants of all the people of a country. Thus, very few people get motor cars in a poor country while most others are left desiring it. There must be some mechanism to decide as to how many of the wants of each individual are to be satisfied. In other words, the society must evolve some method so that total production gets distributed among different individuals in a lawful manner. This is the problem of distribution of national income.

The three basic problems of an economy mentioned above are common to all types of economic system, be it capitalism, socialism, or some other form of economic organisation. However, different economic systems solve these problems differently. Let us now understand how these problems are solved in different economic systems.

4.7 Solution of Basic Problems in a Capitalist Economy

In a capitalist or a free enterprise economy, the means of production are owned by private individuals or groups of individuals (companies, partnership firms etc.). These means of production are used for maximising profit for the owners. Competition is another feature of a capitalist society. These characteristics of a capitalist society must be kept in mind to understand the solution of central problems in it.

Price mechanism is the instrument through which a capitalist society solves its central problems. Producers produce those goods for which consumers are willing to pay prices which, besides covering the cost of production, generate sufficient profit for them. Normally, an increase in the price of a commodity increases its supply and vice versa. Irrespective of the needs of the community, producers will produce those goods which bring them the maximum profit. Millions of producers act independently in taking production decisions without any central guidance. Still, only those goods are produced which the consumers want the most. This is the wonder of price mechanism.

The problem of choice of technology is also solved by the operation of prices, this time the prices of factors of production. Every producer tries to minimise his cost of production. For this purpose, he takes into account the price of labour (wage rate), price of capital services (interest rates) and so on. He will mix different factors of production in such a way that his per unit or average cost is minimised. He will use less of expensive factors of production and more of relatively cheap factors of production. For example, low wage rate of unskilled labour in India is primarily responsible for widespread adoption of labour-intensive technology. Thus, the second fundamental problem is also solved by price mechanism.

Solution of the third problem also lies in the price mechanism. The economy will produce commodities for those who have the money to pay for them. The higher the income of an individual, the more commodities he will get. Those who have less purchasing power will claim a lesser share in the national product. The purchasing power of an individual is determined by: (a) the price of the commodity or service which he is offering in the market, and (b) the prices of commodities and services which he is purchasing in the market. Thus, if the price of his commodity or service remains the same but prices of commodities purchased by him increase, then his share in national product will decrease.

It is clear that price mechanism (fluctuations in prices and the effects thereof) forms the basis of the functioning of a capitalist society.

4.8 Solution of Basic Problems in a Socialist Society

Socialist or a centrally planned economy is an economic system totally different from a capitalist society. In a socialist economy, the means of production are owned by the state, i.e. all land, buildings, factories and machines and equipments are the property of the government. In other words, private property is prohibited. Means of production are used by the state for the general welfare of society. Government enjoys monopoly in the production and distribution of all goods and services. In such a society, prices of commodities and factors of production are fixed by the government. Therefore, price mechanism has no role to play and all decisions regarding production, choice of technology, and distribution are taken by government agencies such as the planning commission. On the basis of past records, the planning commission allocates resources for various uses in such a way that different commodities are produced according to their likely demand. If the actual demand for a commodity exceeds or falls short of the available supply, the administration will revise its production decision for the next year. In short, socialist society works on the basis of *trial and error method.* It is not a flexible system like a free enterprise economy.

Second problem (choice of technology) is also solved by administrative decisions. Unlike a capitalist society, wages are fixed by the government in a socialist society. Government agencies like planning commission take stock of the available factors of production. If the choice of a particular technology leaves part of the labour force unemployed then in the next round the authorities will opt for a more labour-intensive technique of production.

In a socialist society, the distribution of national income is more equitable. Since everybody is a wage earner therefore inequalities of income are modest. The basic philosophy of a socialist society is: from each according to his ability and to each according to his needs. Thus, government ensures equity and fairness in the distribution of available supplies of goods and services. In brief, the role of price mechanism is played by economic planning in a socialist society.

4.9 Solution of Basic Problems in a Mixed Economy

Solution of the central problems in a mixed economy is partly on the basis of price mechanism and partly through administrative decisions of the government. The private sector of a mixed economy behaves in the same way as a capitalist economy (maximising profit). Conversely, the public sector in a mixed economy is not always guided by the objective of profit maximisation. Many public enterprises are set up in backward areas to provide employment and income to the people of that region. Similarly, the prices of public sector products are fixed by the government. Government also interferes in the working of the economy through fiscal and monetary measures and sometimes through physical controls like rationing.

Thus, every economy has to solve the central problems and various methods are adopted for this purpose.

5

Stages of Economic Growth Propounded by W.W. Rostow

Stages of economic growth were advocated by American economist Walt Whitman Rostow in 1960. His model postulates that economic growth occurs in five basic stages of varying length:

1. Traditional society.
2. Transitional stage (or pre-conditions for take-off).
3. Take-off.
4. Drive to maturity.
5. Age of high mass consumption.

Each of these five stages is explained below.

5.1 Traditional Society

An economy in this stage has a limited production function which barely attains the minimum level of potential output. This does not entirely mean that the economy's production level is static. The output level can still be increased, as there was often a surplus of uncultivated land which can be used for increasing agricultural production. Modern science and technology has yet to be introduced. As a result, these pre-Newtonian societies, unaware of the possibilities to manipulate the external world, rely heavily on manual labour and self-sufficiency to survive. States and individuals utilize irrigation systems in many instances, but most farming is still purely for subsistence. There have been technological innovations, but only on ad hoc basis. All of that this can result in increases in output, but never beyond an upper limit which cannot be crossed. Trade is predominantly regional and local, largely done through barter, and the monetary system is not well developed.

Wars, famines and epidemics like plague cause expanding population to halt or shrink, limiting the single greatest factor of production, i.e. human manual labour. Volume fluctuations in trade due to political instability are frequent; historically, trading was subject to great risk and transport of goods and raw materials was expensive, difficult, slow and unreliable. The manufacturing sector and other industries have a tendency to grow but are limited by inadequate scientific knowledge and a backward or highly traditionalist frame of mind which contributes to low labour productivity. In this stage, some regions are entirely self-sufficient.

In settled agricultural societies before the Industrial Revolution, a hierarchical social structure relied on near-absolute reverence for tradition, and an insistence on obedience and submission. This resulted in concentration of political power in the hands of landowners in most cases; everywhere, family and lineage, and marriage ties, constituted the primary social organization, along with religious customs, and the state only rarely interacted with local populations and in limited spheres of life. This social structure was generally feudalistic in nature. Under modern conditions, these characteristics have been modified by outside influences, but the least developed regions and societies fit this description quite accurately.

In short, a traditional society is characterized by the following:

1. Subsistence agriculture or hunting and gathering; almost wholly a primary sector economy.
2. Limited technology.
3. Some advancements and improvements to processes, but limited ability for economic growth because of the absence of modern technologies, lack of class or individual economic mobility, with stability prioritized and change seen negatively.
4. This is where society generally begins before progressing towards the next stages of growth.
5. No centralized nation or political system.

5.2 Transitional Stage (or Pre-conditions for Take-off)

In the second stage of economic growth, the economy undergoes changes for building up of conditions for growth and take-off. These changes in society and the economy have to be of fundamental nature in the socio-political structure and production techniques. There is also a second or third pattern in which there is no need for change in socio-political structure because these economies are not deeply caught up in older, traditional social and political structures. The only changes required are in economic and technical dimensions.

There are three important dimensions to this transition: firstly, the shift from an agrarian to an industrial or manufacturing society begins, albeit slowly. Secondly, trade and other commercial activities of the nation broaden the market's reach not only to neighbouring areas but also to far-flung regions, creating international markets. Lastly, the surplus attained should not be wasted on the conspicuous consumption of the land owners or the state, but should be spent on the development of industries, infrastructure and thereby prepare for self-sustained growth of the economy later on. Furthermore, agriculture becomes commercialized and mechanized via technological advancement; shifts increasingly towards cash or export-oriented crops, and there is a growth of agricultural entrepreneurship.

According to Rostow capital formation depends on the productivity of agriculture and the creation of social overhead capital. Agriculture plays a very important role in this transition process as the surplus quantity of the product is to be utilized to support an increasingly urban population of workers and also becomes a major exporting sector, earning foreign exchange for continued development and capital formation. Increases in agricultural productivity also lead to the expansion of the domestic markets for manufactured goods and processed commodities, which adds to the growth of investment in the industrial sector.

Social overhead capital creation can only be undertaken by the government, in

Rostow's view. Government plays the driving role in the development of social overhead capital as it is rarely profitable, it has a long gestation period, and the pay-offs accrue to all economic sectors, not primarily to the investing entity; thus the private sector is not interested in playing a major role in its development.

All these changes effectively prepare the way for take-off only if there is a basic change in the attitude of society towards risk-taking, changes in the working environment, and openness to change in social and political organizations and structures.

The pre-conditions to take-off begin from an external intervention by more developed and advanced societies, which set in motion ideas and sentiments which initiated the process by which a modern alternative to the traditional society was constructed out of the old culture.

In short, following are the characteristics when an economy is in transitional stage:

1. External demand for raw materials initiates economic change.
2. Development of more productive, commercial agriculture and cash crops not consumed by producers and/or largely exported.
3. Widespread and enhanced investment in changes to the physical environment to expand production (i.e. irrigation, canals, ports).
4. Increasing spread of technology and advances in existing technologies.
5. Changing social structure, with previous social equilibrium now in flux.
6. Individual social mobility begins.
7. Development of national identity and shared economic interests.

5.3 Take-off

This stage is characterized by dynamic economic growth. As Rostow suggests, all is premised on a sharp stimulus that is any or all of economic, political and technological change. The main feature of this stage is rapid, self-sustained growth. Take-off occurs when sector led growth becomes common and society is driven more by economic processes than traditions. At this point, the norms of economic growth are well-established and growth becomes a nation's *second nature* and a shared goal. According to Rostow, there are three main requirements for take-off:

1. The rate of productive investment should rise from approximately 5 percent to over 10 percent of national income or net national product.
2. The development of one or more substantial manufacturing sectors, with a high rate of growth.
3. The existence or quick emergence of a political, social and institutional framework which exploits the impulses to expansion in the modern sector and the potential external economy effects of the take-off.

The third requirement implies that the needed capital must be mobilized from domestic resources and steered into the economy, rather than into domestic or state consumption. Industrialization becomes a crucial phenomenon as it helps to prepare the basic structure for structural changes on a massive scale. Rostow says that this transition does not follow a set trend as there are a variety of different motivations or stimulus which began this growth process.

Take off requires a large and sufficient amount of loanable funds for expansion of the industrial sector which generally come from two sources which are: (a) shifts in income flows by way of taxation, implementation of land reforms and various other fiscal measures, and (b) re-investment of profits earned from foreign trade as has been observed in many East Asian countries.

The take-off also needs a group of entrepreneurs in the society who pursue innovation and accelerate the rate of growth in the economy. For such an entrepreneurial class to develop an ethos of *delayed gratification*, a preference for capital accumulation over expenditure, and high tolerance of risk must be present.

In short, take-off stage exhibits the following features:

1. Urbanization increases, industrialization proceeds, technological breakthroughs occur.
2. Secondary (manufacturing) goods producing sector expands and ratio of secondary to primary (agricultural) sector in the economy shifts quickly towards the secondary sector.
3. Textiles and apparel are usually the first *take-off* industry, as happened in Great Britain's classic Industrial Revolution.
4. Growth is concentrated in few regions of the country.

5.4 Drive to Maturity

After the take-off, there follows a long interval of sustained growth, known as the stage of drive towards maturity. Rostow defines it "as the period when a society has effectively applied the range of modern technology to the bulk of its resources". Now regularly growing economy drives to extend modern technology over the whole front of its economic activity. Some 10-20 percent of the national income is steadily invested, permitting output regularly to outstrip the increase in population. The makeup of the economy changes unceasingly as technique improves, new industries accelerate, older industries level off. The economy finds its place in the international economy. Goods formerly imported are produced at home. The leading sectors in an economy will be determined by the nature of resource endowments and not only by technology.

During this stage a country has to decide whether the industrial power and technology it has generated is to be used for the welfare of its people or to gain supremacy over others. This diversity leads to reduction in poverty rate and increasing standards of living, as the society no longer needs to sacrifice its comfort in order to build up certain sectors.

In short, this stage has the following characteristics:

1. Diversification of the industrial base; multiple industries expand and new ones take root quickly.
2. Manufacturing shifts from investment-driven (capital goods) towards consumer durables and domestic consumption.
3. Rapid development of transportation infrastructure.
4. Large-scale investment in social infrastructure (schools, universities, hospitals etc.).

5.5 Age of High Mass Consumption

The age of high mass consumption refers to the period of contemporary comfort afforded by many western nations, wherein consumers concentrate on durable goods, and hardly remember the subsistence concerns of previous stages.

In the age of high mass consumption, a society is able to choose between concentrating on military and security issues, on equality and welfare issues, or on developing great luxuries for its upper class. Each country in this position chooses its own balance between these three goals. There is a desire to develop an egalitarian society and measures are taken to reach this goal. According to Rostow, a country tries to determine its uniqueness and factors affecting it are its political, geographical and cultural structure and also values present in its society.

In short, this stage is marked by the following features:

1. Industrial base dominates the economy; the primary sector is of greatly diminished weight in the economy and society.
2. Widespread and normative consumption of high-value consumer goods (e.g., automobiles).
3. Consumers typically (if not universally), have disposable income beyond all basic needs for additional goods.
4. Urban society (a movement away from rural country sides to the cities).

5.6 Critical Assessment

According to Rostow countries go through each of these stages fairly linearly. Not all of the conditions were certain to occur at each stage, however, and the stages and transition periods may occur at varying lengths from country to country, and even from region to region.

Rostow's model is a part of the liberal school of economics, laying emphasis on the efficacy of modern concepts of free trade and the ideas of Adam Smith. It disagrees with Friedrich List's argument which states that economies which rely on exports of raw materials may get *locked in,* and would not be able to diversify. Rostow's model states that economies may need to depend on raw material exports to finance the development of industrial sector which has not yet of achieved superior level of the competitiveness in the early stages of take-off. Rostow's model does not disagree with John Maynard Keynes regarding the importance of government control over domestic development which is not generally accepted by some ardent free trade advocates. The basic assumption given by Rostow is that countries want to modernize and grow and that society will agree to the materialistic norms of economic growth.

Rostow's model has been criticized on following grounds:

1. Rostow is historical in the sense that the end result is known at the outset and is derived from the historical geography of a developed, bureaucratic society.
2. Rostow is mechanical in the sense that the underlying motor of change is not disclosed and therefore the stages become little more than a classificatory system based on data from developed countries.

3. His model is based on American and European history and defines the American norm of high mass consumption as integral to the economic development process of all industrialized societies.
4. His model assumes the inevitable adoption of Neo-liberal trade policies which allow the manufacturing base of a given advanced polity to be relocated to lower-wage regions.
5. Rostow's model does not apply to the Asian and the African countries as events in these countries are not justified in any stage of his model.
6. Rostow's thesis is biased towards western model of modernization.

6

Economic Growth Model of Robert Solow

The Solow growth model is a model of economic growth which analyzes changes in the level of output in an economy over time as a result of changes in the population, the savings rate, and the rate of technological progress. The Solow model is the basis for the modern theory of economic growth.

Solow model of growth is a part of macroeconomics, the study of which involves many variables. It is very difficult to construct a model that explains all macroeconomic phenomena. If at all attempted, such a model would be complicated and unwieldy, making it difficult to draw any meaningful conclusions. For this reason, economists tend to adopt a more realistic approach by developing models with few selected variables. The first model of economic growth originally developed by American economist and Nobel laureate Robert Solow in the 1950s is a good example of this approach.

Solow's purpose in developing the growth model was to deliberately ignore some important aspects of macroeconomics, such as short-run fluctuations in employment, in order to develop a model that attempted to describe the long-run evolution of the economy. His paper titled, "A Contribution to the Theory of Economic Growth", published in the *Quarterly Journal of Economics*, 1956, remains highly influential even today and, despite its relative simplicity, it conveys a number of very useful insights about the dynamics of the growth process.

Solow model is also important from a methodological perspective because it provides a simple example of the type of dynamic model that is commonly used in present day macroeconomic theory. The model assumes that gross domestic product (GDP) is produced according to an aggregate production function technology.

6.1 Production Function

It is worth noting that most of the key results for Solow model can be obtained using any of the standard production functions that we come across in microeconomic production theory.

A production function explains the technological relationship between inputs and output.

$P = f(F_1, F_2, ...F_n)$

In the above, P is the quantity of production and F_1, F_2,...F_n are the quantities of different factors of production. Modern economists emphasise the importance of labour (L) and capital (K) in the production process. Land as a factor of production is considered unimportant or as a part of capital and thus ignored. Therefore, the simplified production function becomes:

$P = f(L, K)$

The relationship between inputs and output can be studied in two ways:

1. What happens to output as more of the variable factor is applied to a given quantity of the fixed factor. This is the study of the *law of diminishing returns*. It is also called the *law of variable proportions*.
2. What happens to output when all inputs are increased in a given proportion. This is the study of the *laws of returns to scale*.

A widely used production function takes the Cobb-Douglas form.

6.1.1 Cobb-Douglas Production Function: Named after its authors, Paul H. Douglas and Charles Cobb, it is a linear and homogeneous production function yielding constant returns to a proportionate increase in the use of all inputs. It takes the following form:

$Y = kL^{a}C^{(1-a)}$

Where,

Y represents income (output)

L is the quantity of labour input

C is the capital employed and

k and a are positive constants (and $a < 1$).

6.1.2 Constant Returns to Scale: Solow model assumes that the production function exhibits constant returns to scale. This case refers to that situation where if factors are increased in a given proportion, the output also increases in the same proportion. For example, if capital and labour are doubled, the output is also doubled. We may come across such a production situation in real life. If one worker working on a machine produces 5 units of a commodity, it can be expected that two workers working on two identical machines will produce 10 units of the commodity.

6.2 Assumptions of Solow Model

1. Population grows at a constant rate g. Therefore, the current population (represented by N) and future population (represented by N') are linked through the population growth equation:

   $N' = N(1+g)$

   If the current population is 100 and its growth rate is 3 percent, the future population is 103.
2. All consumers in the economy save a constant proportion (represented by s) of their incomes and consume the rest. Therefore, consumption (represented by C) and output (represented by Y) are linked through the consumption equation:

   $C = (1-s).Y.$

   If a consumer earns 100 units of output as income and the savings rate is 40 percent, then the consumer consumes 60 units and saves 40 units.
3. All firms in the economy produce output using the same production technology that takes in capital and labour as inputs. Therefore, the level of output (represented by Y), the level of capital (represented by K), and the level of labour (represented by L) are all linked through the production function equation

   $Y = aF(K, L).$

4. Present capital stock (represented by K), future capital stock (represented by K'), the rate of capital depreciation (represented by d), and level of capital investment (represented by I) are linked through the capital accumulation equation
   $K' = K(1-d) + I$.

6.3 Solving the Solow Model

In our analysis, we have assumed Cobb-Douglas production function. We also assume that firms are competitive, i.e. they are price-taker. In other words, no market participant is able to dictate the prices in a market. For such a price-taker firm, output per worker is given through the following equation:

$y = ak^b$

Where,

$y = Y/L$ (output per worker)

$k = K/L$ (capital stock per worker)

Coefficient b is the capital share (the share of income that capital receives).

The Solow model does not attempt to explain fluctuations in multiple variables. However, it does characterise the dynamics of the model well enough to be able to figure out what happens if selected variables change. For example, what happens when there is increase in the rate of savings. An increase in the saving rate can raise the growth rate initially by boosting capital accumulation. But diminishing marginal returns implies that during this period capital growth will outstrip output growth. And this will not last because capital growth depends negatively on the capital-output ratio. So higher saving rates can produce temporary increases in the growth rate of output, but cannot get the economy to a path involving a faster steady-state growth rate. Capital-output ratio is the ratio between the book value of plant and machinery and gross value of output of a firm. Also called *capital coefficient,* it measures capacity utilisation and capital intensity of a firm/industry.

There is an important qualification to the decomposition of growth into capital deepening and technological progress. Such decompositions are quite commonly carried out, concluding that a certain fraction of the growth in output per worker over a certain period was due to capital deepening. However, these calculations are based on an arithmetic decomposition of the growth in output per worker, and should not be confused with an economic theory explaining the ultimate sources of growth.

6.4 Implications and Conclusions of the Solow Model

There is no growth in the long-term. If countries have the same g (population growth rate), s (savings rate), and d (capital depreciation rate), then they have the same steady state, so they will converge, i.e. the Solow growth model predicts conditional convergence. Along this convergence path, a poorer country grows faster.

Countries with different saving rates have different steady states, and they will not converge, i.e. the Solow growth model does not predict absolute convergence. When saving rates are different, growth is not always higher in a country with lower initial capital stock.

In particular, the Solow model tells us that we should be careful not to draw from such calculations that policies based solely on encouraging capital deepening are capable of boosting the growth rate in the long-run. Diminishing marginal productivity of capital implies that steady growth can not be maintained based on capital deepening alone. Ultimately, it is technological progress that offsets the effects of diminishing marginal returns, and thus allows capital deepening to play a role along the steady growth path.

In essence, there are two sources of increases in output per worker:

1. Technological progress.
2. Capital deepening (i.e. increases in capital per worker).

The Solow model provides a useful framework to understand how technological progress and capital deepening interact to determine the growth rate of output per worker.

7

Harrod-Domar Model of Economic Growth

An economic model is a statement of relationship among economic variables. It is used to explain the cause and effect relationship among variables. Economic models are helpful in explaining and predicting economic phenomena like rate of growth of an economy. Aggregate models deal with the economy as a whole. Sectoral models examine particular sectors of the economy like industry or agriculture. Inter-industry models explain relationship among various sectors of the economy, using the popular technique of input-output matrices.

Harrod-Domar growth model is a synthesis of the results of two consecutive independent studies by British economist Roy Harrod's *Theory of Dynamic Theory* (1939) and the American economist Evsey Domar's *Capital Expansion, Growth and Jobs* (1946). Harrod-Domar model is used in development economics to explain an economy's growth rate in terms of the level of savings and capital-output ratio. It suggests that there is no natural reason for an economy to have balanced growth.

Harrod-Domar model of growth suggests that the rate of economic growth depends on two things:

1. **Level of Savings:** Higher savings enable higher investment.
2. **Capital-Output Ratio:** A lower capital-output ratio means investment is more efficient and the growth rate will be higher.

7.1 Harrod-Domar Model: An Overview

According to Harrod-Domar model

$g = s/k$

Where,

g is rate of economic growth.

s is level of savings (i.e. average propensity to save which is the ratio of national savings to national income).

k is capital-output ratio (i.e. the amount of capital needed to increase output. A high capital-output ratio means investment is inefficient.

Higher savings enable greater investment in capital stock.

Capital-output ratio (also called capital coefficient), measures the capacity utilisation and capital intensity of a firm.

Thus, suppose that 12 percent of total output is saved annually and that three units of capital are required to produce an additional unit of output. Then the rate of growth in output is 12/3% = 4% per annum. This result is obtained from the basic assumption that whatever is saved will be automatically invested and converted into an increase in output on the basis of a given capital-output ratio. Since a given proportion of this increase in output will be saved and invested on the same basis, a continuous process of growth is maintained.

Growth theory, particularly the Harrod-Domar growth equation, has been frequently applied to the economic planning of developing countries. The planner starts from a desired target rate of growth of perhaps 4 percent. Assuming a fixed overall capital-output ratio of say 3, it is then asserted that the developing country will be able to achieve this target rate of growth if it can increase its savings to 3 × 4 percent = 12 percent of its total output.

7.2 Warranted, Actual and Natural Rate of Growth

According to the Harrod–Domar model there are three kinds of growth: warranted growth, actual growth and natural rate of growth.

Warranted growth rate is the rate of growth at which the economy does not expand indefinitely or go into recession. This is the growth rate at which all saving is absorbed into investment (e.g. ₹ 80 crore of saving = ₹ 80 crore of investment). Let us assume, the saving rate is 10% and the capital-output ratio is 4. In other words, ₹ 10 crore of investment increases output by ₹ 2.5 crore. In this case, the economy's warranted growth rate is 2.5 percent (ten divided by four). This is the growth rate at which the ratio of capital to output would stay constant at four.

Actual growth is the real rate increase in a country's GDP per year.

Natural growth rate is the rate of economic growth required to maintain full employment. If labour force grows at 3 percent per year, then to maintain full employment, the economy's annual growth rate must be 3 percent. This assumes no change in labour productivity which is unrealistic.

7.3 Importance of Harrod-Domar Model

Although the Harrod-Domar model was initially created to help analyse the business cycle, it was later adapted to explain economic growth. Its implications were that growth depends on the quantity of labour and capital. More investment leads to capital accumulation, which generates economic growth. The model carries implications for less developed countries (LDCs), where labour is in plentiful supply but physical capital is not, slowing down economic progress. LDCs do not have sufficiently high incomes to enable sufficient rates of saving. Therefore, accumulation of physical capital stock through investment is low.

The model implies that economic growth depends on policies to increase investment, by increasing saving, and using that investment more efficiently through technological advances. It is argued that in developing countries low rates of economic growth and development are linked to low saving rates. This creates a vicious cycle of low investment, low output and low savings. To boost economic growth rates, it is necessary to increase savings either domestically or from abroad. Higher savings create a virtuous circle of self-sustaining economic growth. The transfer of capital to developing economies should enable higher growth, which, in turn, will lead to higher savings and growth will become more self-sustaining. The model concludes that an economy does not *naturally* find full employment and stable growth rates.

7.4 Criticisms of Harrod-Domar Model

1. Developing countries find it difficult to increase saving. Increasing savings ratios may be inappropriate when you are struggling to get enough food to eat.
2. The model ignores factors such as labour productivity, technological innovation and levels of corruption. Harrod-Domar model is at best an oversimplification of complex factors which go into economic growth.
3. It assumes the existences of a reliable finance and transport system. Often the problem for developing countries is a lack of investment in these areas.
4. Harrod-Domar model assumes there is no reason for the actual growth to equal natural growth and that an economy has no tendency to full employment. This is based on the belief that the relative price of labour and capital is fixed, and that they are used in equal proportions.
5. The effectiveness of foreign capital flows can vary. In the 1970s and 1980s many developing economies borrowed from abroad which led to an inflow of foreign capital. However, there was a lack of skilled labour to make effective use of capital. This led to very high capital-output ratios and growth rates did not increase significantly. However, developing economies were left with high debt repayments and when interest rates rose, a large proportion of national savings was diverted to debt repayments.
6. The model also assumes that savings rates are constant, which may not be true, and assumes that the marginal returns to capital are constant. Furthermore, the model has been criticized for the assumption that productive capacity is proportional to capital stock.
7. The model assumes a fixed overall capital-output ratio, which does away with all the vital problems affecting the developing country's capacity to absorb capital and invest its saving in a productive manner. These problems include the central problem of the efficient allocation of available savings among alternative investment opportunities and the associated organizational and institutional problems of encouraging the growth of a sufficient supply of entrepreneurs.

7.5 Harrod-Domar Model versus Solow Model

Modern growth theory was born after Second World War with the works of Roy Harrod and Evsey Domar. Growth became almost everybody's concern, partly because of the fear of stagnation and also the need for reconstruction of devastated economies during the war.

The second wave of interest in growth theory was launched in the form of neo-classical growth models by Robert Solow, Jan Tinbergen, and James Tobin. Solow's model came into existence as a reaction to the Harrod-Domar model and some deficiencies associated with it. The empirical observations that real economies were not as wildly unstable as the Harrod-Domar model assumed propelled Solow to develop the basic neo-classical model.

Solow noted that the characteristic and powerful conclusion of the Harrod-Domar model was that even for the long-run the economic system was best balanced on a knife-edge of equilibrium growth. Solow attributed this result to dubious assumptions, in particular the assumption of fixed production coefficients for the economy as a whole. Solow abandoned this fixed coefficient technology and replaced it by a technology which allows substitution between the two factors of production, viz. capital and labour.

To sum up, Harrod-Domar model emphasizes economic growth which is interpreted as sustained increase in real per capita income in an economy. However, modern economists distinguish between economic growth and economic development. Economic development is a much wider term. It includes economic growth and at the same time encompasses questions regarding pattern of production, distribution of income and consumption behaviour of the people. In other words, economic development is economic growth plus qualitative changes in productivity, socio-economic institutions and distribution pattern. Hence, Harrod-Domar model falls short of explaining economic progress as it is understood in the present context.

8

Big Push and Critical Minimum Effort Models of Economic Growth

8.1 Big Push Model of Growth

Paul Rosenstein-Rodan propounded this model of growth in 1943. Analysis of this economic model ordinarily involves using game theory.

This model emphasizes that underdeveloped countries require large amounts of investments to embark on the path of economic development from their present state of backwardness. This theory proposes that a 'bit by bit' investment programme will not impact the process of growth as much as is required for developing countries. In fact, injections of small quantities of investments will merely lead to wastage of resources. There is a minimum level of resources that must be devoted to a development programme if it is to have any chance of success. Launching a country into self-sustaining growth is a little like getting an airplane off the ground. There is a critical ground speed which must be passed before the craft can become airborne.

Rosenstein-Rodan argued that the entire industry which is intended to be created should be treated and planned as a massive entity. He supports this argument by stating that the social marginal product of an investment is always different from its private marginal product, so when a group of industries are planned together according to their social marginal products, the rate of growth of the economy is greater than it would have otherwise been.

8.1.1 The Three Indivisibilities: According to Rosenstein-Rodan, there exist three indivisibilities in underdeveloped countries. These indivisibilities are responsible for external economies and thus justify the need for a big push. The indivisibilities are as follows-

1. Indivisibility in production function.
2. Indivisibility of demand.
3. Indivisibility in the supply of savings.

A. Indivisibility in Production Function: Indivisibilities in the production function may be with respect to any of the following: (a) inputs, (b) processes or (c) outputs.

These lead to increasing returns (i.e. economies of scale), and may require a high optimum size of a firm. This can be achieved even in developing countries since at least one optimum scale firm can be established in many industries. But investment in social overhead capital comprises investment in all basic industries (like power, transport or communications) which must necessarily come before directly productive investment activities. Investment in social overhead capital is *lumpy* in nature. Such capital requirements cannot be imported from other nations. Therefore, heavy initial investment necessarily needs to be made in social overhead capital. Social overhead capital is further characterized by four indivisibilities:

1. **Irreversibility in Time:** It must precede other directly productive investments.
2. **Minimum Durability of Equipment:** Any lesser level of durability is either impossible due to technical reasons or much less efficient.
3. **Long Gestation Periods:** The investment in social overhead capital takes time to generate returns and its impact in the economy is not immediately or directly visible.
4. **Irreducible Minimum Social Overhead Capital-Industry Mix:** Investment needs to be of a certain minimum magnitude and spread across a mix of industries, without which it will not significantly impact the process of growth.

B. Indivisibility of Demand: Developing countries are characterized by low per capita income and purchasing power. Markets in these countries are therefore small. In a closed economy, modernization and increased efficiency in a single industry has no impact on the economy as a whole since the output of that industry will fail to find a market. A large number of industries need to be set up simultaneously so that people employed in one industry consume the output of other industries and thus create complementary demand.

To illustrate this, Rosenstein-Rodan gives the example of a shoe industry. If a country makes large investments in the shoe industry, all the disguisedly employed labour from the other industries find work and a source of income, leading to a rise in production of shoes and their own incomes. This increased income will not be expended only on buying shoes. It is conceivable that the increased incomes will lead to increased spending on other products too. However, there is no corresponding supply of these products to satisfy this increased demand for the other goods. Following the basic market forces of demand and supply, the prices of these commodities will rise. To avoid such a situation, investment must be spread out amongst different industries.

The situation may be different in an open economy as the output of the new industry may replace former imports or possibly find its market by way of exports. But even if the world market acts as a substitute for domestic demand, a big push is still needed.

C. Indivisibility in the Supply of Savings: High levels of investment require a corresponding high level of savings. We cannot always rely on foreign aid as the huge levels of investments in the different sectors need to be made not only once, but multiple times. Hence domestic savings are a must. But in an underdeveloped economy, this is a challenge due to the low income levels. The marginal rate of savings needs to be increased following the rise in incomes due to higher investment.

8.1.2 Role of the State: The large-scale programme of industrialization advocated by this model requires huge investments that are beyond the means of the private sector. The investment in infrastructure and basic industries (like power, transport and communications) is *lumpy* and has long gestation periods. The role of the state in this theory is therefore critical for investment in social overhead capital. Even if the private sector had the requisite resources to invest in such a programme, it would not do so since it is driven by profit motives. Many investments are profitable in terms of social marginal net product but not in terms of private marginal net product. Due to this, there is no incentive for individual entrepreneurs to invest and take advantage of external economies.

8.1.3 Criticisms of Big Push Model: The theory has been criticized by Hla Myint and Celso Furtado, among others, primarily on the grounds of the massive effort required to be taken by underdeveloped countries to move along the path of industrialization. Some of the major criticisms are as follows:

1. **Shortage of Resources in Underdeveloped Countries:** Big push theory is criticised on the grounds that underdeveloped countries lack the capital required to provide the big push required for rapid development. If an underdeveloped nation had ample capital supply and scarce factors, it would not be classified as *underdeveloped* at all. Limited resource availability is the first impediment to such countries. Though this problem may be overcome by foreign aids, industrialization may not take off as expected if the aid flows are volatile.
2. **Neglect of Agricultural Sector:** With its heavy emphasis on industry, the model finds no place for agriculture. This is a gaping flaw in the theory, as in most underdeveloped countries it is this sector which is large and has labour surplus. Investments in agriculture need to go hand-in-hand with those in industry so as to stimulate the industrial sector by providing a market for industrial goods. If neglected, it would be difficult to meet the food requirements of the nation in the short run and to significantly expand the size of the market in the long-run.
3. **Difficulties in Execution and Implementation:** The execution of related projects during the course of industrialization may involve unexpected or unavoidable changes due to revisions of plans, delays and deviations from the planned process. Hla Myint notes that the various departments and agencies involved in the process of development need to coordinate closely and evaluate and revise plans continuously. This is a challenging task for the governments of developing countries.
4. **Lack of Absorptive Capacity:** The implementation of industrialization programmes may be constrained by ineffective disbursement, short-term bottlenecks, macroeconomic problems and volatility, loss of competitiveness and weakening of institutions. Credit is often utilized at low rates or after long time lags. There is often a loss of competitiveness due to the Dutch disease effect.
5. **Problems in Mixed Economies:** In a mixed economy, where the private and public sectors co-exist, the environment for growth may not be a conducive one. Unless there is a complementarity between the sectors, there is bound to arise competition between them, with the government departments keeping their plans confidential out of fear of speculative activities by the private sector. The private sector's activities are simultaneously inhibited due to lack of information of government policies and the general economic situation.
6. **Neglect of Techniques of Production:** Rather than capital formation, it is productive techniques which determine the success of a country in economic development. The big push model ignores productive techniques in its support for capital formation and industrialisation.
7. **Historical Inaccuracy:** When viewed in light of historical experience of countries over the last two centuries, no country displayed any evidence of development due to

massive industrialization programmes. Stationary economies do not develop simply by making large-scale investment in social overhead capital.

8.2 Critical Minimum Effort Model

The critical minimum effort theory was propounded by Harvey Leibenstein (1922-1994) in his book *Economic Backwardness and Economic Growth*. He was a Ukrainian-born American economist. One of his most important contributions to economics was the critical minimum effort thesis in development economics. He also introduced the concept of X-inefficiency. [1]

He maintains that underdeveloped countries are characterized by vicious circle of poverty which keeps them around a low income per capita equilibrium state. This circle is believed to be so vicious and deep rooted that no small effort can be expected to break it up. The only way out to develop these countries is to make minimum amount of investments (critical minimum effort) based on relationships between factors, per capita income, population growth, and investment, which would raise the per capita to a level at which sustained development could be maintained.

According to Leibenstein, every economy is surrounded with shocks and stimulants. Shocks (weak point of an underdeveloped country) are understood as a tendency of per capita income to fall initially, whereas stimulants can change the sustainability of underdeveloped countries and tend to increase the per capita income. It is possible that from time-to-time there may be shocks and stimulants to disturb the equilibrium of underdeveloped economies. He explains that in order to raise income, certain minimum amount of effective measures are required. Also, if per capita income is not raised at once above a certain level, certain income depressing forces will be set in operation during the process of development, and these forces will in the end outrun the income-raising forces and bring per capita income back to its previous level.

There are many factors that are responsible for depressing of per capita income in under developed countries. These include the following:

1. Conservative activities of organized and unorganized labour.
2. Resistance to new knowledge and ideas and attachment to old ideas.
3. Increase in consumption.
4. Unproductive use of those resources which could be used for capital accumulation.
5. Increase in population.
6. High capital-output ratio.

In order to overcome these influences which keep an economy in backwardness, a sufficiently large critical minimum effort is required to sustain a rapid rate of economic growth. As a result of critical minimum effort, the per capita income will ultimately rise, leading to increase in the level of savings and investments. They will in a turn lead to an expansion of growth agents, the capital-output ratio will come down and the income depressing forces wil! get weaken. Such a social environment will be created which will promote social and economic mobility. He assumed that the most important induced income-depressing force is population growth and for backward economy there exist a positive functional relation between per capita income and population and that population growth always means an increase in the labour force. Further on the above statement, additions to the labour force are subject to the law of diminishing returns [2] because of the relative scarcity of land and capital. Thus, an upward or downward change in income will lead to a change in population in the same direction, with little change in the long-run.

Endnotes

1. In economics, X-efficiency is the effectiveness with which a given set of inputs are used to produce outputs. If a firm is producing the maximum output it can, given the resources it employs, such as men and machinery, and the best technology available, it is said to be technical-efficient. X-inefficiency occurs when technical-efficiency is not achieved.
2. Historically, the law of diminishing returns is associated with agricultural operations, with land being the fixed factor and labour the variable factor. However, this law holds good for all those productive activities where increasing quantities of a variable factor are applied to a given quantity of a fixed factor. Modern economists regard labour (L) and capital (K) to be the most significant factors of production, considering land as either unimportant or a part of capital.

   The law of diminishing returns states that if increasing quantities of a variable factor (labour) are applied to a given quantity of fixed factor (land), the marginal product of the variable factor will eventually decline. The law is based on the following assumptions:

- If one factor is kept fixed and increasing quantities of the other factor are applied, variations in the proportions of the two factors are implicitly assumed. This law will apply only to those cases where possibilities of variable proportions exist.
- Since it is assumed that some factors are fixed therefore this law pertains to short-run.
- Production technology is assumed to be given. A change in technology may postpone the operation of the law for sometime.
- Different units of the variable factor are assumed to be homogenous.

9

Theories of Balanced and Unbalanced Economic Growth

9.1 Ragnar Nurkse's Balanced Growth Theory

Balanced growth theory is an economic theory pioneered by the economist Ragnar Nurkse (1907-1959). The theory hypothesises that the government of any underdeveloped country needs to make large investments in a number of industries simultaneously. This will enlarge the market size, increase productivity, and provide an incentive for the private sector to invest.

Nurkse was in favour of attaining balanced growth in both the industrial and agricultural sectors of the economy. He recognised that the expansion and inter-sectoral balance between agriculture and manufacturing is necessary so that each of these sectors provides a market for the products of the other and, in turn, supplies the necessary raw materials for the development and growth of the other.

Nurkse's theory discusses how the poor size of the market in underdeveloped countries perpetuates its underdeveloped state. Nurkse has also clarified the various determinants of the market size and puts primary focus on productivity. According to him, if the productivity levels rise in a less developed country, its market size will expand and thus it can eventually become a developed economy. Apart from this, Nurkse has been nicknamed an export pessimist, as he felt that the finances to make investments in underdeveloped countries must arise from their own domestic territory. No importance should be given to promoting exports.

9.1.1 Size of Market and Inducement to Invest: The size of a market assumes primary importance in the study of what induces investment in a country. Nurkse asserts that inducement to invest is limited by the size of the market. The original idea behind this was put forward by Adam Smith, who stated that division of labour is limited by the extent of the market.

According to Nurkse, underdeveloped countries lack adequate purchasing power. Low purchasing power means that the real income of the people is low, although in monetary terms it may be high. If the money income were low, the problem could easily be overcome by expanding the money supply. However, since the meaning in this context is real income, expanding the supply of money will only generate inflationary pressure. Neither real output nor real investment will rise. A low purchasing power means that domestic demand for commodities is low. Apart from encompassing consumer goods and services, this includes the demand for capital as well.

The size of the market determines the incentive to invest irrespective of the nature of the economy. This is because entrepreneurs invariably take their production decisions by taking into consideration the demand for the concerned product. For example, if an automobile manufacturer is trying to decide which countries to set up plants in, he will naturally only invest in those countries where the demand is high. He would prefer to invest in a developed country, where though the population is lesser than in underdeveloped countries, the people are prosperous and there is a definite demand.

Private entrepreneurs sometimes resort to heavy advertising as a means of attracting buyers for their products. Although this may lead to a rise in demand for that entrepreneur's good or service, it does not actually raise the aggregate demand in the economy. The demand merely shifts from one provider to another. Clearly, this is not a long-term solution.

9.1.2 Determinants of Size of Market: According to Nurkse, expanding the size of the market is crucial to increasing the inducement to invest. Only then can the *vicious circle of poverty* be broken. He mentioned the following pertinent points about how the size of the market is determined:

A. Money Supply: Nurkse emphasised that Keynesian theory should not be applied to underdeveloped countries because they do not face a lack of effective demand in the way that developed countries do. Their problem is to do with a lack of real purchasing power due to low productivity levels. Thus, merely increasing the supply of money will not expand the market but will in fact cause inflationary pressure.

B. Population: Nurkse argued against the notion that a large population implies a large market. Though underdeveloped countries have a large population, their levels of productivity are low. This results in low levels of per capita real income. Thus, consumption expenditure is low, and savings are either very low or completely absent. On the other hand, developed countries have smaller populations than underdeveloped countries but by virtue of high levels of productivity, their per capita real incomes are higher and thus they create a large market for goods and services.

C. Geographical Area: Nurkse also refuted the claim that if a country's geographical area is large, the size of its market also ought to be large. A country may be extremely small in area but still have a large effective demand as, for example, Japan. In contrast, a country may cover a huge geographical area but its market may still be small. This may occur if a large part of the country is uninhabitable, or if the country suffers from low productivity levels and thus has a low national income.

D. Transport Cost and Trade Barriers: The notion that transport costs and trade barriers hinder the expansion of the market is age-old. Nurkse emphasised that tariff duties, exchange controls, import quotas and other non-tariff barriers to trade are major obstacles to promoting international cooperation in exporting and importing. More specifically, due to high transport costs between nations, producers do not have an incentive to export their commodities. As a result, the amount of capital accumulation remains small. However, Nurkse, as an export pessimist, did not agree with this view. Export pessimism is a trade theory which is governed by the idea of *inward looking growth* as opposed to *outward looking growth*.

E. Sales Promotion: Often, it is true that a company's private endeavour to increase the demand for its products succeeds due to the extensive use of advertisement and other sales promotion technique. However, Nurkse argues that such activities cannot succeed at the macro level to increase a country's aggregate demand level. He calls this the *macroeconomic paradox*.

F. Productivity: Nurkse stressed productivity as the primary determinant of the size of the market. An increase in productivity (defined as the output per unit input) increases the flow of goods and services in the economy. As a response, consumption also rises. Hence, underdeveloped economies should aim to raise their productivity levels in all sectors of the economy, in particular agriculture and industry. For example, in most underdeveloped economies, the *technology* used to carry out agricultural activities is backward. There is a low degree of mechanisation coupled with rain dependence. This can be done if the government provides irrigation facilities, high-yielding variety seeds, pesticides, fertilisers, tractors etc. The positive outcome of this is that farmers earn more income and have a higher purchasing power (real income). Their demand for other products in the economy will rise and this will provide industrialists an incentive to invest in that country. Thus, the size of the market expands and improves the condition of the underdeveloped country.

Nurkse concluded, "The limited size of the domestic market in a low income country can thus constitute an obstacle to the application of capital by any individual firm or industry working for the market. In this sense the small domestic market is an obstacle to development generally".

9.1.3 Export Pessimism: Citing the limited size of the market as the main impediment in economic growth, Nurkse reasons that an increase in productivity can create a virtuous circle of growth. Thus, a large scale investment programme in a wide array of industries simultaneously is the answer. The increase in demand for one industry will lead to an increase in demand for another industry due to *complementarity of demands*. As Say's Law states, *supply creates its own demand*.

However, Nurkse clarified that the finance for this development must arise to as large an extent as possible from the underdeveloped country itself i.e. domestically. Any strategy of financing development from outside the home country is undertaken, it creates a number of problems. For example, the foreign investors may carelessly misuse the resources of the underdeveloped country. This would in turn limit that economy's ability to diversify, especially if natural resources were plundered. This may also create a distorted social structure. Apart from this, there is also a risk that the foreign investments may be used to finance private luxury consumption. People would try to imitate Western consumption habits and thus a balance of payments crisis may develop, along with economic inequality within the population.

Another reason exports cannot be promoted is because in all likelihood, an underdeveloped country may only be skilled enough to promote the export of primary goods, say agricultural goods. However, since such commodities face inelastic demand, the extent to which they will sell in the market is limited. Although when population is at a rise, additional demand for exports may be created, Nurkse implicitly assumed that developed countries are operating at the replacement rate of population growth. For

Nurkse, then, exports as a means of economic development are completely ruled out.

Thus, for a large-scale development to be feasible, the requisite capital must be generated from within the country itself, and not through export surplus or foreign investment. Only then can productivity increase and lead to increasing returns to scale and eventually create virtuous circles of growth.

9.1.4 Role of State: After First World War, a debate about whether a country should introduce *financial planning* to develop itself or rely on *private entrepreneurs* emerged. Nurkse believed that the subject of who *should* promote development does not concern economists. It is an administrative problem. The crucial idea was that a large amount of well dispersed investment should be made in the economy, so that the market size expands and leads to higher productivity levels, increasing returns to scale and eventually the development of the country in question. However, most economists who favoured the balanced growth hypothesis believed that only the state has the capacity to take on the kind of heavy investments the theory propagates. Further, the gestation period of such lumpy investments is usually long and private sector entrepreneurs do not normally undertake such high risks.

9.1.5 Criticisms: Ragnar Nurkse's balanced growth theory has been criticised on a number of grounds. His main critic was Albert O. Hirschman, the pioneer of the strategy of unbalanced growth. Hans W. Singer also criticised certain aspects of the theory.

Hirschman stressed the fact that underdeveloped economies are called underdeveloped because they face a *lack of resources*, maybe not natural resources, but resources such as skilled labour and technology. Thus, to hypothesise that an underdeveloped nation can undertake large scale investment in many industries of its economy simultaneously is unrealistic due to the paucity of resources. To quote Hirschman, "If a country were ready to apply the doctrine of balanced growth, then it would not be underdeveloped in the first place".

Hans Singer asserted that the balanced growth theory is more applicable to cure an economy facing a cyclical downswing. Cyclical downswing is a feature of an advanced stage of sustained growth rather than of the vicious cycle of poverty. Hirschman also stated that during conditions of slack activity in developed countries, the stock of resources, machines and entrepreneurs are merely unemployed, and are present as idle capacity. So in this situation, simultaneous investment in a large number of sectors is a well-suited policy. The various economic agents are temporarily unemployed and once the inducement to invest starts operating, the slump will be overcome. However, for an underdeveloped economy, where such resources are absent, this principle does not fit.

Another contention was Nurkse's approval of Say's Law, which theorises that there is no overproduction or glut in the economy. Supply (production of goods and services) creates a matching demand for the output and this results in the entire output being sold and consumed. However, Keynes stated that Say's Law is not operational in any country because people do not spend their entire income, i.e. a part of it is saved for future consumption. Thus, according to Nurkse's critics, his assumption of Say's Law being operational in underdeveloped countries needs greater justification.

Nurkse states that if demand for the output of one sector rises, due to the complementary nature of demand, the demand for the output of other industries will also experience a rise. Paul Rosenstein-Rodan spoke of a similar concept called "indivisibility of demand" which hypothesises that if large investments are made in a large number of industries simultaneously, an underdeveloped economy can become developed due to the phenomenon of complementary demand. However, both Nurkse and Rosenstein-Rodan only took into consideration the situation of industries that produce complementary goods. There are substitute goods too, which are in competition with each other. Thus, if the state pumps in large investments into the car industry, for example, it will naturally lead to a rise in the demand for petrol. Conversely, if the state makes large scale investments in the coffee sector of a country, the tea sector will suffer.

Hans Singer suggested that Nurkse's theory makes dubious assumptions about the underdeveloped economy. For example, Nurkse assumes that the economy starts with nothing at hand. However, an economy usually starts at a position which reflects the previous investment decisions undertaken in the country, and at any given moment, an imbalance already exists. So the logical step would be to take on those investment programmes which complement the existing imbalance in the economy. Clearly, such an investment cannot be a balanced one. If an economy makes the mistake of setting out to make a balanced investment, a new imbalance is likely to appear which will require still another *balancing investment* to bring equilibrium, and so on and so forth.

Hirschman believed that Nurkse's balanced growth theory was not in fact a theory of growth. Growth implies the gradual transformation of an economy from one stage to the chronologically next stage. It entails the series of actions which leads the economy from a stage of infancy to that of maturity. However, the balanced growth theory involves the creation of a brand new, self-sufficient modern industrial economy being laid over a stagnant, self-sufficient traditional economy. Thus, there is no transformation. In reality, a dual economy will come into existence, where two separate economic sectors will begin to coexist in one country. They will differ on levels of development, technology and demand patterns. This may create inequality in the country.

9.2 Albert Hirschman's Theory of Unbalanced Growth

Some tend to think that unbalanced growth is harmful to the long-term prospects of the economy. However, one theory of unbalanced growth suggests that it is not harmful but actually a necessary part of economic development.

The theory of unbalanced growth is associated with Albert O. Hirschman who propounded it in his book *The Strategy of Economic Development,* published in 1958.

Hirschman maintains that it is not possible to always have broad growth across different sectors. He argues that as long as there is growth in some sector, it will create a dynamic pressure to grow other sectors at a later stage. Hirschman even argues that unbalanced growth and the dynamic tensions it creates helps to speed up economic development. For example, if there is growth in primary product sector, this creates a complementary investment in transport to get the goods to the export market. Secondly, if there is growth in one sector, there will be a multiplier effect, and this will cause induced investment in related industries. For example, if mining jobs are created, miners will demand more retail services. Thirdly, if the mining industry develops and creates more infrastructure, this will later benefit different industries which can make use of the same infrastructure. Thus, if railways are built to transport raw materials, the same railways infrastructure can be used by commuters to get into the city and work in the service sector.

Unbalanced growth is a natural path of economic development. Situations that countries are in at any one point in time reflect their previous investment decisions and development. Accordingly, at any point in time desirable investment programmes that are not balanced investment packages may still advance welfare. Unbalanced investment can complement or correct existing imbalances. Once such an investment is made, a new imbalance is likely to appear, requiring further compensating investments. Therefore, growth need not take place in a balanced way. Besides Hirschman, supporters of the unbalanced growth doctrine include Hans Singer, Paul Streeten, and J. Sheehan.

Hirschman contends that deliberate unbalancing of the economy according to the strategy is the best method of development and if the economy is to be kept moving ahead, the task of development policy is to maintain tension, disproportions and disequilibrium. Balanced growth should not be the goal but rather the maintenance of existing imbalances, which can be seen from profit and losses. Therefore, the sequence that leads away from equilibrium is precisely an ideal pattern for development. Unequal development of various sectors often generates conditions for rapid development. More developed industries provide undeveloped industries an incentive to grow. Hence, development of underdeveloped countries should be based on this strategy.

9.2.1 Complementarity: Complementarity is a situation where increased production of one good or service builds up demand for the second good or service. When the second product is privately produced, this demand will lead to imports or higher domestic production of the second product, as it will be in the interests of the producers to do so. Otherwise, the increased demand takes the form of political pressure. This is the case for such public services such as law and order, education, water and electricity that cannot reasonably be imported.

The desirable investment programmes always exist within a country that represents unbalanced investment to complement the existing imbalance. These investments create a new imbalance, requiring another balancing investment. One sector will always grow faster than another, so the need for unbalanced growth will continue as investments must complement existing imbalance. Hirschman states "If the economy is to be kept moving ahead, the task of development policy is to maintain tensions, disproportions and disequilibrium". This situation exists for all societies, developed or underdeveloped.

9.2.2 Induced Investment: Complementarity allows investment in one industry or sector to encourage investment in others. This concept of induced investment is like a multiplier, because each investment triggers a series of subsequent events. Convergence occurs as the output of external economies diminishes at each step. Growth sequences tend to move towards convergence or divergence and the policy is usually concerned with preventing rapid convergence and promoting the possibility of divergence.

9.2.3 Backward and Forward Linkages: Hirschman introduced the concept of backward and forward linkages. A backward linkage is created when a project encourages investment in facilities that enable the project to succeed. A forward linkage is created when investment in a particular project encourages investment in subsequent stages of production. Normally, projects create both backward and forward linkages. Investment should be made in those projects that have the greatest total number of linkages. Hirschman called the industries with greatest complementarities as the *leading sectors*. Projects with many linkages will vary from country to country. Knowledge about project linkages can be obtained through input and output studies.

Example of an industry that has excellent backward and forward linkages is the steel industry. Backward linkages include coal and iron ore mining. Forward linkages include items such as steel utensils. While this industry has strong linkages, it is not a good leading sector. Any industry that has a high capital/output ratio and causes significant costs to other businesses has the potential to hurt the developing economy more than it helps it.

Most underdeveloped economies are primarily agrarian. Agriculture is typically at a primitive stage and hence possesses few linkages, as most output goes for consumption or exports. Therefore, it is said that underdeveloped countries are lacking in interdependence and linkages.

The development of an economy using the unbalanced method depends on the linkages between sectors. Hirschman suggests that the best strategy is induced industrialization. This type of development will create more backward and forward linkages and should be the first step taken. Industries that transform semi-manufactured goods into goods needed by final demand are called *last industries* or *enclave import industries*.

In underdeveloped countries, industrialization takes place through such industries, through plants that add final touches to unfinished imported products. Examples are metal fabricating industries, pharmaceutical laboratories and assembly and mixing plants. Such industries have many advantages, as they often require the smaller amounts of capital available in such economies and without having to rely on unreliable domestic producers. Therefore, underdeveloped countries set up such *last industries* first. These industries create long chains of backward linkages. Brazil and Mexico are examples of countries that followed this path.

Protection and subsidy of import-replacing industries should come, but at a later stage. The last industry strategy has certain disadvantages. It can slow the creation of domestic production. Industrialists who have begun working with imports may not accept domestic alternative products that reduce demand for their output. Creating last industries first can create loyalty toward foreign products and distrust of domestic products and their quality.

10

Inequalities of Income, Lorenz Curve and Kuznet's Inverted U Hypothesis

10.1 The Issue of Inequalities of Income

Income inequalities in economics mean significant disparities in the distribution of income between individuals, groups, populations, social classes, or countries. Income inequalities are a major dimension of social stratification. They affect and are affected by many other forms of inequalities, such as inequalities of wealth, political power, and social status. Income is a major determinant of quality of life, affecting the health and well-being of individuals and families, and varies by social factors such as sex, age, and race or ethnicity.

In a free enterprise economy, an individual's income is determined by the factors of production owned by him and the prices of those factors in the market. An individual who has no capital or land and is unable to work will receive no income. Distribution of income and wealth based on this method is socially undesirable. Moreover, the development process generally brings in its wake proportionately large benefits for certain select groups like industrialists, real estate owners, exporters and importers, traders, speculators, big landlords, and the like. If no corrective measures are adopted, the gulf between the rich and the poor goes on widening, threatening political stability and social order.

Perfect equality is not found anywhere and there are many reasons why it may not even be a feasible objective. However, there can be no two opinions on the fact that inequality must be kept within tolerable limits. Some increase in inequality in a developing country during a period of rapid growth and transformation may be unavoidable and it may even be tolerated if it is accompanied by sufficiently rapid improvement in the living standards of the poor. However, an increase in inequality with little or no improvement in the living standards of the poor is a recipe for social tensions. Static measures of inequality do not capture the phenomenon of equality of opportunity which needs special attention. Any given level of inequality of outcomes is much more socially acceptable if it results from a system which provides greater equality of opportunity.

Income inequality can be studied within countries, between countries, or across the world's population without regard to national boundaries.

10.2 Measurement of Income Inequalities

10.2.1 Lorenz Curve: In economics, the Lorenz curve is a graphical representation of the distribution of income developed by Max Lorenz in 1905. The graph plots percentiles of the population on the horizontal axis (or x-axis) according to income and plots cumulative income on the vertical axis (or y-axis). The Lorenz curve is accompanied by a straight diagonal line with a slope of 1, which represents perfect equality in income distribution. A perfectly equal income distribution would be one in which every person has the same income. This can be depicted by the straight line, called the *line of perfect equality*.

The Lorenz curve lies beneath it, showing the observed or estimated distribution of income. The area between the straight line and the curved line, expressed as a ratio of the area under the straight line, is called the Gini coefficient, a scalar measurement of inequality. The farther the curve moves from the baseline, represented by the straight diagonal line, the higher the level of inequality.

Gini coefficient is used to express the extent of inequality in a single figure. It can range from 0 (or 0%) to 1 (or 100%). Complete equality, in which every individual has the exact same income, corresponds to a coefficient of 0. Plotted as a Lorenz curve, complete equality would be a straight diagonal line with a slope of 1. A coefficient of 1 means that one person earns all of the income.

The Lorenz curve is important because it represents one of the best and simplest ways to illustrate the level of income inequality in a society.

A typical Lorenz curve is shown in Figure 10.1.

Figure 10.1: Lorenz Curve

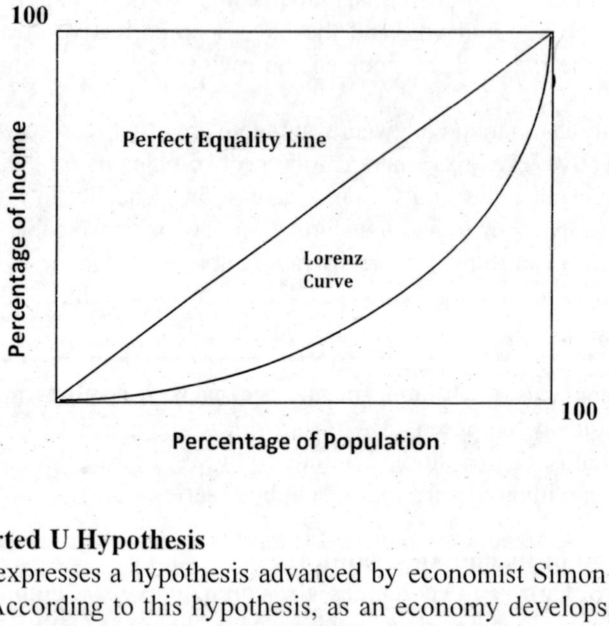

10.3 Kuznets Inverted U Hypothesis

Kuznets curve expresses a hypothesis advanced by economist Simon Kuznets in the 1950s and 1960s. According to this hypothesis, as an economy develops, market forces first increase and then decrease economic inequality.

The relationship between income inequality and economic development has popularly been characterized by the Kuznets' inverted U curve, which argued that income inequality tends to increase at an initial stage of development and then decrease as the economy develops, implying that income inequality will fall as income continues to rise in developing countries. However, when income has kept rising and reached a high level, income inequality increases again. The intuition of the inverted U curve is that when an economy's income is at a low level, there are only a few rich individuals, and the Gini coefficient will be quite extreme. As the overall income increases, it is accompanied by a rise in employment and job opportunities. This will result in upward mobility on the income ladder, and a middle class of income earners will emerge, thereby improving the Gini coefficient. This is the prediction of the Kuznets' relationship that inequality improves as income expands. However, when an economy's income level keeps rising to a high level, there are more people who could achieve high incomes. Portfolio investment and windfall gains from speculation in stocks and property, for example, can result in the rise of super-rich individuals. And while the majority of the population is engaged in paid jobs, income inequality will deteriorate as a result. The inverted U curve actually describes income at different stages of economic development.

One can conclude that the lack of economic development could be the reason for the higher level of income inequality among developing countries. Very often, the modern form of employment could not increase and mobility could not occur if the level of economic development was below a certain threshold level. For example, economic openness has been considered as an important element in economic development. A certain level of industrialization and infrastructure achievement are needed before employment can occur and income can increase which, in turn, could have multiplying impact on upward mobility. Indeed, it is the reduction of poverty that is more crucial than the lessening of income inequality. Ultimately, it is economic growth that will reduce poverty, though in the process of poverty reduction there is the possibility of creating income inequality. The rise in income should permit mobility, but while it can generate inequality in the process, the more important principle is the equality in opportunity. Kuznets inverted U curve is shown in Figure 10.2.

10.3.1 Criticism: The Kuznets curve appeared to be consistent with experience at the time it was proposed. However, since the 1960s, inequality has risen in the USA and other developed countries.

The East Asian miracle (EAM) has been used to criticize the validity of the Kuznets theory. The rapid economic growth of eight East Asian countries—Japan; South Korea, Taiwan, Singapore, Hong Kong (Four Asian Tigers), Indonesia, Thailand, and Malaysia—between 1965 and 1990, was called the East Asian miracle. Manufacturing and export grew quickly and powerfully. Yet simultaneously, life expectancy was found to increase and population levels living in absolute poverty decreased. This development process was contrary to the Kuznets curve theory. Many studies have been done to identify how the EAM was able to ensure that the benefits of rapid economic growth were distributed broadly among the population, because Kuznets' theory stated that rapid capital accumulation would lead to an initial increase in inequality.

Figure 10.2: Kuznets Inverted U Curve

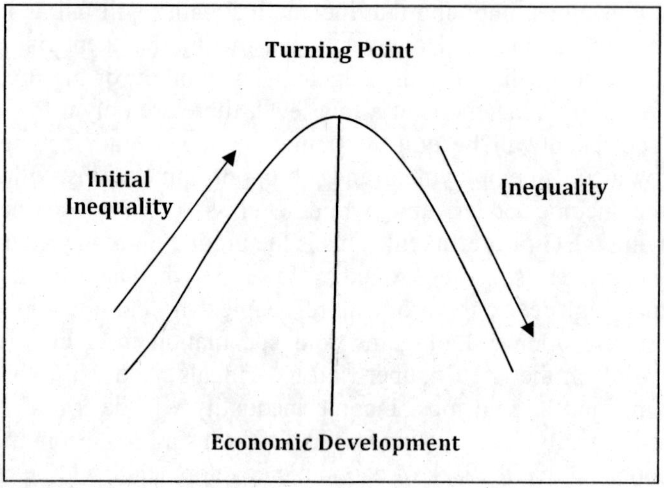

10.4 Causes of Income Inequalities

One's occupation is a central basis for differences in income for most people. In more-developed countries such as the US, wages and salaries are the major source of income for most households, while property, including capital gains, is the major source for the most affluent.

Wages are the reward for the services of labour. However, wages of all types of workers are not the same. Differentials in wage rate are due to a host of factors.

1. Wages differ with the type of job. Generally, more risky jobs carry more wages than less risky jobs involving same skills. Coal miners get more wages than ordinary ditch-diggers.
2. Wages depend on the length of education and training required to perform a particular job. A surgeon gets more than a typist because the job of the former requires education and training for a much longer period than the job of the latter.
3. Wages vary with experience in a particular job. An airline pilot with 20 years experience gets more than a newly recruited pilot.
4. Wage differentials may exit due to sexual and racial prejudices. Very often women get lesser wages than men for doing the same job. Similarly, black workers may be paid less than the white workers.
5. Wages also differ according to the structure of the labour market. In a competitive market, wages are less than in an imperfect labour market. Members of strong trade unions earn more than their less organised counterparts.

Despite popular belief that income inequalities largely reflect individual differences in talent and motivation, there are also significant structural and cultural causes, such as segmented labour markets, discrimination, institutionalized racism and sexism, gender roles, and family responsibilities. Other legal, political, and economic factors—such as corporate power, degree of private versus public ownership and control of resources, collective bargaining frameworks, and minimum wage laws—also affect income levels independently of individual traits. Income inequalities can have different implications for levels of well-being in different countries, depending on whether other basic needs such as housing, healthcare, and food are largely market-based and on whether people have access to productive resources such as land, water, and technology.

10.5 How to Reduce Income Inequalities?

How should income be distributed? It should be distributed as fairly or justly as possible. Unfortunately, it is difficult to define what is precisely meant by fairness or justness. These ideas involve considerations of value judgement and social philosophy.

Policies to address income inequalities can focus narrowly on individual skills, opportunities, and aspirations or may focus more broadly on altering the social, political, and economic structures that create and maintain income inequalities. Income inequality can be reduced directly by decreasing the incomes of the richest or by increasing the incomes of the poorest. Policies focusing on the latter include increasing employment or wages and transferring income.

10.5.1 Tax Policy: Income distribution is affected by patterns of taxation. Tax policy is a democratic method to influence the distribution of income and wealth on desired lines. The main ingredients of this policy can be the following.

1. Progressive direct taxation of income, wealth and property transactions.
2. Taxation of commodities (customs duties, excise levies, and sales taxes) purchased largely by high-income groups.

For every rupee raised as tax, there is a corresponding reduction in the disposable real income of someone or another. Reduction in one's disposable real income is taken to be equivalent to the tax realisation by the government. Tracking down individuals or households whose real incomes are truncated when taxes are imposed is called incidence of taxation. It deals with the diffusion of tax burden among different economic classes in a country.

Incidence in economics refers to the distributional effects of a fiscal measure. Thus, tax incidence means 'who bears the burden of taxes'? While expenditure incidence means 'who benefits from public expenditure?' Similarly, budget incidence relates to the combined effects of an equal increase in tax and public expenditure on the distribution of income. It is also called net incidence and is obtained by summing, algebraically, both the tax incidence (negative) and expenditure incidence (positive) for each of the sub-groups.

More specifically, incidence of taxation refers to the final resting place of tax burden as against the impact which means the first place where a tax is imposed. The incidence of a tax is on the person who ultimately pays it, i.e. who cannot shift it any further.

Due to economic transactions, a tax percolates through many parts of the economy and its burden can be shifted, forward or backward, by the original taxpayer to other entities.

When taxes are imposed, disposable real incomes of the people get reduced. Real incomes may be reduced either because there is reduction in disposable money income (direct taxes) or because the prices of products purchased are enhanced (indirect taxes).

To use the Musgravian formula [1], the disposable real income (DRY) of a household may be defined as:

$$DRY = \frac{E - Ty}{P + Ts} = \frac{DY}{GP}$$

Where, E is earning, Ty is income tax, P is the price (at factor cost) of products bought, and Ts is the sales tax (or some other commodity tax) addition thereto. DY is disposable or after-tax money income, and GP is the gross (or market) price.

Changes in Ty operate on the earnings (as producers) side of the household account. Changes in Ts operate on the expenditure (as consumers) side of the account. Thus, an increase in income tax lowers DRY via an increase in Ty and hence a fall in DY. An increase in sales tax lowers DRY via an increase in Ts and hence in GP. It is clear now how disposable real income of a household is subject to both direct and indirect tax effects. The total incidence of a tax system on an individual is equal to the sum of tax burden borne by him as a producer and as a consumer.

For reducing income inequalities the incidence of taxes should be on the rich. Low income groups should be exempted from taxation to the extent possible. It might be argued that taxation of the rich will reduce savings and thus retard developmental efforts. The conflict between equity and growth can be reduced by incorporating suitable provisions in tax laws to encourage savings and investments.

10.5.2 Public Expenditure Policy: Overall economic inequality is affected by policies that provide public goods, such as healthcare and education, leaving a larger proportion of individuals' incomes to be spent on other goods. Subsidies (negative taxation) on goods purchased by low income groups are a case in point.

Public expenditure is an important instrument of the economic policy of a government. The size and pattern of public spending has great relevance in the growth process and in the reduction of economic disparities. The pressure on public expenditure is particularly great in developing countries because of growing population and the consequent need for medical, educational, housing and employment facilities. In the emerging developing economies of Asia and Africa, people are aspiring for a better standard of living after centuries of subjugation. Public expenditure is an effective policy instrument in this context.

The political and economic thinking has stressed the establishment of welfare societies within democratic framework. Left to itself, the market mechanism may not produce that distribution of income and wealth which is desired by society. Due to imperfections of the market and other malpractices by the owners of the means of production, economic inequalities may increase. If no corrective measures are taken, this may lead to social tensions. Public expenditure is a powerful and democratic method to realise distributive justice.

The provision of beneficial public services constitutes an addition to the real income of the citizens. Free/subsidised medical, educational and transport facilities, and slum improvement schemes are examples of positive additions to the real income of beneficiaries. Pensions, annuities, scholarships and unemployment allowances directly add to the money incomes of the receivers. The pattern of public expenditure should be such that its effect on reducing economic inequalities is the strongest.

It is important that benefits intended for the poor should preferably be given in kind rather than cash grants. Aid given in kind, e.g. medicines, books, clothes etc. cannot be turned into cash and diverted for other purposes. However, money given for a particular purpose may not be used to that end.

Highlighting the importance of taxation and public expenditure policies in the context of redistribution of economic power, Alejandro Foxley has opined, "modern public finance studies have de-emphasised the analysis of the normative considerations of theory and focused on the very basic question of incidence; who pays and who benefits from government action? Thus, we can say that focus has shifted from the question of 'What should the State do?' to the question of knowing 'What in fact it has been doing'?" [2]

10.5.3 Employment-related Policies: Enforcement of affirmative action and non-discrimination policies by employers, governments, and educational institutions and policies such as government-subsidized childcare that enable people to enter the labour market should also affect income inequalities through facilitating greater access to higher-income jobs. The range of employment-related policies includes strengthening collective-bargaining rights, full-employment schemes, living-wage policies, stronger minimum-wage laws, and wage subsidies. Direct income transfer policies include traditional cash welfare payments. Globally, debt forgiveness and reform of trade agreements so that they do more to benefit the least advantaged in each country can also reduce income inequalities.

The present upsurge of interest in the distributional aspects of economic policy in developing countries is a reaction against the growth-oriented development theories propounded by Western economists. The state, far from being a neutral entity, has to act to correct distortions, and to change the distributive content of the development efforts.

Endnotes

1. Richard Musgrave and Peggy Musgrave, *Public Finance in Theory and Practice* (New York: McGraw-Hill Book Company, 1989), p. 240.
2. Alejandro Foxley, Eduardo Aninat, and J.P. Arellano, *Redistributive Effects of Government Programmes: The Chilean Case* (Pergamon Press, 1979), p. 18.

11

Factors Affecting Location of Industry

There are various economic and social criteria to determine location of industries. Economic criteria include availability of raw materials, nearness to market and infrastructural facilities. These may be available in already developed areas. Social criteria include employment opportunities and laying of social and economic overheads in backward areas. Zoning and land use regulations as well as environmental legislations in different countries also regulate industrial locations.

Location of industry refers to establishment of an industry or cluster of industries in a particular location or region due to availability of cheap factors of production, transport and infrastructural facilities, demand incentives, raw materials etc. These are some of the factors which attract entrepreneurs to set up their plants in a particular area. Once the process starts, it has a tendency to accelerate.

A series of location factors influence the location patterns of various individual industries during their respective periods of evolution. No single location factor on its own absolutely determines or clearly indicates the right location of a given industry. Among the principal factors enumerated by the theorists, transportation costs in general, and those of finished products in particular, seem decisive in the choice of the location of most industrial plants. Importance of each locational factor varies for different geographic areas and for different types of industries. In general, following are the factors which affect the location of industry.

11.1 Land Cost and Climate

The issue of land and its attributes is of initial concern to an industrialist. Although land cost may be a major cost item in the initial setting up of a firm, it becomes much less important when considered over a long period and may be relatively insignificant in determining choice between comparable sites. Nonetheless it may rule out certain very expensive locations. It is also important that the land be physically suitable for its intended purpose or at least adaptable to development. Climatic, geological and other physical attributes may affect the location of some industries while others remain indifferent.

Of considerable advantage is land which is already serviced prior to development. Industries will be attracted to sites where infrastructure, public utilities and amenities are easily accessible. Other industries will be drawn to the occurrence of large quantities of water while others will be concerned with the deposit of industrial effluence. Also significant to location is the size of land parcels and their related costs. Sites that are otherwise desirable may have to be eliminated either because they are not of adequate proportions or due to the prohibitively high cost of the land. This is generally true of city or town-centre locations where plots are small or a manufacturer is not able to outbid commercial users.

Climate of the area selected for the industry is important. Very harsh climate is a discouraging factor in the location of industry.

11.2 Sources of Power and Water

Power is a necessity condition for any industrial establishment. Electricity is one of the key inputs for the overall economic development of the country. The basic responsibility of the power supply industry is to provide adequate electricity at economic cost, while ensuring reliability and quality of the supply. The demand for power in both rural and urban areas is increasing rapidly.

Electricity is the main source of power for most industries today. It is more mobile geographically than the earlier forms of industrial energy (water and steam power) since it can be transmitted from one place to another at little cost. This means that over fairly large areas the cost of electricity may not vary much if there are no significant differences in local production costs, and in those circumstances its influence on industrial location will be negligible. However, there can be instances where large supplies of cheap power are necessary and this will have an important effect on industrial location. Certain metallurgical and chemical industries such as aluminium and copper processing and the production of fertilizers are especially sensitive to the cost of power. Areas that can produce electricity cheaply have been able to attract important manufacturing industries of this type.

Some industries like iron and steel, textiles and chemical require large quantities of water for their proper functioning. Such industries are established near rivers, canals, and lakes.

11.3 Availability of Raw Materials

This is one of the important factors in an industrial location. The mere location of industries itself may be determined by the availability or location of the raw materials. The essence of industrial process is the conversion of one thing into another of greater value, hence all manufacturing activities require raw materials. Industrial raw materials can be grouped into organic and inorganic. The leading organic raw materials are those derived from agriculture, i.e. agro-industrial raw materials. Inorganic materials include minerals and water-power resources for hydroelectric generation. The effects of raw materials on industrial location arise from the issue of transportation costs. Materials vary enormously in terms of bulk, weight, and perishability, while others need special treatment in transport, handling or storage.

The outlay incurred in acquiring raw materials involves the costs of both production and transportation to the factory. The cost of extracting a mineral or manufacturing a component will affect locational choice only if there are significant variations in the price from different places. Owing to a dependence on transport charges, the cost of raw materials varies with distance from the source in a fairly regular manner. However, where a uniform delivered price is adopted, the cost of the particular raw materials would be the same anywhere and its effects on plant location insignificant.

11.4 Transport Facilities

Transport always influences the location of the industry. So the junction points of waterways, roadways and railways become humming centres of industrial activity. Transport is often considered to be the most important determinant of plant location. Few firms can overlook the transport factor when making their location decision, and for many the total freight charge will be the largest difference between costs at alternative sites. Important innovations undertaken in the recent past have had considerable impact on the factor of transportation and its related costs with regard to raw materials and finished goods. The use of pipelines for moving tricky commodities like petroleum and oil, and the development of container systems have greatly facilitated the transfer of goods by road, rail, air and water. The more efficient transportation becomes in terms of decreasing costs of overcoming distance, the more flexible the manufacturer's choice of location.

The nature of material or product to be transported affects the means of transport to be adopted. Bulky goods of relatively low value such as iron ore and coal are cheaply shipped on water. A commodity of high value in relation to its weight and volume, on the other hand, may justify air transport. If it is crucial that goods are moved quickly, then road is preferable to rail which is preferable to water. Other goods require special facilities such as refrigeration or careful handling and the selected mode of transport should cater to these needs. The distance over which the goods are to be moved is also important. For a majority of items trucking is the cheapest mode of transport over relatively short distances, railway suitable for medium distances and waterway best for long hauls. All in all, a good transport system with direct access to primary distributor roads is a prerequisite for industrial areas.

11.5 Access to Capital and Market

The accessibility of a proposed industrialist to finance capital is another factor of industrial location. Finance capital is necessary before land or other inputs like machinery, equipment, buildings and so forth, are acquired. For small firms and those just getting established, capital may be obtainable more easily in some places than in others. Frequently too, industrialists would prefer to locate within easy reach of financiers.

The finished goods should reach the market at the end of the process of manufacturing. Thus, nearness to the market is an important factor in the process of selecting a location for industry. For many industries the significance of the market is growing in relation to such considerations as the cost of labour and materials. Freed from the original necessity of being close to sources of raw materials, many firms now show a distinct preference for a location close to major urban centres. The market is not the only attraction of a metropolitan location. The large concentration and relatively affluent body of final consumers found in the city, together with its large industrial market, is certainly one of the main reasons for relatively rapid industrial growth in and around major urban areas. The market can also influence plant location through its effects on costs. Finished products have to be transported to the consumer and for many industries the outgoing freight bill can be a substantial addition to the cost incurred in acquiring the inputs and conducting the process of manufacture. Proximity to the market if it is spatially concentrated, or a central location if consumers are dispersed, can thus be an advantage.

11.6 Skilled Workforce and Managerial Skills

The amount and type of labour necessary for operation varies from one industry to another and one firm to another. Some industries require thousands of employees while others can run with a few operatives. Some industries need a highly skilled labour force, some a large clerical and managerial staff, and others need numerous unskilled manual workers. The distinctive labour requirements of some concerns make certain locations more suitable them others. A firm needing a large labour force supplying a diverse range of skills would find it easier to obtain in a metropolitan area than in a small town. However, labour is likely to be more costly to the industry in large cities or national core regions than in the periphery where the cost of living is lower. However, if the right labour is not available at an otherwise attractive location, it is possible to obtain it from elsewhere since labour is mobile both geographically and in terms of occupation.

Skilled labour is important because of its contribution to enhancing productivity at the individual, industry and also national levels. Complementarities exist between physical capital and human capital on the one hand and between technology and human capital on the other. Fast changing knowledge economies call for new core competencies among all learners in the society. Managerial skill is a category of labour and has a vital bearing on the success or failure of a business. Other than the policy-making function and organization structuring, management has the important decision-making task beginning with the initial choice on location, the balancing of various considerations and the assessment of *local business climate*. The need for skilled managerial employees may bestow locational advantages to areas best able to supply them. A firm requiring a range of managerial personnel with specific skills is more likely to locate where it can find it which would probably be in major urban area rather than in a small town.

11.7 Area Concentration of Industrial Activity

The area concentration of industrial activity (called agglomeration) often provides firms with collective benefits that they would not enjoy in an isolated location. These collective benefits take the form of external economies or agglomeration.

The advantages of a new firm locating among other firms engaged in the same activity include a pool of labour with particular skills and special educational institutions geared to the needs of the particular industry, both of which reduce the cost of training workers. Firms may also join together to develop a research institute, a marketing organization, and other collective facilities that individual manufacturers would be unable to provide for themselves. In addition, a region specializing in one industry will often have machine-makers, repair-works, suppliers of components etc., and other activities ancillary to the main one and providing goods and services for it. All these benefits of agglomeration when added together offer considerable cost advantages over alternative locations.

There are also benefits that arise in any large urban industrial area and which are potentially available to any firm irrespective of the industry to which it belongs. The main advantages of a large city or industrial region arise from the existence of a relatively well-developed infrastructure, i.e. highways, railways, airports, utilities, commercial facilities, educational institutions, research organizations and many other services that might not exist or would be less developed in a smaller place. However, a city location is not always to the advantage of the firm which may instead experience diseconomies of urbanization. In addition to the high price for land, taxes, labour etc., a firm may also have to contend with traffic congestion, lack of space, pollution and so forth. Nevertheless the balance of advantages still appears to favour the city.

11.8 Backward and Forward Linkages

It is important to make a clear distinction between industrial linkage and agglomeration. Linkages, both within and between firms, may encourage the geographical concentration, i.e. agglomeration of interdependent activities. More often than not such activities are separated by considerable distances. This suggests that linkages only reflect other factors and conditions that are the explanatory variables in industrial location. One of the key determinants of an industry's actual and potential importance for industrial development is the range of its backward and forward linkages.

Backward linkages occur when finished goods of a firm are used in the manufacturing process of another firm. Backward linkage is extremely common because so much of the activity in any region is producing for and oriented to the regional market.

Forward linkages occur when a firm produces raw materials or intermediate products that are used in the manufacture of finished goods by another firm. This means that an impact of change is transmitted to an activity further along in the sequence of operations. Large food processing industry can develop linkages with agricultural producers, transporters and packaging suppliers. The agro-related industry has probably the most significant linkages. For instance the textile industry is mainly cotton-based and is linked to primary cotton production via cotton-growing enterprises, to suppliers of dyes, printing and finishing chemicals and producers of synthetic fibres for blended textiles. The main forward linkages are to tailors and to final consumers through retail outlets. Significant potential exists for other linkages of the textile industry to engineering workshops for machines parts, to specialised tailors, hotels and service for curtain and upholstery materials, and for exports to regional and world markets. The motor vehicle assemblers and coach builders can establish some linkages with smaller workshops for a few components.

11.9 Public Policy

Many countries now seek to actively direct industry to particular problem regions or when they believe that certain economic, social or strategic objectives can be achieved more readily by planning than by leaving manufacturers to locate where they please. National or local government bodies can influence industrial location in two ways:

1. Freedom of choice of site may be restricted through land use zoning or by some tax

penalty in an area where new industrial development is to be discouraged.

2. Encouraging firms to locate in certain areas which need new development by offering financial inducements in the form of loans, subsidies or tax incentives. Aid at the local level is more often organizational than financial. Local help with regard to matters such as housing requirements and planning permission can be a real factor in the choice between alternative locations. In addition, many local authorities band together to sponsor regional scale industrial development associations, each seeking to lure the limited supply of mobile industry to its own constituent authority through a combination of publicity campaigns, industrial promotion and political pressure.

In countries where industry is state-owned or where the positive direction of industry to selected areas is possible, public action can modify existing location patterns speedily and effectively. In a free-enterprise economy, however, the adjustment is likely to be less rapid and predictable since whatever the national government may think is best for the nation, and whatever inducements are offered, location decisions are still subject to the capriciousness of the individual entrepreneur.

11.10 Personal Considerations

Almost any industry reveals cases of plant location that cannot be explained by obvious economic factors. The choice of one site over possible alternatives might seem to be entirely a matter of chance, with historical accident or the personal whim of the entrepreneur as the only possible explanation. The random factor in the diffusion of industrial innovation can also have a bearing on the spatial pattern of the adoption of new techniques, with some places and some entrepreneurs being more receptive to change than others. Once a plant has been built, personal factors as well as immobility of fixed capital may prevent relocation, even if it seems desirable on other economic grounds. In addition to leaving familiar surroundings, a move involves an increase in managerial effort while it is planned and undertaken, with some degree of risk and uncertainty as to the outcome. Some manufacturers may simply prefer to stay put, no matter how attractive an economic proposition an alternative location may be. Such attitudes make an important contribution to industrial inertia and existing industrial location patterns a degree of stability and permanence that economics alone may not justify.

11.11 Theories of Industrial Location

A discussion of theories of industrial location seeks an answer to the question of what is the most rational location or pattern of land use for industries, describing why and how industries choose their actual sites or situations. Basically, location theory attempts to idealise the rational factors which ought to be considered before any use can be given a specific location. Concern would be to find that pattern of locational decisions which give the maximum amount of real goods and services from the sources available.

Industrial location analysis is structured around three approaches:

1. Least-cost approach which attempts to explain location in terms of the minimisation of factor costs.

2. Market area analysis where there is more emphasis on the demand or market factors.
3. Profit maximisation approach which is the logical outcome of the two.

Least-cost location theory rests upon the work of Alfred Weber who began on the premise that the best location was the one at which costs are minimized. Considerable emphasis was placed upon the transport costs involved in assembling materials at the manufacturing site and in delivering the finished product to the market, although Weber also recognised the influence of labour costs and the possibility that economies may be achieved as a result of the agglomeration of several plants in close proximity to one another.

One of the fundamental weaknesses of the least cost approach is the over-emphasis of the input side (cost minimisation) and the under-emphasis of the output or demand side, simply assuming that the firm can sell all it produces wherever it locates. However, the market is a variable: buyers are scattered over a wide area and the intensity of demand varies from place to place. Firms will seek to gain access to the market and serve the greatest demand. Both these approaches are nonetheless one-sided, holding either the input supply or market demand constant.

In practice, both costs and revenue vary with location and the optimum location is the one which yields the greatest profit as upheld by the profit maximisation approach.

11.12 William Launhardt's Location Triangle Model

The analysis of William Launhardt provided the basis for the theory of industrial location. It was his contention that the decision to locate in a particular place would be based on transport costs of raw materials, inputs, finished goods etc. Using a simple model called the *location triangle* and the concept of ton-mileage, Launhardt suggested that as bulky products incur high transportation costs, the profits of finished goods should make these costs worthwhile. If not, a rational manufacturer would opt to relocate, always seeking the point of least transportation costs.

In his contribution, Alfred Weber considered transportation costs, labour costs and agglomeration forces as the major factors of industrial location given the location of raw material and market, assuming that raw material locations are sporadic. On the basis of the *location triangle*, Weber concluded that transportation costs were the primary determinants of industrial location. A new aspect in Weber's refashioned *triangle* was the use of isodapanes. He described these as hypothetical lines joining places of equal additional transportation costs from the least cost location of the industry that would be located somewhere within the *triangle*. An industry would face increasing costs the further away it was located from the least cost location.

Weber extended his analysis using isodapanes to include the effect of labour costs on industrial location, showing how cheap labour productivity would influence the decision of entrepreneurs in selecting the location of their industry. Through the same model Weber introduced the concept of raw material and market orientation where an industry would be attracted to the factor input product that is most costly to transport. If the finished product demanded in a particular market were bulky and thus costly to transport, the industry would be drawn to locate near the market, i.e. market orientation. Conversely, the industry would be raw material or resource-oriented if its finished product were *weight-losing* through the process of manufacture. Thus, furniture-making and saw-milling would be market and raw material oriented respectively.

11.13 Alfred Weber's Theory of Industrial Location

Alfred Weber, a German economist, enunciated a systematic theory of industrial location in 1909. Weber's theory of location is purely deductive in its approach. He formulated a theory of industrial location in which an industry is located where the transportation costs of raw materials and final product is a minimum. He singled out two special cases. In one the weight of the final product is less than the weight of the raw material going into making the product.

He analyzed the factors that determine the location of industry and classified these factors into two divisions. These are as under:

1. Primary causes of regional distribution of industry (regional factors).
2. Secondary causes (agglomerative and deglomerative factors) that are responsible for redistribution of industry.

11.13.1 Primary Causes: According to Weber, transport costs and labour costs are the two regional factors on which his pure theory is based. Assuming that there are no other factors that influence the distribution of industry, except transportation costs, then it is clear that the location of industry will be pulled to those locations which have the lowest transportation costs. The key factors that determine transportation costs are as follows:

1. The weight to be transported.
2. The distance to be covered.

Weber lists some more factors which influence the transportation costs such as: (a) the type of transportation system and the extent of its use, (b) the nature of the region and kinds of roads, and (c) the nature of goods themselves, i.e. the qualities which, besides weight, determine the facility of transportation.

However, the location of the place of production must be determined in relation to the place of consumption and to the most advantageously located material deposits. Thus, *locational figures* are created. These locational figures depend upon: (a) the type of material deposits, and (b) the nature of transformation into products.

11.13.2 Secondary Causes: We have so far been discussing primary causes of industrial location. Weber has also discussed secondary causes responsible for industrial location. He has taken into account agglomerative and deglomerative factors. An agglomerative factor, according to him is a factor which provides an advantage in production or marketing a commodity simply because industry is located at one place. On the other hand, deglomerative factor is one which gives such advantage because of decentralization of production.

Agglomerative factors include gas, water etc. and are conducive for concentration of industry and deglomerative factors include land values and taxes and lead to decentralisation. Pulls of agglomerative factors are index of manufacture and locational weight. According to

Weber, ratio of manufacturing cost of locational weight is co-efficient of manufacture. According to Weber, agglomeration is encouraged with high co-efficient and deglomeration with low. According to him, we shall do well to bear in mind that labour orientation is one form of deviation from the minimum point; agglomeration to another.

When agglomerative forces appear in an industry oriented towards labour, there takes place a competition between the agglomerative deviation and the labour deviation, a struggle to create, locations for agglomeration, as compared with labour locations, both bearing upon the foundations of the transport ground work. The contribution of Alfred Weber was monumental and subsequent location theorists have upheld his analysis, emphasising transport costs as the basic factor of location.

11.14 Sargent Florence's Theory of Industrial Location

Sargent Florence started with the idea that some of Weber's assumptions are not realistic. According to him geographical location of an industry is not as important as the distribution of occupied population. His main consideration is that occupational distribution of population should be the main and primary factor for taking into consideration the location of an industry.

His theory is mainly based on inductive analysis and while explaining location factor of an industry he has taken into consideration location factor and co-efficient of localisation. According to him, location factor is an index of the degree of concentration of an industry in a particular region. This index is calculated by taking into consideration two ratios, namely the percentage of workers of the industry in question found in the region under consideration and the percentage of all industrial workers in the country. In calculating index to find out the location factor the first one is divided by the second and if the quotient is one, the location factor is said to be unity and it can be said that the industry is evenly distributed over the whole country. If quotient is above unity, then it means the region under reference has higher share of industry.

11.14.1 Co-Efficient of Localisation: By this he meant prosperity of an industry for concentration. It indicates an industry's tendency for localisation anywhere in the country. It is primarily concerned with a particular industry and not a particular region. It will thus be a single figure for the industry and also for the country as a whole. On the basis of coefficients it becomes possible to divide the industries into three categories namely high, medium and low. Thus, coefficient helps in classifying industries according to their dispersion or concentration.

However, his theory is not in a position to explain the causes responsible for the choice of location of an industry. It can only help in finding out the existing state of industrial distribution in a country. It can be said that the theory is only the investigation of status quo and nothing beyond that. According to his theory, the number of workers is the only factor as the indicator of concentration of an industry. Choosing this one factor alone for finding out concentration of an industry is unrealistic assumption. Still, his theory is of considerable use for studying location dynamics and guiding the trends of industrial development in a country.

12

Role of Infrastructure and Logistics

Availability of adequate efficient and affordable infrastructural facilities constitutes the core of development strategy and efforts. By their very nature, infrastructure projects (power, railways, ports, civil aviation, roads and telecommunications) involve huge initial investments, long gestation periods and high risk. The demand for infrastructural services has increased rapidly after industrial liberalisation of the Indian economy. Unfortunately, infrastructural bottlenecks remain the biggest stumbling block of industrial progress in the country.

12.1 What is Infrastructure?

Infrastructure is generally defined as the physical framework of facilities through which goods and services are provided to the public. Its linkages to the economy are multiple and complex, because it affects production and consumption directly, creates positive and negative spill over effects (externalities), and involves large flows of expenditure.

In economic literature, infrastructure is popular by the name *overhead capital* which represents basic services without which primary, secondary and tertiary productive activities cannot function. The very success of social and economic transformation of an economy lies in providing inclusive and sustainable infrastructure amenities to the people and the pace of economic growth depends on how competently and judiciously an economy is able to address its infrastructure bottlenecks.

Generically, infrastructure has the following distinct components:

1. Energy (electricity, coal, petroleum and natural gas, renewable energy sources and atomic power for civil use).
2. Transport (railways, roads and road transport, shipping and ports and civil aviation).
3. Telecommunications and information technology.
4. Special economic zones (SEZs).
5. Harnessing water resources (irrigation).
6. Rural infrastructure (housing, transport, telephony, water supply and sanitation.
7. Urban infrastructure (housing, transport, slum clearance/development, water supply, sanitation and sewerage and solid waste management).

12.2 Why is Infrastructure Important?

The availability of adequate infrastructure facilities is imperative for the overall economic development of a country. Infrastructure adequacy has a productivity-enhancing and employment-generating impact. It helps determine success in diversifying production, expanding trade, coping with population growth, reducing poverty and improving environmental conditions. Infrastructure contributes to economic development both by increasing productivity and by providing amenities which enhance the quality of life. The services provided lead to growth in production in several ways.

1. Infrastructure services are intermediate inputs to privatisation and any reduction in these input costs raises the profitability of production, thus permitting higher levels of output, income, and/or employment.
2. They raise the productivity of other factors, including labour and other capital. Infrastructure is thereby often described as an 'unpaid' factor of production, since its availability leads to higher returns obtainable from other capital and labour.

The infrastructure sector covers a wide spectrum of services. Some of these services have a direct impact on the working of a business enterprise, while others are more important from a societal point of view. Each sub-sector of an infrastructural service is inherently unique in terms of its administration and operational structure, the regulatory framework governing its operations, the level of technology and the degree of commercialisation. In addition, while some services such as telecommunications can be provided on a strictly commercial basis, others like roads are expected to be fully provided by the State or at least part-subsidised.

Typically, as incomes rise, the composition of infrastructure changes significantly. For low-income countries, basic infrastructure is more important—water, irrigation, and transport. As economies mature, most of the basic consumption demands for water are met, the share of agriculture in the economy shrinks, and more transport infrastructure is provided. The share of power and telecommunications is greater in high-income countries.

Most directly, productive activities in industry, agriculture and services use electricity, telecommunications, water and transport as intermediate inputs. Even in the informal sector, infrastructure can be a major share of business expenses. A measurable benefit of investment in infrastructure is the reduced cost to users of each service unit consumed. This benefit is greater, the more the service is characterised by economies of scale.

If enterprises are unable to realise the benefit of efficient generation of infrastructure services, they are forced to seek higher-cost alternatives that may have unfavourable impacts on profits and production levels. Unreliability (erratic water pressure, call interruptions etc.) and lack of access to infrastructure services lead to under-utilisation of existing productive capacity and constrains short run productive efficiency and output growth. Users are forced to invest in alternative sources such as captive power plants and tube wells, thereby raising capital costs. This has ripple effects, creating bottlenecks and slack capacity utilisation in other sections of the economy. Problems like under-maintenance of facilities and poor service quality shifts the burden of infrastructure provision and increase overall costs to produce outcomes which are not the most economically efficient.

Infrastructure is central to the basic patterns of demand and supply, and to the economy's ability to respond to changes in prices or endowments of other resources. The expansion of service, high-technology and financial sectors relative to manufacturing industries increases the demand for telecommunications, but decreases the relative requirements for industrial waste disposal and transportation of manufacturing inputs and outputs.

The ultimate goal of infrastructure policy is to effectively deliver infrastructure services of high quality and at low prices, to households and firms in the country. The success of policies in infrastructure must be judged by the quality, quantity and prices that end-users are charged for these services, and comparisons with global standards on each of these three fronts. Provision of quality infrastructure services at reasonable cost is a necessary condition for achieving sustained economic growth. In fact, one of the major challenges being faced by the Indian economy is to enhance infrastructure investment and to improve the delivery system and quality of services. Investment in infrastructure involves high risk, low return, lumpiness of huge investment, high incremental capital/output ratio, long payback periods and superior technology. These prerequisites pose a constraint on the Government's efficient delivery of quality infrastructure services. Government is moving away from its traditional role as a *provider* of services to one of *facilitator* and *regulator* by ensuring that infrastructure services are actually delivered in a desirable manner. A robust economic and social infrastructure creates conducive environment for private investment and enterprise. This, in turn, leads to more production and employment.

12.3 Nature of Infrastructure Services

Infrastructure projects are characterised by large financial outlay requirements and long generation periods. Investment involves high upfront costs and long-term financing since the payback period is long. Infrastructure services are often monopolistic in nature, they usually involve high upfront costs and long payback periods, and investments are typically bulky and lumpy. They are also characterised by the existence of externalities which make it difficult for infrastructure entities to recoup investment costs and operational expenses through the levy of user charges. Consequently, infrastructure services have been predominantly provided by the public sector in almost all countries for most of the 20th century.

Historically, initiatives to implement infrastructure projects in India have generally been vested in the public sector. With infrastructure services being perceived as natural monopolies, it was argued that only the government should be entrusted with its provision. There was also the view that the financial outlays involved were beyond the resources available with the private sector. Both these views have since undergone a change. In the current fiscal situation, the government will be very constrained to raise resources from the market for providing budgetary support to departments or public sector enterprises engaged in infrastructure development. Technological improvements and organizational innovations have enabled unbundling of services and this, in turn, has debunked the view about economies of scale and the purely monopolistic nature of infrastructure activities.

A solution to the problems associated with the traditional approach to infrastructure can be found in commercialising these projects. The recovery of investments should be through a system of user charges which bears a direct relation to the specific benefits that the facility provides to the user.

12.4 Financing of Infrastructure

The importance of infrastructure financing towards economic growth can hardly be overemphasized. It has remained a principal area of government intervention in India and many other countries, given the sector's fundamental contribution to economic growth and social welfare. Developing countries have to make massive investments of financial, human and managerial resources in infrastructure.

Future investment needs are expected to be much higher, because of demand created by economic growth, rising population, rapid urbanisation as well as the need to reconstruct some economies and make up for lack of adequate investment in others in the recent past. This is particularly true for the East Asia Region, whose increasing investment needs are driven by its very high economic growth rate. The need for investment in infrastructure rises exponentially with economic growth rate.

Till recently, as the government implemented and financed the bulk of infrastructure outlays, all the attendant project risks were also borne by the government. Resource mobilisation, mainly domestic, was through pre-emption of funds from banks and insurance companies backed by issue of dated securities. Foreign funds, mainly in the form of project-specific aid from bilateral and multilateral sources, supplemented domestic resources. Hence, infrastructure financing was relatively simple and straightforward, but undoubtedly inefficient and lacking accountability.

The pattern of financing witnessed in the past will undergo a change as the transition from predominant state investment in infrastructure to increasing private/foreign participation occurs. While the reliance on domestic sources would continue as in the past, these would need to be augmented by foreign funds in the form of equity as well as debt.

12.4.1 Role of Financial Institutions: The nature of infrastructure projects and their inherent complexities make them different from traditional industrial projects with which the financial institutions (FIs) have been familiar. In addition to traditional financial, technical and economic appraisal capabilities of project financing, infrastructure projects require deep understanding of the legal, regulatory and institutional arrangements under which the project promoters would operate. Most infrastructure projects are limited-resource financing and hence bear higher risk compared to traditional industrial lending where the risk is covered by the balance sheet of the sponsor, with tangible assets as security.

Privately financed infrastructure projects need well developed domestic capital markets and provide an opportunity to develop them. Since most of these investments generate revenues in local currency, it may not be sustainable in the long run to finance these investments out of foreign savings. There is both the scope and the need to develop financial instruments and the market systems to tap domestic capital markets to finance infrastructure investments.

Private investment and financing while offering the benefit of additional funds, will also importantly encourage better risk sharing, accountability, monitoring and management. Empirical evidence suggests that infrastructure projects, irrespective of their sectoral characteristics, have high leverage ratios. Since the level of retained earnings over and above the depreciation provisions is low, infrastructure firms typically fund projects through debt finance. They also tend to diverge from the conventional pecking order of corporate finance, i.e. using retained earnings in preference to debt and debt in preference to public issues of equity capital to fund asset acquisition. Not only is the initial recourse to debt funding very high for infrastructure investments, but subsequent expansion, renovation, and modernisation are also funded substantially through debt finance. The central financial issue in infrastructure investment is not adequacy of funds, but more importantly the institutional framework and other related mechanisms which facilitate convergence of investment horizons of ultimate savers and borrowers in the economy.

In developed countries, infrastructure projects raise financing from institutional investors (insurance companies, pension funds, endowments, and the like) either through the bond markets, or through direct private placements. In India also, the contractual savings institutions [like Life Insurance Corporation of India (LIC), and General Insurance Corporation of India (GIC)] that have long-term liabilities, make natural investors in private infrastructure projects. Apart from these institutions, other institutional investors such as charitable and religious trusts can also be a source of substantial funds. With the development of an active and liquid market for securitised corporate debt, mutual funds, commercial banks and financial institutions, they could also emerge as potentially large investors. However, all this calls for substantial reform in the debt market.

At present all the contractual savings institutions are under the control of the government which largely pre-empts their funds. If infrastructure has to be financed through the capital markets, it is necessary to initiate major reforms in the area of contractual savings institutions, allowing for the entry of private companies and institutions in each of these areas. The government's programme to reduce its fiscal deficit would also bring down its pre-emption of funds in existing institutions. The more widespread availability of contractual savings instruments which provide good returns can be expected to lead to increasing financial savings rates of the households.

In order to leverage their core competence of project appraisal, the FIs would need to adopt a number of strategies, such as taking of loans onto their books and then syndicating them, or lending to projects during the construction and start-up stages, and securitising the loans or selling down the bonds, once operations have begun and the project is investment graded. FIs would thus bear their risk-assessment capabilities during the riskier pre-operative phase, with securitisation made easier in the post completion phase. Such turnover of portfolio would have a salutary effect on the quantum of funds mobilised. However, securitisation as a financing mechanism would require a fair amount of reforms in the legal framework.

12.4.2 Debt Market: If the trend towards private investment in infrastructure is to continue, financial markets will have to respond by providing the necessary long term resources. Parallel to the innovations in the structuring of contractual agreements, which are critical in making a project finance worthy, delivering long-term finance through alternative institutions and instruments would be critical success factors. Overall balance of payments constraints and the sheer size of infrastructure investments imply that a sustained infrastructure programme will have to be accompanied by a strategy for mobilising domestic funds. In turn, an increasing share of domestic savings will need to come from private sources as the government reduces its involvement in infrastructure.

Synergistic links can develop between private infrastructure projects and domestic financial intermediation through capital markets. Infrastructure developments and private (especially contractual) savers share a long term horizon. Bringing compatible savers and investors together is the task of the capital markets. At the same time, the financing of infrastructure projects improves appraisal capabilities and expands risk-diversification possibilities for local commercial banks, equity and bond markets, and institutional investors such as insurance companies and pension funds.

Successful implementation of the envisaged investment would call for reforms in all segments of the financial system. The major areas, where comprehensive polity and procedural changes would be necessary would largely be in the institutional segment of contractual savings—insurance, pension and provident funds and the debt market. The policies relating to the equity and forex markets, external commercial borrowings (ECBs) and fiscal concessions to infrastructure projects also need to be reviewed. Deepening and widening of the market in debt instruments through financial innovations are expected to go a long way in stepping up the overall domestic savings rate. This of course, also crucially hinges on the speed with which the policy framework is made conducive. International experience suggests that the traditional approaches to financing that involve term loans from FIs and banks and equity offerings in the domestic capital markets, are inadequate to match the risk returns profile and payback periods of infrastructure projects. FIs and banks are constrained by the time profile of their own liabilities and hence cannot prudently lend large volumes of debt. Hence, an intermediary would be needed to provide credit enhancements to extend the maturity of the funding raised for infrastructure projects.

In most countries, special arrangements have been made to make possible the issuance of different kinds of bonds meant mainly for raising resources from the capital market at the lowest possible cost and with the longest possible debt maturities. For example, in the US, much of urban infrastructure is financed through the sale of municipal bonds which have been given tax-free status by the Federal Government. A complex market structure exists to make these bonds marketable. The availability of credible ratings, financial guarantees, bond insurance and the like helps in this respect.

12.4.3 Value Guarantees: Governments are increasingly providing guarantees to private lenders rather than directly financing infrastructure projects. Though government guarantees targeted at specific sovereign risks are relatively new, loan guarantees that cover some or all of the repayment risk have been frequently used by governments to pursue policy objectives. It has been observed that such loan guarantees are of significant value, particularly when the underlying risk is high and the term of the loan exceeds 10 years. As such, when governments give guarantees, they are providing substantial comfort to lenders.

However, government guarantees for infrastructure projects involve risks which are often unexpectedly high for both the government, and the private investor. The government faces the risk of such unforeseen liabilities that may occur when the guarantee is called and when it may possibly lack the necessary budgetary resources to honour the commitment.

Similarly, because of this possibility of unforeseen future risk, the private investor also funds such guarantees to be less than credible, particularly at lower levels of government. Often, the market may not also attach much value to them and hence the credit enhancement provided by government guarantees is negligible. It is, therefore, suggested that government at both central and state levels should consider setting up Contingent Valuation Funds for providing additional back-up to any infrastructure project guarantees that are given. It is possible to value guarantees and thereby set aside specific funds from the budget on an annual basis so that the Contingent Valuation Fund has adequate resources to fund the guarantees in case they are called. Such a mechanism would provide both safety to the government as well as additional comfort to creditors.

12.5 Commercialisation of Infrastructure Services

With greater demand, changing technology, increasing complexity for financing the infrastructure projects and the budgetary constraints, the public sector is no longer able to discharge efficiently its role as a provider of infrastructure services. The Government has recognised that private sector participation including foreign investment is required to supplement the public sector efforts. Various reforms have been made in infrastructure sectors, and rules and procedures for investment have been liberalised in order to provide an enabling environment conducive for private participation.

A wave of privatisation and deregulation has been sweeping infrastructure sectors around the globe over the last decade or so. These bold new approaches promote improvement in efficiency and service quality. Whereas the specific motivations and circumstances vary by countries, and in countries by sectors, there are five factors that are leading economies all over the world to consider enhanced commercialization of infrastructure provision.

1. The massive investment requirement arising from sharply rising economic growth rates are pushing countries to look for additional sources of financing against the backdrop of fiscal stringency in most countries.
2. The rising awareness of the importance of efficiency in investment and delivery in the context of tight fiscal conditions, is leading to rethinking on the ability of government owned entities to supply infrastructure services in a business like manner.
3. Changes in technology now make it easier to charge for marginal use of infrastructure services. Such technological changes are making possible the introduction of competition horizontally and unbundling of services vertically.
4. The increasing need for countries to compete in the global marketplace is putting additional pressure on countries to provide efficient infrastructure services to their businesses in a cost-effective and competitive manner. Higher infrastructure costs in terms of both price and time delays can make the difference between firms being globally competitive or otherwise.
5. The new dynamism and integration of world capital markets have vastly increased

the possibility of raising large funds for infrastructure investment on a commercial basis whereas earlier, it was governments which had better access to resources. In many cases, it is now the private sector which has the capability of sourcing large funds internationally.

While these forces are pushing most countries towards the commercialisation of infrastructure investment services, there is also increasing understanding of the social dimension of infrastructure in poor countries in particular. The state bears a responsibility to provide the impoverished, access to basic services such as health, education, water supply, sanitation and sewerage.

Moreover, despite the new possibilities of competition mentioned above, most infrastructure services retain very strong monopolistic elements. As such, the State continues to be responsible for providing appropriate regulatory frameworks which assist investors and infrastructure entities on the one hand and protect consumers from monopolistic exploitation on the other. The commercialisation of infrastructure and unbundling also lead to a considerable increase in transaction costs which have to be mitigated through transparent and appropriate regulation.

The general condition is that whereas the possibility of commercialisation of infrastructure investment and services has increased tremendously over the last decades, the role of the public sector in investment delivery of services and in regulation will continue to be vital. The future therefore, suggests the introduction of a new framework for public-private-partnership (PPP) in different forms so that appropriate infrastructure investment can fructify.

12.5.1 Involvement of Private Sector in Infrastructure Projects: A major problem in the commercialisation of infrastructure projects is the appropriate allocation of risk. When infrastructure is provided by the public sector, all the risks are internalised within the government and hence the issue of risk allocation does not arise. Successful design of an infrastructure project involves the appropriate demarcation and allocation of risks to the different stakeholders in the project. Clarity in this allocation is essential to avoid confusion in the financing and implementation of commercialised infrastructure projects as the tendency of each stakeholder is to shift the risk to others. In other words, the question is what recourse the lenders have if investments fail to produce the expected returns. The financing is usually non-recourse, with lenders being repaid only from the cash flow generated by the project.

These days, financial markets have growing experience of non-recourse financing where the focus is not to down the balance sheet of the promoter. The assessment of the cash flow stream of an infrastructure project determines the eventual financing structure and the range of instruments required to realise it. In all cases, the viability of the project should be assessed at commercial rates of return.

Of late, different countries have adopted various methods for attracting private sector funds for infrastructure development. The most prominent, and possibly the most widely used, is the build-operate-transfer (BOT) arrangement. As the term suggests, the private investor (concessionaire) builds, operates and transfers the facility back to the government at the end of a specified period, called the concession period. A transparent regulatory framework is needed to make BOT type projects easier to negotiate and implement.

Recent years have witnessed substantial progress from the old paradigm of public monopoly provision of infrastructure services to the new paradigm which also encourages private investment and provision of infrastructure services within a stable, predictable and commercially viable regulatory framework.

12.6 Logistics: Meaning and Importance

Logistics refers to a series of services and activities, such as transportation, warehousing, and brokerage that help to move goods and establish supply chains across and within borders. Although these services and activities are carried out by private firms for the benefit of private firms, service delivery and the efficiency of supply chains depend on public sector provisions and interventions in a number of domains. Logistics uses publicly funded or regulated infrastructure. International trade is processed by border agencies. Services and logistics activities are regulated with fiscal, environmental, safety, land use, and competition objectives.

Logistics organizes the movement of goods through a network of activities and services operating at global, regional, and local scale. Logistics encompasses more than freight transportation. Traders delegate increasingly sophisticated tasks to networks of specialized service providers. Efficient logistics connects people and firms to markets and opportunities and helps achieve higher levels of productivity and welfare. Crucially, logistics is not only a private endeavour, but also a public policy concern. The performance and reliability of supply chains depend on an array of interventions, ranging from trade facilitation at the border to infrastructure and regulations and to urban planning and skills. Empirical evidence confirms that logistics and connectivity-related interventions have the highest potential to reduce the cost of trade and to boost integration in global value chains. Policy makers know that logistics matters and that they can improve the efficiency of the supply chains connecting their countries internally and externally.

Logistics performance both in international trade and domestically is central to the economic growth and competitiveness of countries, and the logistics sector is now recognized as one of the core pillars of economic development. Policy makers not only in the best performing countries, but also in emerging economies, increasingly see the need to implement coherent and consistent policies to foster seamless and sustainable supply chain operations as an engine of growth. Efficient logistics connects firms to domestic and international markets through reliable supply chain networks. Conversely, countries characterized by low logistics performance face high costs, not merely because of transportation costs but also because of unreliable supply chains, a major handicap in integrating and competing in global value chains.

Logistics firms have a strong incentive to provide predictable deliveries in both the developed and the developing world. Supply chain reliability continues to be a major concern among traders and logistics providers. In a global environment, consignees require a high degree of certainty on when and how deliveries will take place. This is much more important than the speed of the delivery. Predictability also carries a premium, which many shippers are willing to pay. In other words, supply chain predictability is a matter not merely of time and cost, but also of shipment quality.

Efficient clearance procedures at the border are critical to eliminating avoidable delays and to improving supply chain predictability. To achieve this, governments need to facilitate trade, while safeguarding the public against harmful activities ranging from health hazards to crime and terrorism. Realizing these two objectives—facilitating trade and safeguarding the public interest—is a challenge for policy makers and authorities, especially in countries with a low performance record, where delays and unexpected costs are more common.

Trade facilitation tools and principles have taken hold in many countries thanks to growing awareness and international initiatives to support trade facilitation reforms in developing countries. Co-ordination among government-controlled agencies continues to require attention, including the need to introduce best practices in automation and risk management in non-customs control agencies.

Implementation of trade and transport reform is lagging in the logistically constrained countries that are most in need of attention from the international community. Many landlocked developing countries and small island states also fall into this category because their connectivity with global markets is severely challenged by their economic size or geography. In logistics-friendly countries, manufacturers and traders already outsource much of their basic transport and logistics operations to third-party providers and focus on their core business, while managing more complex supply chains. The more such advanced services are available at a reasonable price-cost ratio, the more shippers will outsource their logistics. The demand for environmentally friendly logistics solutions, or green logistics, is gradually becoming a common feature in most advanced logistics environment.

12.7 Strategies to Improve Logistics

Comprehensive strategies increasingly focus not merely on looking at the sources of costs, but on steering a sector with a large footprint in the economy and with links to concerns about the environment, jobs, land use, urban planning, and other issues.

Logistics performance depends on the availability to traders of reliable supply chains and predictable service delivery. Global supply chains are becoming more complex, and the safety, social, environmental, and other regulations affecting traders and operators are becoming more demanding. Efficient management and information technology (IT) solutions in both the private and public sectors are vital tools of the trade in high-quality logistics. The ability to manage logistics processes in today's global business environment is a crucial factor in national competitiveness. More than ever, comprehensive reform and long-term commitments from policy makers and private stakeholders are needed.

The two main objectives of current logistics strategies in all types of economies are as follows. First, logistics is an input to much of the economy, i.e. industry, commerce, and so on. The performance of logistics impacts productivity in other sectors. This is most often presented in negative language in terms of average costs of logistics.

Secondly, logistics can be a sector of development in and of itself, where countries with high global or regional connectivity expect to play the role of a logistics and trade hub, such as the Netherlands in Europe and Dubai or Singapore in Asia.

12.7.1 One Belt, One Road: Led by China, this initiative targets 60+ countries. This ambitious programme seeks to improve trade connectivity among Silk Road economies and also countries on the main sea routes from China. It is likely to have significant implications for logistics operators. Though in its early stages, the initiative has an ambitious scope. It will target physical infrastructure in a variety of locations, catalyzing finance and investment resources. The initiative can help develop a broad, business-focused programme that can work on multiple fronts to bring improvements in trade facilitation and logistics to participating countries. However, hard infrastructure is not enough. There also needs to be a soft component, involving regulatory reform in service markets such as transport, logistics, and telecommunications.

13

Agriculture and Economic Development

Achievement of rapid and sustainable growth in any country is critically dependent on its ability to use and manage its natural resources effectively. The most important natural resource of any country is land which is the base for agricultural production. Land, a non-renewable resource, is central to all primary production systems.

Land is a fixed resource. There is a conflict regarding the allocation of available land between agriculture, industry and urban use. It is important to recognise that diversion of land from agricultural to non-agricultural uses is inevitable in any development process since industry must expand and so also cities and in both cases land needed can only come from agriculture. Concern is often raised in this context about the impact on food security. This problem is greatly exaggerated because the productivity of land in agriculture in less developed countries (LDCs) at present is very low and the shift of some land from agriculture to non-agricultural use can easily be offset by productivity increases, which are feasible and have been seen in many other developed countries.

There is inter-dependence between agriculture and industry. The development of the agricultural sector depends, to a large extent, on such core industries as power, petroleum, fertilisers and machine tools. Agricultural sector provides market for capital goods (tractors, pump sets and other agricultural machinery), inputs (fertilisers, insecticides), and light consumer goods.

As a country develops economically, the relative importance of agriculture declines. The primary reason for that was shown by the 19th century German statistician Ernst Engel, who discovered that as incomes increase, the proportion of income spent on food declines.

13.1 Why is Agriculture Important for Less Developed Countries (LDCs)?

In looking back on the history of the present day developed countries, one can see that agriculture played an important part in the process of their enrichment. For one thing, if development is to occur, agriculture must be able to produce a surplus of food to maintain the growing non-agricultural labour force. Since food is more essential for life than are the services provided by merchants or bankers or insurers, an economy cannot shift to such activities unless food is available for barter or sale in sufficient quantities to support those engaged in them. Unless food can be obtained through international trade, a country does not normally develop industrially until its farm areas can supply its towns with food in exchange for the products of their factories.

Economic development also requires a growing labour force. In an agricultural country most of the workers needed must come from the rural population. Thus, agriculture must not only supply a surplus of food for the towns, but it must also be able to produce the increased amount of food with a relatively smaller labour force. It may do so by substituting animal power for human power or by gradually introducing labour-saving machinery.

Agriculture may also be a source of the capital needed for industrial development to the extent that it provides a surplus that may be converted into the funds needed to purchase industrial equipment or to build roads and provide public services. A strong agricultural economy brings social progress by increasing productivity, employment and income. Agriculture is the main driver of development in most rural areas. Demand for staple foods, agricultural commodities and processed food is growing in developing countries. To meet these needs, the agricultural and food sectors must be modernized.

For these reasons, a country seeking to develop its economy may well be advised to give a significant priority to agriculture. Experience in the developing countries has shown that agriculture can be made much more productive with the proper investment in irrigation systems, research, fertilizers, insecticides, and herbicides. Fortunately, many advances in applied science do not require massive amounts of capital, although it may be necessary to expand marketing and transportation facilities so that farm output can be brought to the entire population.

One difficulty in giving priority to agriculture is that most of the increase in farm output and most of the income gains are concentrated in certain regions rather than extending throughout the country. The remaining farmers are not able to produce more and actually suffer a disadvantage as farm prices decline. There is no easy answer to that problem, but developing countries need to be aware of it.

As economic development proceeds, a large proportion of the farm labour force must shift from agriculture into other pursuits. That fundamental shift in the labour force is made possible, of course, by an enormous increase in output per worker as agriculture becomes modernized. That increase in output stems from various factors. Where land is plentiful, the output per worker is likely to be higher because it is possible to employ more fertilizer and machinery per worker.

13.2 Characteristics of Agriculture in LDCs

13.2.1 Subsistence Agriculture: As against the commercialised nature of agricultural operations in the developed countries, farming in LDCs still remains a source of livelihood for most farmers. The main reason for this is the low per capita availability of land. As a result of population growth, there is tremendous pressure on available cultivable land. This has led to overcrowding and hence sub-division and fragmentation of holdings. Small-sized and scattered holdings imply wastage of time and labour, difficulties in the use of modern techniques, and quarrels and litigation among farmers. The existence of these problems is also responsible for poor farm yield.

Farm families consume a substantial part of what they produce. While some of their output may be sold in the market, their total production is generally not much larger than what is needed for the maintenance of the family. Not only is productivity per worker low under those conditions, but yields per unit of land are also low. Even where the land was originally fertile, the fertility is likely to have been depleted by decades of continuous cropping. The available manures are not sufficient, and the farmers cannot afford to purchase them elsewhere.

13.2.1 Small-sized Holdings: The average size of farms is small and this is often in fragments. There are also those who are entirely landless, although agriculture is their main source of livelihood. They have inadequate financial resources to purchase land and often depend on leasing at insecure terms and for short periods. Hence many face insecurity of tenure and the growing threat of land alienation.

Small farmers are unable to take advantage of the economies of scale, or invest in lumpy inputs such as irrigation, technology or machinery. They have limited access to formal credit. Hence, they have few resources for land improvement or crop insurance or adequate inputs (seeds, fertilisers etc.). They are often ignored by extension agencies and seldom receive information on new technologies or training in skill-intensive agricultural practices.

Sub-division of holdings leads to loss of cultivable land due to boundaries. Too many boundaries cause disputes, often leading to litigation. Instead of investing their precious resources in improving the productivity of land, farmers waste their limited funds in settling claims and counter claims. This tendency has created tensions in rural areas.

What is the ideal size of a holding? The ideal size of a holding (called economic holding or optimum holding) is one which allows the most efficient use of land, labour and capital with a given technique of production. It is difficult to prescribe a uniform size of economic holding for all crops and for all regions. In fact, the size of economic holding depends upon a host of factors such as nature of the crop, fertility of soil and technique of production.

There is a great debate among agricultural economists regarding the relationship between size of farms and productivity/profitability. Productivity simply means output per hectare of land while farm-profitability relates to the value of output over all costs of cultivation. Some experts have argued that as farm size increases, productivity also increases. However, some researchers hold the opposite view and maintain that productivity declines as farm size increases.

13.2.3 Fragmented Holdings: Fragmented holdings create difficulties in the management of land resources. When a farmer has to shift from one piece of land to another, it involves wastage of manpower and extra expenses. Similarly, fragmented farms restrict opportunities for the use of modern science and technology. Proper arrangements for irrigation cannot be made if farms belonging to a farmer are scattered here and there. Modern agricultural machines cannot be successfully operated on tiny farms. Absence or limited use of modern agricultural practices keeps farm productivity low.

13.3 Causes of Low Productivity of Agriculture

Although per hectare yield of major crops has increased in developing countries over the years yet it is far below the international levels. Statistical evidence suggests that farm productivity in LDCs is low as compared to developed countries of the world. The low productivity of the agricultural sector is attributable to a host of technological and institutional factors. Some of the important factors are described hereby.

13.3.1 Lack of Good Quality Seeds: One of the most outstanding achievements of agricultural research is the production of improved varieties of seeds for different crops. One of the main reasons for the low levels of yields in agriculture in LDCs has been the unsatisfactory spread of new technological practices, including the adoption of high yielding varieties of seeds (HYV). The adoption of new technology, mainly the HYV seeds requires intensive use of fertilisers and pesticides under adequate and assured water supply. The scope for securing increased production from the use of improved seed is very considerable.

13.3.2 Lack of Irrigation Facilities: Most of the farmers depend on uncertain rainfall for irrigation of their fields. Rainfall is uncertain in terms of quantity, place and time. Agriculture is still a gamble for millions of farmers in LDCs.

13.3.3 Limited Use of Fertilisers: Adequate use of fertilisers is crucial for improving the farm productivity. Unfortunately, the use of fertilisers by farmers in LDCs is much below the level achieved in developed countries. Manures and fertilizers play the same part in relation to the soil as food in relation to the body. Just as a well-nourished body is capable of the maximum effort, a well nourished soil will have the best fertility. Organic matter, nitrogen, phosphorus and potash are the chief constituents which must be supplied to the soil.

13.3.4 Inadequate Plant Protection Schemes: Another reason for low productivity is the damage caused to crops by insects, pests, and plant diseases. The use of pesticides and insecticides is not widespread, particularly among the small and marginal farmers. The triple alliance of pests, pathogens and weeds is the cause of substantial crop losses every year. Plant protection is an important component of crop production programme. Plant protection activities encompass plant quarantine, regulation of pesticides, activities aimed at minimizing crop losses due to pests (including locust control in desert areas), and training and capacity building in plant protection.

13.3.5 Lack of Farm Mechanisation: Most farmers in LDCs still use age-old farming techniques like wooden plough, cattle power, and sickle. The use of modern farm machinery is limited to affluent farmers. Use of modern methods of production is conditioned by the institutional framework of a production sector. If the institutional set up is exploitative, it will discourage the adoption of efficient technology. Unfortunately, the institutional setting of the farm sector in most LDCs is not congenial for the use of modern agricultural technology.

There is a great deal of controversy regarding mechanisation of agriculture in view of widespread unemployment and disguised unemployment in rural areas. Therefore, the policy regarding mechanisation of agriculture has to be cautious and selective. It is true that by using modern agricultural machines productivity of land can be raised. However, there are fears that such an approach will displace labour, adding to the already huge army of unemployed/underemployed people. Whatever may be the arguments for and against mechanization of agriculture, the fact of the matter remains that farmers in many LDCs are adopting modern mechanical devices to boost their farm productivity. To keep pace with improved production and productivity, different machines have been developed for effective cultivation, intercultural operations, harvesting, grading, packaging and value addition.

13.3.6 Marketing Difficulties: Marketing is the last ring in the production chain. If the marketing system is inefficient and denies the farmers a reasonable return for their efforts, they will be discouraged to produce more. Unfortunately, the present marketing system of agricultural produce is not favourable to the interests of the farmers. The preponderance of intermediaries and the malpractices of commission agents deny remunerative prices to the farmers.

13.3.7 Lack of Agricultural Research: Agricultural research is of a continuing nature. New knowledge has to be gained, and fresh problems tackled. The role of universities in promoting agricultural research is a question which needs attention. Although universities are eminently suited for such research, especially of the more fundamental type, they have not taken it up to any significant extent in the past, owing perhaps to lack of funds and other causes. Limitations in the way of the universities to take an appropriate part in agricultural research should be removed and the universities encouraged to make their contribution to research. This will benefit the universities also by bringing their scientific staffs into direct contact with real problems which are in urgent need of solution for the betterment of the vast majority of rural people.

Extension is another element needing urgent attention alongside research. New methods and approaches need to be devised for agricultural extension using information technology and mobile technology. Local participation of progressive farmers, self-help groups and agricultural co-operative societies should be leveraged to help transfer technology through one-to-one exchange of information.

13.3.8 Skewed Cropping Pattern: Cropping pattern refers to the distribution of cultivated land among different crops grown in a country. Cropping pattern reveals the nature of agricultural operations, e.g. the importance of food crops vis-à-vis cash crops. Cropping pattern is influenced by a host of factors which can be broadly classified into two categories: (a) physical factors, and (b) economic factors.

The existing cropping pattern in most LDCs is skewed towards cultivation of sugarcane, paddy and wheat. Crop diversification can be used as a tool to promote sustainable agriculture, reduction in import dependence and higher incomes for the farmers. Shifting some area from staple cereals to high value produce can lead to a sizable increase in the returns for farmers. This would also bring in water use efficiency and sustainability of soil health.

13.4 Agro Forestry

Agro forestry means practice of agriculture and forestry on the same piece of land. It has been defined as a sustainable management system for land that increases overall production, combines agricultural crops and animals simultaneously. It also connotes a land use system that integrates trees, crops and animals in a way that is scientifically sound, ecologically desirable, practically feasible and socially acceptable to the farmers.

Another widely used definition given by the International Centre for Research in

Agro-forestry (ICRAF) Nairobi, Kenya reads: "Agro-forestry is a collective name for all land use systems and practices where woody perennials are deliberately grown on the same land management unit as agricultural crops or animals in some form of spatial arrangement or temporal sequence".

13.4.1 Advantages of Agro Forestry: It is only too obvious that government owned forests cannot meet the current requirement of the country, let alone in the future. Forests, even at the optimum level of conservation and productivity, would find this task not possible. With forests under increasing pressure, agro forestry is the only segment that can record growth in production—in timber, fuel wood, industrial wood, fodder and grass, medicinal plants and the rest. The current situation and future prospects must alter the role of forests and forestry, and with it the forest personnel would also have to change their recruitment, training, attitudes and mindset. Needs of timber, fuel wood, fodder, industrial wood and medicinal plants must also be met from private lands and community lands. This can only happen if the farmers get remunerative returns and there are no hassles in harvesting, transport and market access.

Timber and fuel wood produced under agro forestry meet the local demands in rural areas and thus the problems and expenditure related to transport is avoided. Productivity of agro forestry plantations is much higher than that of natural forests or plantations in forest areas. Production and processing of wood produced under agro forestry is estimated to generate substantial employment in rural areas, major part of which is in processing of timber such as sawing, joinery, furniture making etc. Agro forestry thus offers great potential of providing off farm employment, which is strategically needed to take surplus labour off agriculture.

Agro forestry is capable of meeting the present challenges of resource conservation and improvement of environmental quality. In low rainfall areas, agro forestry increases rainfall utilization by extending the growing season. Agro forestry provides insurance against risks caused by weather aberrations and erosion hazards and ensures sustainable production of the land. In agro forestry, maintenance of a sufficient ground cover during the period of erosive rains has a high potential to reduce erosion.

Following are the tangible and intangible benefits of agro forestry system:

1. Improvement in soil structure and fertility with increasing effects on crop yield.
2. Reduction in losses from soil erosion.
3. Creation of better micro climatic conditions for the growth of agricultural crops.
4. Greater efficiency of tree species for photosynthesis.
5. Meeting the demand of fuel, fodder and timber for the increasing population.
6. Development of wasteland/degraded lands by planting suitable tree species with agricultural crops.
7. Reduction in the biotic pressure on existing forests.

Thus, agro forestry can help in poverty alleviation in rural areas.

13.4.2 Constraints of Agro Forestry: In spite of its various benefits, agro forestry is not widespread in most underdeveloped countries due to the following reasons:

1. Lack of appropriate machinery and infrastructure at the ground level for generating

data on agro forestry area, production and prices by species and regions.

2. Market imperfections.
3. Lack of adequate policy and institutional infrastructure for promotion of agro forestry.
4. Lack of awareness on the part of farmers.

Farmers would grow commercially important species only if they get remunerative prices for their produce. Non-availability of quality planting stock of commercially important species, inadequate extension services on the benefits of planting tree species, restrictions on felling and transport, lack of market linkages etc. are some of the constraints which discourage bringing more area under farm forestry.

14

Public Goods and the Problem of Free-riding

14.1 Public versus Private Goods

Harvey Rosen and Ted Gayer have given the following illustration to make clear the distinction between public goods and private goods, "What's the difference between national defence and pizza? The question seems silly, but thinking about it leads to a useful framework for determining whether public or private provision of various commodities makes sense. To begin, one big difference between the two commodities is that two people cannot consume a pizza simultaneously—if I eat a piece, you can't. In contrast, your consumption of the protective services provided by the army does nothing to diminish my consumption of the same services. A second major difference arises because I can easily exclude you from consuming my pizza, but excluding you from the benefits of national defence is all but impossible. National defence is an example of a pure public good, defined as follows.

- Once it is provided, the additional resource cost of another person consuming the good is zero, i.e. consumption is non-rival.
- To prevent anyone from consuming the good is either very expensive or impossible, i.e. consumption is non-excludable.

In contrast, a private good like pizza is rival and excludable". [1]

14.2 Pure and Impure Public Goods

The production of public goods results in positive externalities for which producers do not receive full payment. Pure public goods are those that are perfectly non-rivalrous in consumption and non-excludable. Impure public goods are those that satisfy the two conditions to some extent, but not fully.

By the traditional definition, a pure public good is *equally available* to all members of the relevant community. A single unit of the good, as produced, provides a multiplicity of consumption units, all of which are somehow identical. Once produced, it will not be efficient to exclude any person from the enjoyment (positive or negative) of its availability. According to Richard Musgrave, the principle of exclusion characteristic of goods produced in the market breaks down here. Non-exclusion applies in the extreme or polar sense. Additional consumers may be added at zero marginal cost.

Strictly speaking, no good or service fits the extreme or polar definition in any genuinely descriptive sense. In real-world fiscal systems, those goods and services that are financed publicly always exhibit less than such pure publicness. The standard examples such as national defence come reasonably close to descriptive purity, but even here careful consideration normally dictates some relaxation of the strict polar assumption. It is evident that the whole theory would be severely limited if it were to stand or fall on the correspondence of this purity assumption with observations from the real world.

A pure public good is a good which satisfies both non-excludability and non-rivalry assumptions.

14.3 Public Goods and the Free Riding Problem

Public goods include roads, public parks, and street lights etc. Public goods may give rise to the *free rider problem.* A free-rider is a person who receives the benefit of a good without paying for it. In other words, people free ride on the efforts of others to recycle. This may lead to the under-provision of certain goods or services.

The free rider problem is an economic concept of a market failure that occurs when people are benefiting from resources, goods, or services that they do not pay for. If there are too many free riders, the resources, goods, or services may be underprovided. Therefore, this would create a free rider problem. The problem is commonly seen with public goods (goods with non-excludable benefits).

Suppose a shipping company builds a lighthouse on the coast to serve as a navigational aid for its sailors. As a result, all sailors (including non-company sailors) are now able to benefit from the lighthouse even if they are not paying towards its upkeep. If too many sailors are free riding, there would be no incentive for the shipping company to maintain the lighthouse, as it is the only entity contributing to its upkeep.

Public goods commonly face a free rider problem due to the two characteristics of a public good:

1. **Non-rival:** Consumption of the good or service by one individual does not reduce the availability of the good to others.
2. **Non-excludable:** It is impossible to prevent other consumers from consuming the good or service.

In the above example, use of light house by non-company sailors does not reduce the availability of navigational aid from the light house for company sailors. Secondly, it is not possible to exclude non-company sailors from availing the services of light house.

Take another example. A residents' welfare association collects ₹ 500 from every household as maintenance charges to provide security and other facilities in the locality. If one householder refuses to pay the charges, he will still be enjoying the facilities and security environment provided by the association. By all accounts, he will be free rider.

Other examples of public goods where consumption is non-rival and exclusion is not possible include national defence, fresh air and street lighting.

14.4 Limitations of Market Mechanism

Left to itself, market mechanism cannot perform all economic functions optimally. The premise that market mechanism leads to efficient use of resources, i.e. it produces in the cheapest way what consumers want the most, is based on the following assumptions:

1. There is perfect competition in the factor market as well as in the commodity market.
2. Individuals can be excluded from consuming goods if they do not pay for them.

These conditions are rarely fulfilled in practice. Monopolistic and oligopolistic tendencies replace competitive forces to rob capitalism of its virtues. To quote, "in reality, various difficulties arise. Markets may be imperfectly competitive, production may be subject to decreasing cost, consumers may lack sufficient information or be misled by advertising, and so forth. For these reasons, market mechanism is not as ideal a provider of private goods as it might be". [2] State intervention becomes necessary to curb such tendencies to protect consumers' interests. Even if it is assumed that competition is assured in the factor and commodity markets, still certain goods, because of their peculiar production and consumption characteristics, cannot be provided through market mechanism. In view of the problem of externalities, certain services (like defence, and street lighting) have to be provided through the public sector. This leads us to the discussion of public or social goods. [3]

14.5 Market Failure for Public Goods

Market mechanism operates almost successfully in the case of private goods. The two chief characteristics of private goods are: (a) benefits derived are internalised, and (b) consumption is rival. In other words, market for private goods functions on the basis of exclusion principle. According to this principle, he who pays the price gets the commodity, and he who does not pay the price is denied the same. The principle applies in the case of private goods like food, furniture, houses, cycles, and hundreds of other marketable goods. As we see in our daily life, the nature of these goods is such that the exclusion principle can be readily applied. When A pays the price, he is handed over the shirt but B is refused the same if he fails to make the payment. This is so because benefits derived are internalised and consumption is rival.

However, market mechanism fails in the case of public goods. The production and consumption characteristics of social goods are such that they cannot be provided through the market economy. To quote, "Social goods are goods the consumption of which is non-rival. That is, they are goods where A's partaking of the consumption benefits does not reduce the benefits derived by all others". [4] Two appropriate examples of non-rival consumption are: (a) defence services, and (b) anti-pollution measures. It would be inefficient to apply exclusion principle in the case of such services. Efficient resource use requires that price should equal marginal cost. Since the marginal cost in this case is zero, the additional consumer should be admitted even if he pays zero price. It is noteworthy that exclusion, even if desired, is not possible in the case of services mentioned above. In short, market may fail due to non-rival consumption or due to non-excludability or both of these reasons.

14.6 Allocative Inefficiency

Allocative inefficiency (also known as excess burden or deadweight loss) is a loss of economic efficiency that can occur when the free market equilibrium for a good or a service is not achieved. Price ceilings and rent controls can also create deadweight loss by discouraging production and decreasing the supply of goods, services, or housing below what consumers truly demand. Consumers experience shortages, and producers earn less than they would otherwise.

A deadweight loss is a cost to society created by market inefficiency, which occurs when supply and demand are out of equilibrium. In other words, market inefficiency occurs when goods within the market are either overvalued or undervalued. While certain members of society may benefit from the imbalance, others will be negatively impacted by a shift from equilibrium.

Mainly used in economics, deadweight loss can be applied to any deficiency caused by an inefficient allocation of resources. Price ceilings, such as price controls and rent controls; price floors, such as minimum wage and living wage laws; and taxation can all potentially create deadweight losses. With a reduced level of trade, the allocation of resources in a society may also become inefficient. Overvalued prices may lead to higher profit margins for a company, but it negatively affects consumers of the product. For goods the demand of which is relatively inelastic, the increased cost may prevent consumers from making purchases in other market sectors. In addition, some consumers may purchase a lower quantity of the item when possible. For goods the demand of which is relatively elastic, consumers may reduce spending in that market sector, though unwillingly.

Minimum wage laws can create a deadweight loss by causing employers to overpay for employees and preventing low-skilled workers from securing jobs. Price ceilings and rent controls can also create deadweight loss by discouraging production and decreasing the supply of goods, services, or housing below what consumers truly demand. Consumers experience shortages, and producers earn less than they would otherwise.

Taxes also create a deadweight loss because they prevent people from engaging in purchases they would otherwise make because the final price of the product is above the equilibrium market price. If taxes on an item rise, the burden is often split between the producer and the consumer, leading to the producer receiving less profit from the item and the customer paying a higher price. This results in lower consumption of the item than previously, which reduces the overall benefits the consumer market could have received while simultaneously reducing the benefit the company may see in regard to profits.

14.7 Models of Allocative Efficiency

Allocative efficiency is a state of the economy in which production represents consumer preferences. In particular, every good or service is produced up to the point where the last unit provides a marginal benefit to consumers equal to the marginal cost of producing.

In contract theory, allocative efficiency is achieved in a contract in which the skill demanded by the offering party and the skill of the agreeing party are the same.

An efficient allocation of resources occurs when those goods and services are produced which people value most highly. Resources are allocated efficiently when it is not possible to produce more of a good or service without giving up some other good or service that is valued more highly. In other words, an efficient allocation of resources is: that combination of inputs, outputs and distribution of inputs, outputs such that any change in the economy can make someone better off only by making someone worse off (called Pareto efficiency).

Although there are different standards of evaluation for the concept of allocative efficiency, the basic principle asserts that in any economic system, choices in resource allocation produce both *winners* and *losers* relative to the choice being evaluated. The principles of rational choice, individual maximization, utilitarianism and market theory further suppose that the outcomes for winners and losers can be identified, compared and measured. Under these basic premises, the goal of attaining allocative efficiency can be defined according to some principle where some allocations are subjectively better than others. For example, an economist might say that a change in policy is an allocative improvement as long as those who benefit from the change (winners) gain more than the losers lose.

An allocatively efficient economy produces an *optimal mix* of commodities. A firm is allocatively efficient when its price is equal to its marginal costs (P = MC) in a perfect market. When a market fails to allocate resources efficiently, there is said to be market failure. Market failure may occur because of externalities, imperfect knowledge of market, differentiated goods, and concentrated market power (e.g. monopoly or oligopoly).

Allocative efficiency is the main tool of welfare analysis to measure the impact of markets and public policy upon society and subgroups being made better or worse off.

14.8 Pareto Optimality Criterion

This famous criterion of social welfare was suggested by the Italian economist Vilfredo Pareto (1848-1923). It refers to economic efficiency which can be objectively measured. The Pareto optimality (or Pareto efficiency) criterion may be defined in the following different ways.

Any change which makes at least one individual better-off and no one worse-off is an improvement in social welfare. Conversely, any change which makes no one better-off and at least one worse-off is a decrease in social welfare. To put it differently, a situation in which it is impossible to make anyone better-off without making someone worse-off is said to be Pareto-optimal or Pareto-efficient.

There are three marginal conditions which must be satisfied for the attainment of Pareto-efficient situation. These are: (a) efficiency in exchange, (b) efficiency of production, and (c) efficiency in the composition of output.

There are important limitations of Pareto-criterion. For example, it cannot evaluate a change which makes some individuals better-off and others worse-off. Since most government policies involve changes which benefit some and harm others therefore Pareto criterion has limited applicability in real world situations. Moreover, Pareto-optimal situation does not guarantee the maximisation of the social welfare. Pareto-optimal situation is a necessary but not a sufficient condition for maximum social welfare.

14.8.1 Pareto Optimality and Externalities in the Real World: The problem with Pareto optimality is that it is possibly inapplicable to the real world entirely. All economic value is subjective and, by its nature, impossible to compare interpersonally. Even if it were possible, it is unlikely that anyone could possess the adequate knowledge of timing and circumstance to know how each individual values any given transaction. In practical terms, this means it is not possible to move markets towards a Pareto Optimal solution through a top-down approach.

Endnotes

1. Harvey Rosen and Ted Gayer (2008), *Public Finance* (Eighth edition), McGraw-Hill, International, pp. 52-53.
2. Richard Musgrave and Peggy Musgrave (1985), *Public Finance in Theory and Practice,* McGraw-Hill Book Company, New York, p. 48.
3. The terms public goods and social goods are used interchangeably here. For niceties of the distinction between the two, see *ibid*, pp. 50-51.
4. Richard Musgrave and Peggy Musgrave, op. cit., p. 49.

15

Good Governance and Economic Development

In its most abstract sense, governance is a theoretical concept referring to the actions and processes by which stable practices and organizations arise and persist. These actions and processes may operate in formal and informal organizations of any size; and they may function for any purpose, good or evil, for profit or not. Conceiving of governance in this way, one can apply the concept to states, corporations, NGOs, partnerships, and any number of humans engaged in some purposeful activity.

Most theories of governance as process arose out of neo-classical economics. These theories build deductive models, based on the assumptions of modern economics, to show how rational actors may come to establish and sustain formal organizations, including firms and states, and informal organizations, such as networks and practices for governing the commons. Many of these theories draw on transaction cost economics

15.1 Governance Defined

Governance is a very general concept that can refer to all manner of entities. Equally, this generality means that governance is often defined more narrowly to refer to a particular *level* of governance associated with a type of organization (including public governance, global governance, non-profit governance, corporate governance, and project governance), a particular *field* of governance associated with a type of activity or outcome (including environmental governance, internet governance, and information technology governance), or a particular *model* of governance, often derived as an empirical or normative theory (including regulatory governance, participatory governance, multi-level governance, meta-governance, and collaborative governance). Governance can be used not only to describe these diverse topics but also to define normative or practical agendas for them. Normative concepts of fair governance or good governance are common among political, public sector, voluntary, and private sector organizations.

The World Bank defines governance as "the manner in which power is exercised in the management of a country's economic and social resources for development." The Worldwide Governance Indicators project of the World Bank defines governance as "the traditions and institutions by which authority in a country is exercised".

According to the United Nations Development Programme's Regional Project on Local Governance for Latin America, "Governance has been defined as the rules of the political system to solve conflicts between actors and adopt decision (legality). It has also been used to describe the proper functioning of institutions and their acceptance by the public".

15.2 Importance of Governance

Better governance is crucial for translating the large development and welfare expenditure of the public authorities into enduring outcomes on the ground. While there is general appreciation that development programmes have the right objectives, their implementation on the ground is poor. Implementation of programmes can be improved through a multi-faceted approach relying on professionalization of public service delivery, total quality management (TQM), innovative use of digital and other technologies which improve monitoring and supervision. It can also be improved through: (a) greater emphasis on social mobilisation and capacity building, (b) strengthening of local institutions, and (c) building deeper partnerships with civil society organisations and the community to determine the needs and aspirations of the people.

Implementation in many areas—particularly in infrastructure development involving large projects—is held up for a variety of reasons. Co-ordination needed across different agencies to facilitate progress in project implementation is often lacking and can lead to long delays and cost over-runs. Project management capabilities must be improved for the country to get better returns from public investment in infrastructure and also in the social sectors.

Corruption distorts the decision-making mechanism and leads to an inefficient distribution of resources. Improving anti-corruption efforts is one of the highest rated priorities of the business leaders. India should work closely with the relevant international organizations and give particular importance to the fight against corruption in the public and private sectors. Measures to increase transparency in government-business relations will have a corrective impact on corruption.

A number of initiatives need to be urgently pursued to rid the system of corruption, which is both morally abhorrent and imposes economic costs. Several legislative measures are needed. These include the establishment of an effective Lokpal, introduction of a law on public procurement and transparency, and the creation of a legislative framework governing the functioning of regulatory institutions so as to ensure both functional autonomy and accountability.

To combat corruption, it is imperative to ensure speedy prosecution and trial in corruption cases. The long delays in the judicial process are an important factor behind the growing cynicism about the rule of law in our system. Reforms in the legal process need to be put in place without further delays.

The use of information technology (IT)—world's fastest growing economic activity—to improve governance cannot be over-emphasized. It is transforming resource-based economies to knowledge-based economies. IT has become the greatest agent of change and promises to play this role even more dramatically in future. IT changes every aspect of human life, apart from impacting changes in the field of communications, trade, manufacturing, services, culture, entertainment, education, research and national security. IT has broken old barriers and is building new interconnections in the emerging concept of a single global village. It has also become one of the critical indicators of the progress of nations, communities and individuals.

The advent of IT offers opportunities to overcome historical disabilities. IT is a tool that will enable nations to achieve the goal of becoming a strong, prosperous and self-confident state. IT promises to compress the time it would otherwise take for countries to advance rapidly in their march towards faster development.

15.3 Three Broad Dimensions of Governance

A variety of entities (known generically as *governing bodies*) can govern. The most formal is a *government*, a body whose sole responsibility and authority is to make binding decisions in a given geo-political system (such as a state) by establishing laws. Other types of governing bodies are possible. These include an organization (such as a corporation recognized as a legal entity by a government), a socio-political group (chiefdom, tribe, family, religious denomination, etc.), or another, informal group of people. Whatever form the entity takes, its *governance* is the way the rules, norms and actions are produced, sustained, regulated and held accountable. The degree of formality depends on the internal rules of a given organization. As such, governance may take many forms, driven by many different motivations and with many different results. For instance, a government may operate as a democracy where citizens vote on who should govern and the public good is the goal, while a non-profit organization may be governed by a small board of directors and pursue more specific aims.

In addition, a variety of external actors without decision-making power can influence the process of governing. These include lobbies, political parties, and the media.

15.3.1 Public Governance: It is useful to note the distinction between the concepts of governance and politics. Politics involves processes by which a group of people (perhaps with divergent opinions or interests) reach collective decisions generally regarded as binding on the group, and enforced as common policy. Governance, on the other hand, conveys the administrative and process-oriented elements of governing rather than its antagonistic ones. Such an argument continues to assume the possibility of the traditional separation between *politics* and *administration*. Contemporary governance practice and theory sometimes questions this distinction, premising that both *governance* and *politics* involve aspects of power and accountability.

In general terms, public governance occurs in three broad ways:

1. Through networks involving public-private-partnerships (PPPs) or with the collaboration of community organisations;
2. Through the use of market mechanisms whereby market principles of competition serve to allocate resources while operating under government regulation;
3. Through top-down methods that primarily involve governments and the state bureaucracy.

15.3.2 Private Governance: Private governance occurs when non-governmental entities, including private organizations, dispute resolution organizations, or other third party groups, make rules and/or standards which have a binding effect on the quality of life and opportunities of the larger public. Simply put, private—not public—entities are making public policy. For example, insurance companies exert a great societal impact, largely invisible and freely accepted, that is a private form of governance in society. In turn, reinsurers, as private companies, may exert similar private governance over their underlying carriers. The term *public policy* should not be exclusively associated with policy that is made by government. Public policy may be created by either the private sector or the public sector. If one wishes to refer only to public policy that is made by government, the best term to use is *governmental policy*, which eliminates the ambiguity regarding the agent of the policy making.

15.3.3 Global Governance: Global governance is defined as the complex of formal and informal institutions, mechanisms, relationships, and processes between and among states, markets, citizens and organizations, both inter- and non-governmental, through which collective interests on the global plane are articulated, right and obligations are established, and differences are mediated. In short, global governance denotes the regulation of interdependent relations in the absence of an overarching political authority. The best example of this is the international system or relationships between independent states. The term, however, can apply wherever a group of free equals needs to form a regular relationship.

15.4 Forms of Governance

15.4.1 Non-profit Governance: Non-profit governance has a dual focus: achieving the organization's social mission and ensuring that organization is viable. Both responsibilities relate to fiduciary responsibility that a board of trustees has with respect to the exercise of authority over the explicit actions the organization takes. Public trust and accountability is an essential aspect of organizational viability so it achieves the social mission in a way that is respected by those whom the organization serves and the society in which it is located.

15.4.2 Corporate Governance: Corporate organizations often use the term governance to describe: (a) the manner in which boards or their like direct a corporation, and (b) the laws and customs (rules) applying to that direction.

Corporate governance consists of the set of processes, customs, policies, laws and institutions affecting the way people direct, administer or control a corporation. Corporate governance also includes the relationships among the many players involved (the stakeholders) and the corporate goals. The principal players include the shareholders, management, and the board of directors. Other stakeholders include employees, suppliers, customers, banks and other lenders, regulators, the environment and the community at large.

15.4.3 Regulatory Governance: Regulatory governance reflects the emergence of decentred and mutually adaptive policy regimes which rests on regulation rather than service provision or taxing and spending. The term captures the tendency of policy regimes to deal with complexity with delegated system of rules. It is likely to appear in arenas and nations which are more complex, more global, more contested and more liberally democratic. The term builds upon and extends the terms of the regulatory state on the one hand and governance on the other. While the term regulatory state marginalize non-state actors (NGOs etc.) in the domestic and global level, the term governance marginalizes regulation as a constitutive instrument of governance. The term regulatory governance, therefore, refers to governance beyond the state and governance via regulation.

15.4.4 Participatory Governance: Participatory governance focuses on deepening democratic engagement through the participation of citizens in the processes of governance with the state. The idea is that citizens should play a more direct role in public decision-making or at least engage more deeply with political issues. Government officials should also be responsive to this kind of engagement. In practice, participatory governance can supplement the roles of citizens as voters or as watchdogs through more direct forms of involvement.

15.4.5 Meta-governance: Meta-governance is widely defined as the *governing of governing*. It represents the established ethical principles, or *norms,* that shape and steer the entire governing process. It is important to note that there are no clearly defined settings within which meta-governing takes place, or particular persons who are responsible for it. While some believe meta-governing to be the role of the state which is assumed to steer actors in a particular direction, it can potentially be exercised by any resourceful actor who wishes to influence the governing process. Examples of this include the publishing of codes of conduct at the highest level of international government, and media focus on specific issues at the socio-cultural level. Despite their different sources, both seek to establish values in such a way that they become accepted *norms*. The fact that *norms* can be established at any level and can then be used to shape the governance process as a whole, means meta-governance is part of both the input and the output of the governing system.

15.4.6 Fair Governance: When discussing governance in particular organisations, the quality of governance within the organisation is often compared to a standard of good governance. In the case of a business or of a non-profit organization, for example, good governance relates to consistent management, cohesive policies, guidance, processes and decision-rights for a given area of responsibility, and proper oversight and accountability.

15.4.7 Good Governance: Good governance implies that mechanisms function in a way that allows the executives to respect the rights and interests of the stakeholders, in a spirit of democracy. Good governance is an indeterminate term used in international development literature to describe various normative accounts of how public institutions ought to conduct public affairs and manage public resources. These normative accounts are often justified on the grounds that they are thought to be conducive to economic ends, such as the eradication of poverty and successful economic development. Unsurprisingly different organizations have defined governance and good governance differently to promote different normative ends.

15.5 Measuring Governance

Several efforts have been made to assess and measure the quality of governance of countries all around the world. In recent years, measuring governance is inherently a controversial and political exercise. A distinction is, therefore, made between external assessments, peer assessments and self-assessments.

Examples of external assessments are donor assessments or comparative indices produced by international non-governmental organisations. An example of a peer assessment is the African Peer Review Mechanism. Examples of self-assessments are country-led assessments that can be led by government, civil society, researchers and/or other stakeholders at the national level.

One of these efforts to create an internationally comparable measure of governance —and an example of an external assessment—is the Worldwide Governance Indicators project, developed by members of the World Bank and the World Bank Institute. The project reports aggregate and individual indicators for more than 200 countries for 6 dimensions of governance:

1. Voice and accountability.
2. Political stability and lack of violence.
3. Government effectiveness.
4. Regulatory quality.
5. Rule of law.
6. Control of corruption.

To complement the macro-level cross-country Worldwide Governance Indicators, the World Bank Institute developed the World Bank Governance Surveys, which are country-level governance assessment tools that operate at the micro or sub-national level and use information gathered from a country's own citizens, business people and public sector workers to diagnose governance vulnerabilities and suggest concrete approaches for fighting corruption.

A new Worldwide Governance Index (WGI) has been developed and is open for improvement through public participation. The following domains, in the form of indicators and composite indexes, were selected to achieve the development of the WGI:

1. Peace and security.
2. Rule of law.
3. Human rights and participation.
4. Sustainable development.
5. Human development.

In 2009 the Bertelsmann Foundation published the Sustainable Governance Indicators (SGI), which systematically measure the need for reform and the capacity for reform within the Organisation for Economic Co-operation and Development (OECD) countries. The project examines to what extent governments can identify, formulate and implement effective reforms that render a society well-equipped to meet future challenges, and ensure their future viability.

15.5.1 Governance Analytical Framework (GAF): GAF is a practical methodology for investigating governance processes, where various stakeholders interact and make decisions regarding collective issues, thus creating or reinforcing social norms and institutions. It is postulated that governance processes can be found in any society, and unlike other approaches, that these can be observed and analysed from a non-normative perspective. It proposes a methodology based on five main analytical units: problems, actors, norms, processes and nodal points. These logically articulated analytical units make up a coherent methodology aimed at being used as a tool for empirical social policy research.

Part II
Aspects and Approaches to Economic Development

16

Demographic Transition Theory and Demographic Dividend Hypothesis

Human resources in terms of demographic trends are important, as also the development of human resources through programmes in education, health, social welfare and science and technology.

According to one view, the high growth rate of population in less developed countries (LDCs) is a drag on available economic resources. It is hindering the development process and defeating the twin objectives of removal of poverty and unemployment. The pressure of population is being felt in a variety of ways. Such dizzying rate of population growth negates whatever gains a country has been able to achieve in agriculture, industrial and services sectors. Also, this leads to an unbearable burden on health, education, and housing sectors. If this trend is not halted, it will never be possible to render social and economic justice to millions of people in developing countries. The current rate of population growth is simply not sustainable. In nutshell, the population explosion has proved a damper on the developmental efforts of these economies. The alarming growth of population calls for a systematic and effective population policy to curb the undesirable trend.

There is another view (called demographic dividend hypothesis) which maintains that if the population of LDCs is properly educated and trained, it can prove a boon for the national economy.

16.1 Characteristics of Population

16.1.1 Age Composition: Age composition of population is important because it indicates the dependency ratio of the population. Dependency ratio is defined as the ratio of children below 15 years to population above 15 years. The age composition also determines the proportion of the labour force (15-60 years) in the total population.

16.1.2 Overall Sex Ratio: It refers to the number of females to every 1,000 males across all ages. In many underdeveloped countries, the number of females per thousand males is low. There were many reasons for excess of male over female population. The lack of pre-natal and post-natal care is the major cause of high death-rate among women in reproductive age. The persistent tendency towards low sex ratio can be attributed to lack of attention and care given to female children, sex selective female abortions, and the higher death-rate among women in the reproductive age. It is noteworthy that in Western countries, the sex ratio favours the feminine population.

16.1.3 Life Expectancy: Life expectancy at birth or longevity is an overall indicator of the economic and social well being of the people. As a society advances, the life expectancy of its people also increases. The life expectancy has improved in most countries of the world owing to decline in infant mortality, control of epidemics, and general improvement in the standard of living.

The most fundamental of all human capabilities is life itself and the steady rise in life expectation in a country suggests that significant progress has been made in this dimension. Increasing longevity will inevitably bring in its wake increase in the prevalence of non-communicable diseases. The growing number of senior citizens in the country poses a major challenge and the cost of providing socio-economic security and healthcare to this population has to be met. Currently several region and culture-specific innovative interventions to provide needed care to this population are underway and among these are efforts to reverse the trend of break up of joint families.

16.1.4 Literacy Rate: Literacy is an important factor in judging the quality of population. Illiteracy is widespread in rural areas as compared to urban areas of LDCs. Therefore, concerted efforts are needed to direct literacy programmes towards rural areas with particular emphasis on female literacy.

16.1.5 Degree of Urbanisation: Urbanisation is directly associated with economic development. In fact, a shift of population from rural to urban areas is an indicator of economic development. With prospect of industrialization and the consequent migration of rural population to urban areas, the trend toward urbanization is gaining momentum in LDCs. As the proportion of the urban population continues to grow, investments in urban infrastructure for the provision of services such as roads, water supply and sewerage, urban transportation and the like will need to be much higher than they have been in the past. There will be heavy demand for better quality infrastructure in urban areas, especially water, sewerage, public transport and low cost housing. Since it takes time to create urban infrastructure, it is necessary to have a sufficiently long-term focus on urban planning.

16.1.6 Density of Population: Density of population means the average number of persons living per squire kilometre of area. Geographical area remaining the same, an increase in population means increase in the density of population.

16.2 Theory of Demographic Transition

According to the theory of demographic transition, propounded by A.J. Coale and E.M. Hoover, every country passes through the following three stages of demographic transition.

16.2.1 First Stage: During the first stage, the economy is rural and agriculture is the main occupation of the people. Techniques of production are primitive and per capita income is low. This type of economy is characterised by high birth rate and high death rate. High birth rate is attributable to widespread illiteracy, superstitions, absence of family planning methods and deep-rooted social and religious beliefs about family size. Likewise, death rate is also high on account of lack of medical facilities, poor sanitation and malnutrition. Thus, high birth rate is balanced by high death rate, and population remains stable or increases marginally. The first stage is marked by high growth potential of population but low actual growth.

16.2.2 Second Stage: It marks the beginning of the process of economic development. Living standard of the people starts improving. In this stage, death rate declines sharply owing to improved medical facilities, particularly eradication of mass-killing diseases like smallpox, cholera and plague. However, birth rate continues to remain at high levels because social and religious beliefs about marriage and family size take much longer time to change. Hence, high birth rate and falling death rate accelerate the growth of population. This stage is termed as the stage of *population explosion*. The high growth potential of the first stage is realised in the form of high actual growth of population.

16.2.3 Third Stage: In this stage, the economy moves from an agrarian to an industrial society. There is an increasing trend toward urbanisation and small families for achieving a higher standard of living. The economy is characterised by low birth rate and low death rate. Birth rate declines due to the spread of education and family planning methods. Otherwise also, a large family is a burden in urban industrial areas. Thus, the third stage is marked by low birth rate and low death rate, resulting in stable or marginally increasing population.

These three stages of demographic transition explain the transformation of a primitive high birth and high death rate economy into a low birth rate and low death rate economy.

16.3 Population as a Retarding Factor in Development

High growth rate of population in most underdeveloped countries has nullified, to a large extent, the gains of developmental efforts. Unabated growth of population in has offset to a significant extent the fruits of economic growth and used up part of the potential savings which could have been utilized to raise capital per head and the productivity of the labour force at a faster pace. The pressure of population is being felt in a variety of ways.

1. **Population and Per Capita Income:** A strong relationship exists between population and per capita income (per capita income = national income/population). Economic development is generally defined in terms of increase in real per capita income. The high growth rate of population has depressed the increase in per capita income in LDCs.
2. **Population and Food Supply:** The rapid increase in population has called for tremendous efforts to augment food supplies. Food shortages are felt in many developing countries.
3. **Population and Land-Man Ratio:** The pressure of population has adversely affected the land-man ratio. The growing pressure of population has also led to sub-division and fragmentation of holdings. The widespread disguised unemployment in the agricultural sector is also indicative of the burden of population on land.
4. **Population and Unemployment:** An increase in population is invariably accompanied by an increase in labour force. The growing unemployment in most underdeveloped countries reflects the failure of the economy to absorb the net additions to the labour force. Given the present backlog of unemployment, the continuing increase in population will further aggravate unemployment situation in the years to come.

5. **Population and Basic Amenities:** Unabated growth of population has exerted great pressure on the demand for basic amenities of life such as housing, and medical and educational facilities. Considerable resources are diverted to meet basic needs of the teeming millions. This has adversely affected the availability of resources for developmental projects.
6. **Population and Environment:** Rapid population growth is leading to environmental deterioration. Developed countries are less densely populated and contribute very little to population growth. However, they cause massive ecological damage by the wasteful, unnecessary and unbalanced consumption the consequences of which are adversely affecting both the developed and the developing countries. In developing countries, continued population growth has resulted in pressure on land, fragmentation of land holding, shrinkage of forests, and loss of plant and animal species.

Effective measures to reduce the rate of growth of population are imperative and must command priority of action. Apart from the expansion of family welfare services, sustained improvement in education and healthcare facilities and improved status of women in social and economic life are essential for the success of the family welfare programme and voluntary acceptance of the small family norm.

16.4 Demographic Dividend Hypothesis

Population growth and its relation to economic growth has been a matter of debate for a long time. The earlier view was that population growth impedes economic growth because it puts pressure on the available resources, resulting in reduction in per capita income and resources. This, in turn, results in deterioration in quality of life.

Contrary to this view, several of the East Asian countries have been able to achieve economic prosperity and improvement in quality of life in spite of population growth. This has been attributed to the increase in productivity due to development and utilization of innovative technologies by the young educated population who formed the majority of the growing population. These countries have been able to exploit the dynamics of demographic transition to achieve economic growth by using the human resources as the engine driving the economic development; improved employment with adequate emoluments has promoted saving and investment which in turn stimulated economic growth.

It was earlier assumed that population growth during demographic transition will lead to overcrowding, poverty, under-nutrition, environmental deterioration, poor quality of life and increase in disease burden. Experience in the last few decades has shown that this may not always be correct.

LDCs can reap this demographic dividend only if there is massive investment in human resources development in terms of healthcare, higher education and skill formation. Simultaneously, an environment must be created in which the economy not only grows rapidly, but also enhances good quality employment and livelihood opportunities to meet the needs and aspirations of the youth. Demographic dividend can add to growth potential, provided three conditions are fulfilled.

1. Higher levels of health, education and skill development must be achieved.
2. An environment must be created in which the economy not only grows rapidly, but also enhances good quality employment/livelihood opportunities to meet the needs and aspirations of the youth.
3. Current size of the population is stabilized at the earliest.

16.5 Population, Social Security and Social Justice

Economic growth alone cannot be relied upon to deal either with the promotion, or with the protection of living standards. Many view social security as a system of proper distribution of income and also a right mechanism of wage fixation. Social security is an essential ingredient in the protection, development and full utilisation of human resources.

Millions of people in developing countries live on the edge of disaster. Joblessness is a major source of insecurity, undermining people's entitlement to income and other benefits. For too long the ideal of security has referred to military security or the security of states. One of the most basic needs is security of livelihood, but people also want to be free from chronic threats, such as disease or repression, as well as from sudden and hurtful disruptions in their daily lives.

The objective of social justice is the attainment of social health which implies the realisation of such objectives as adequate living standards, opportunities for cultural development through individual and group self-expressions, and re-adjustment of human relations leading to social harmony. A comprehensive concept of living standards includes the satisfaction of basic needs like food, clothing and shelter as well as normal satisfactions of family life, enjoyment of physical and mental health, opportunities for the expression of skills and recreational abilities, and active and pleasurable social participation.

The achievement of social justice demands co-operative and concerted effort on the part of the state and the people. These objectives are to be achieved mainly by revitalising the nation's life by creating well-organised and active regional communities in rural and urban areas to work co-operatively for national development. Such decentralised community groups should release national energy, extend the scope for leadership, and help to create initiative and organisation extensively in the remotest parts of the country.

The aim of social welfare in the past was essentially curative, and efforts were directed towards relief for the handicapped and the uplift of the under-privileged sections of society. It is essential to maintain vigilance over weaknesses and strains in the social structure and remedy the deficiencies by organising social service programmes/schemes. The aim of all social policies now is the gradual rehabilitation of all weak, handicapped and anti-social elements in society.

The notion of human well-being itself is more broadly conceived to include not only consumption of goods and services in general but more specifically to ensure that the basic material requirements of all sections of the population, especially those below the poverty line, are met and that they have access to basic social services such as health and education. Specific focus on these dimensions of social development is necessary because experience shows that economic prosperity, measured in terms of per capita income, alone does not always ensure enrichment in quality of life, as reflected, for instance, in the social indicators on health, longevity, literacy and environmental sustainability.

To sum up, population stabilisation is crucial for the achievement of the goal of sustainable development and an equitable distribution of resources and opportunities. Though government initiatives exist in the form of suitable public policies on education, health and family welfare along with economic incentives and facilities for small and micro-families, these measures have had a limited impact on the fertility, net reproduction rates and the family size. Improved access to primary and secondary education extension of basic amenities, the empowerment of women, awareness generation and a better standard of living would ultimately contribute towards inculcation of the required consciousness regarding the desirability of a small family size.

17

Harris-Todaro Model of Rural-Urban Migration

17.1 Economic Development and Rural-Urban Migration

Urbanization is a natural process associated with economic growth. It is well-known that agglomeration and densification of economic activities in urban areas stimulate economic efficiency and provide more opportunities for earning livelihoods. Possibilities for entrepreneurship and employment increase when urban concentration takes place, in contrast to the dispersed and less diverse economic possibilities in rural areas.

Urbanization is a key indicator of economic development and should be seen as a positive factor for overall development. As an economy grows, its towns and cities expand in size and volume. Urbanization is a natural consequence of economic changes that take place as a country develops. At the same time, urbanization helps to contribute to the growth process at large. This is manifest in the increasing contribution of urban sector to national income.

Cities and towns have become the engines of social change and rapid economic development. Urbanization is associated with improved access to education, employment, and healthcare, resulting in increase in the age at marriage, reduction in family size and improvement in health indices. As people have moved towards and into cities, information has flowed outward.

The positive role of urbanization is often over shadowed by the evident deterioration in the physical environment and quality of life in the urban areas caused by widening gap between demand and supply of essential services and infrastructure. This results from increasing population, pressure on urban centres, most of which are financially and organisationally ill-equipped to respond to infrastructural needs.

Better communication and transportation now link urban and rural areas both economically and socially, creating an urban-rural continuum of communities with improvement in some aspects of lifestyle of both. The ever increasing reach of mass media communicates new ideas, points of reference, and available options are becoming more widely recognized, appreciated and sought.

The rural hinterland has played a critical role in sustaining urbanization. This is reflected in the indicators of sources of primary inputs, competitively priced labour for urban economic activities, primary funds as reflected in comparative urban and rural credit-deposit ratios and market for urban products. However, the unending migration of the rural poor to urban areas may have a destabilising effect on urbanization and its sustainability.

Attention needs to be focussed not only on the growing challenges of urbanization but on the relationship between urban and rural development. Rapid transformation in urban scenario must be taken into account and provided for, in order that urban growth becomes compatible with healthy socio-economic development of the country. It will be necessary to take note of the prevailing dichotomy in rural and urban development and evolve a mechanism for bringing about rural-urban cohesion in the management of growth.

Although the theme of a *rural-urban divide* still colours some policy discourse in many countries, there is a growing recognition that urbanization is necessary to realise growth potential of the country, and that rural-urban linkages must be strengthened. Indeed this will accelerate growth of the rural sector also.

In France, for instance, there is a north to south movement. Scandinavian countries have seen movements from peripheral regions and industrial areas to metropolitan areas. In Sweden and Finland, for example, there has been large-scale rural depopulation of more remote areas and the main cities have expanded, so that increasing proportions of the population live in cities. This has resulted in some places with largely emptied villages and the loss of rural services. These areas now tend to be dominated by, for example, industrial forestry.

Counter-urbanisation is another type of internal migration and represents the movement of people from urban to rural areas. In England, contradicting the world's tendency, this movement is increasing and has been observed since the 1980s. This phenomenon is characterised mainly by the in-migration of older couples and "relatively well-off families", which balance the rates of younger groups moving into cities.

17.2 Harris-Todaro Model: An Overview

Harris-Todaro model, named after John R. Harris and Michael Todaro, is an economic model developed in 1970 and used in development economics and welfare economics to explain some of the issues concerning rural-urban migration. It is considered one of the starting points of the classic rural-urban migration theory. The hypothesis and predictions of Harris-Todaro model have been subjected to econometric evaluation and have been corroborated by several studies. The key hypothesis of Harris-Todaro model is that migrants react mainly to economic incentives, earnings differentials, and the probability of getting a job at the destination. The rural-urban migration will occur when the urban expected wage exceeds the rural wage.

The formal statement of the equilibrium condition of the Harris-Todaro model is as follows:

Let w_r be the wage rate (marginal productivity of labour) in the rural agricultural sector.

Let l_e be the total number of jobs available in the urban sector, which should be equal to the number of employed urban workers.

Let l_{us} be the total number of job seekers, employed and unemployed, in the urban sector.

Let w_u be the wage rate in the urban sector, which could possibly be set by government with a minimum wage law.

Rural to urban migration will take place if:

$w_r < l_e/l_{us} \times w_u$

Conversely, urban to rural migration will occur if:

$w_r > l_e/l_{us} \times w_u$

At equilibrium,

$w_r = l_e/l_{us} \times w_u$

With the random matching of workers to available jobs, the ratio of available jobs to total job seekers gives the probability that any person moving from the agricultural sector to the urban sector will be able to find a job. As a result, in equilibrium, the agricultural wage rate is equal to the expected urban wage rate, which is the urban wage multiplied by the employment rate.

In the model, equilibrium is reached when the expected wage in urban areas is equal to the marginal product of an agricultural worker. In equilibrium, the rural to urban migration rate will be zero since the expected rural income equals the expected urban income. However, in this equilibrium there will be positive unemployment in the urban sector.

17.3 Assumptions of the Model

Harris-Todaro model is based on the following assumptions:

1. Migration decision is based on *expected* income differentials between rural and urban areas rather than just wage differentials. This implies that rural-urban migration in a context of high urban unemployment can be economically rational if expected urban income exceeds expected rural income.
2. Rural agricultural production and the subsequent labour market are perfectly competitive. As a result, the agricultural rural wage is equal to agricultural marginal productivity.
3. The model studies the migration of workers in a two-sector economic system, namely rural sector and urban sector. The difference between these sectors is the type of goods produced, the technology of production and the process of wage determination. The rural sector is specialized in the production of agricultural goods. Similarly, the urban sector is specialized in the production of manufactured goods.
4. Both goods and labour markets are perfectly competitive.
5. In the urban sector, a minimum wage is assumed fixed institutionally at a level above equilibrium in this labour market.
6. The relative price of the agricultural good in terms of the manufactured good varies according to the relative scarcity between agricultural and manufactured goods.
7. The overall population of workers in the economy is is kept constant during the whole period of analysis.
8. There are only two sectors and rural prices are wholly flexible, which implies that there is full employment in the rural area, i.e. all workers living at the rural sector are employed at any period.

17.4 Conclusion

Rural-urban allocation of workers is a process of social learning by imitation. Harris-Todaro model is set in a two-sectorial economy composed of individuals who grope over time for best sectorial location in terms of earnings. There will be a migratory flow from the rural to the urban sector when the expected urban wage is higher than the rural wage. Thus, the long run equilibrium is attained when the urban worker population reaches a level such that the expected urban wage equates the rural wage. This equality is known in the economic literature as the *Harris-Todaro condition.* Harris-Todaro model, in determining the long run equilibrium, i.e., the absence of a net rural-urban migratory flow, argues that the rural workers, in their decision on migrating to the urban area, estimate the expected urban wage.

However, even though this migration creates unemployment and induces informal sector growth, this behaviour is economically rational and utility-maximizing in the context of the Harris-Todaro model. As long as the migrating economic agents have complete and accurate information concerning rural and urban wage rates and probabilities of obtaining employment, they will make an expected income-maximizing decision.

Therefore, migration from rural areas to urban areas will increase if:

1. Urban wages increase in the urban sector, increasing the expected urban income.
2. Agricultural productivity decreases, lowering marginal productivity and wages in the agricultural sector, decreasing the expected rural income.

18

Dualism and Economic Development

A dual economy is the existence of two separate economic sectors within one country, divided by different levels of development, technology, and different patterns of demand. The concept was originally created by Julius Herman Boeke to describe the coexistence of modern and traditional economic sectors in a colonial economy.

Dual economies are common in less developed countries, where one sector is geared to local needs and another to the global export market. Dual economies may exist within the same sector, for example a modern plantation or other commercial agricultural entity operating in the midst of traditional cropping systems.

Arthur Lewis used the concept of a dualistic economy as the basis of his labour supply theory of rural-urban migration. Lewis distinguished between a rural low-income subsistence sector with surplus population, and an expanding urban capitalist sector. The urban economy absorbed labour from rural areas (holding down urban wages) until the rural surplus was exhausted.

It can be argued that a dualistic development is not a specific feature of some individual country, since it has been observed in many transition economies albeit at different periods of time in the course of transformation.

18.1 Dualism and Economic Transition

A concept of dualism in economic development was originally proposed by Julius Herman Boeke in 1953 to study the Indonesian economy and society. A typical dual economy consists of two sectors: a small urban-industrial and a big rural-agricultural sector. The manufacturing sector displays features of any modern industrial economy, while a much bigger agricultural sector surrounding the advanced one is characterised by a primitive mode of production. As a result, labour market is split into two parts: one is comprised of relatively well-paid and skilled urban workers and the other is full of poorly paid and low-productive rural workers.

It is widely recognized that model developed by Lewis can be considered a pioneering model of rural-urban migration. In this framework, the backward rural sector is the supplier of cheap labour to the advanced industrial sector. The rapid capital accumulation in industry that drives growth depends on savings. It is argued that the central problem in the theory of economic development is to understand the process by which a community which was previously saving and investing 4 or 5 percent of its national income or less, converts itself into an economy where voluntary saving is running at about 12 or 15 percent or more.

Commercialisation of the traditional sector results in the elimination of dualism. Other formulation consider diminishing—and not disappearing—differences in production conditions through time that result in the mere attenuation of dualism. It is argued that dualism cannot fully elapse since some degree of dualism exists in virtually every economy. Even the most advanced countries, such as Canada and the United States, have areas in which techniques lag behind those of the most advanced sectors, and in which standards of economic and social welfare are correspondingly low. This conception, however, emphasizes the simultaneous presence of well-performing and poorly-performing sectors, reflecting different stages of their development as the economy evolves. In similar vein, contemporary explorations of dualism stress the existence of factor market inefficiencies that lower the overall productivity and income.

18.2 Colonialism and Dualism

Most LDCs have a colonial heritage. For example, India was under the British rule for more than two centuries and it inherited a colonial structure at the time of Independence. It is often felt that the heritage of colonialism is partly responsible for the present-day backwardness and underdevelopment in LDCs like India. The colonial era before Second World War created the problem of economic dualism which implies the coexistence of traditional and modern sectors with the same economy or region.

Colonialism brought in its wake enclaves of modernised sector the population was literate, worked for wages or engaged in commerce and have learned how to use modern technology such as railroads, motor cars, electric power and simple machines. By contrast, in the traditional sector, the population was largely illiterate and engaged in subsistence agriculture. These were not used to wage labour (as in share-cropping) and accustomed to traditional methods of production and pre-industrial technology.

18.3 Characteristics of Dualistic Society

On economic basis the dualistic society is classified as by giving the names: (a) traditional sector, and (b) modern sector. There are certain characteristics of traditional sector of a dualistic economy which distinguish it from modern sector. They are as under:

1. The needs of traditional sector are limited. People pass a contented life.
2. People work for social needs rather for economic gains.
3. Crops are cultivated according to their prestige value rather on their use value.
4. The native industries have neither organization nor capital and they are ignorant of modern technology and market conditions.
5. People indulge in speculative activities rather in business enterprises. They do not take risk by making productive investment.
6. They lack the initiative and organizational skill which is a feature of modern sector of dual economy.
7. Labour is unorganized, passive and unskilled. They are reluctant to leave their village and community.
8. The urban development takes place at the cost of rural life.

Due to these features of traditional society, modern economic theory is not applicable as far as LDCs are concerned. The Western economic theory is meant to explain capitalistic society whereas traditional sector is pre-capitalistic. The modern sector is based on unlimited wants and money economy etc.

There are different dimensions of dualistic character of LDCs.

18.4 Economic Dualism

Economic dualism, a characteristic feature of most less developed countries (LDCs) of the world, means the coexistence of a modern industrial sector and a traditional agricultural sector in an economy. Dualism in LDCs is the result of colonial domination. Historically, dualism crept into these countries when the colonial powers introduced a modern sector into the traditional economies of subjugated countries.

A dual economy is characterised by surplus labour in the subsistence agricultural sector. By expanding the modern sector through transfer of surplus labour from the traditional sector, economic development can be speeded up in LDCs. Given the sectoral differential in productivity of modern sector and traditional sector, transfer of labour from the latter to the former will be a step towards sectoral productivity equalisation. Through this process, economic dualism is overcome and the economy is said to be integrated. Hence, growth with employment is achieved.

Let us divide an underdeveloped economy into modern sector and a traditional sector. The economic development of this economy involves the process of surplus labour transfer from the traditional sector to the modern sector. The speed of labour transfer is determined by the rate of industrial investment and capital accumulation in the modern sector.

The traditional sector is non-capitalist. It is self-employment sector with massive surplus labour or disguised unemployment. The modern sector is capitalist, using reproducible capital. The process starts when demand for industrial goods expands autonomously, may be due to foreign markets. Consequently, the derived demand for labour increases. As a result, workers move from agriculture to industry. Abundant labour supply at the existing wage rate keeps labour cost of the industries low. Meanwhile, rising demand and higher industrial prices lead to greater profits. When these profits are reinvested for capital formation, the demand for industrial output rises in two categories: (a) consumption goods demanded by newly employed workers, and (b) capital goods demanded by owners of capital.

Rising demand for industrial production leads to further shift of labour out of agriculture into industry. As the shift from agriculture to industry proceeds, agricultural productivity rises while the number of farmers falls. Labour migration would stop when the point of equal attraction is reached, i.e. when the marginal product of labour in the two sectors is equal.

18.5 Technological Dualism

Technological dualism refers to the use of different production functions in *modern* and *traditional* sectors of an economy. It is widely believed that labour employment problems of less developed countries (LDCs) are due to this dualism rather than due to lack of aggregate demand.

Traditional sector consists of peasant agriculture, handicrafts and cottage industries. Production can take place with a wide range of techniques, i.e. with various alternative combinations of labour and capital. Farmers can use simple tools and implements or heavy machinery for agricultural operations. Choice between capital-intensive and labour-intensive technology is available. Thus, this sector has *variable technical coefficients of production.*

Since labour is relatively abundant factor in LDC-, the technique of production is usually labour-intensive. The modern sector comprises large-scale industries, oil fields and mines. The technique of production is almost fixed. For example, if a modern oil refinery is to be set up, the proportion in which labour and capital are to be used is almost given (fixed). In other words, there is limited degree of technical substitutability. The technique of production in this sector is usually capital-intensive.

Technological dualism has been instrumental in aggravating disguised unemployment in the traditional sector. As surplus labour cannot be absorbed by the modern sector, it has to fall back on the traditional sector for survival.

18.6 Social Dualism

J.H. Boeke, a Dutch economist, studied Indonesian economy and presented his theory of social dualism bases on the following three characteristics:

1. Social spirit.
2. Organizational form.
3. Techniques dominating them.

Their inter-relationship and interdependence is called the social system or social style. A society is homogeneous if there is only one social system in the society. But the society which has two or more social systems is known as dual or plural society. Boeke says that the dual society is a society which has two full grown social styles which represent pre-capitalism and post-capitalism. Such a dual society is furnished with the existence of an advanced imported western system on the one side and endogenous pre capitalistic agricultural system on the other side. The former is under the western influence which uses the advance techniques and where standard of living is high. The later is native and it is furnished with the outdated techniques and low social and economic life. This is called social dualism and these two systems are clashing. The imported social system is highly capitalistic and it may be socialistic as well as communistic system.

18.7 Financial Dualism

Hala Myint has developed the theory of financial dualism. Such dualism rises because of division of money markets in unorganized and organized money markets in LDCs. The rate of interest in unorganized market is higher than the rate of interest in organized money market which is concerned with modern sector. The unorganized money market consists mainly of village money lenders and landlords. They charge the high interest because of the following reasons.

1. The lenders have monopoly and position of the borrowers is very weak.

2. There is a shortage of savings in the traditional sector because most of the savings are made in terms of land or gold.
3. Due to natural calamities etc. the risk attached with such lending are very high.

Thus, we find that the high interest rate which the farmers have to pay not only consists of formal interest charges but also the concealed charges obtained through under-pricing the grains purchased by the farmers. On the other hand, in the organized markets of LDCs the interest rates are low and credit facilities are abundant. The loans are advanced to manufactured sector, export industry and modern commerce sector. Professor Myint says that there was an old financial dualism which used to exist in the open economy of colonial period and the financial dualism which now exists.

Under colonial system there was perfect convertibility at fixed exchange rate. Consequently there was no shortage of foreign exchange and there were no balance-of-payments problems. These days the LDCs have to face internal as well as external balance. Thus the poor traders and small peasants not only have to face high interest rates, but also the shortage of foreign exchange. Then they are not in a position to get advanced machinery etc. Under the colonial system, organized money market of LDCs consisted of the branches of western commercial banks which were linked with international financial market. In colonial system, the modern sector, consisting of mines, plantation and foreign trade, borrowed at low interest rates both from western banks and the world capital markets.

Presently, LDCs have attained monetary independence by establishing their own central banks. They have introduced the exchange control. As a result, the organized money market of the LDCs has been separated from the world capital market. Hence, their central banks are following the cheap monetary policy even when they are having shortage of funds. They are maintaining over-valued exchange rate on the ground that devaluation will create inflation. On the other hand, there is chronic excess demand for foreign exchange in these poor countries. To meet this situation, these countries depend upon exchange controls, direct controls, monetary and fiscal policies. This has led to enhance the economic dualism between the traditional sector and modern industrial sector. The cheap monetary policy by maintaining artificial low interest rates has become helpful for the large industrial sector. The low interest rates have discouraged the flow of funds from abroad and savings from within the country. But it has created an excess demand for loans. Thus, the major part of domestic savings is flowing towards industrial sector. This has reduced the capital to traditional and agriculture sector which have to get at higher interest rate. The foreign exchange control to correct deficit in balance-of-payments has also benefited the modern industrial sector against the traditional sector. It is because that the major share of available foreign exchange is allocated to the industrial sector to import capital intensive goods.

On the other hand, the agricultural and small-scale sectors fail to get foreign exchange and import permits because of red-tapism and corruption in the LDCs. Most of the LDCs have established agricultural banks and cooperative societies. But these institutions have been found providing loans to the influential people and to the model villages. All this has led to misallocation of resources between the modern and traditional sector. So money markets in the LDCs remain backward. Domestic inflation along with over-valued exchange rate has encouraged flight of capital. The countries where this is checked, the capital moved in the purchase of gold, jewellery, real estates and other speculative activities. This is because of low rate of interest against investment. Hence the money market remains ineffective.

Government controls over the scarce supply of capital have also retarded the growth of financial intermediaries in the LDCs. These controls favour the large manufacturing units and the banks. They discriminate against the small borrowers and the money lenders who provide credit to the small borrowers. In the LDCs governments believe that capital funds invested in durable capital goods are productive while those invested in financing agriculture and trading activities are unproductive. According to Myint the cheap and easy credit to the traditional sector is not provided because of following reasons:

1. High over head costs and salaries of officials of commercial banks in the rural areas.
2. Red-tapism in dealing with small borrowers according to the rigid rules.
3. Lack of coordination between the head office and the branches.
4. Lack of subsidized loans supplied by the agricultural banks etc.

Hala Myint has suggested two types of policies to reduce financial dualism in LDCs:

1. Official interest rate in the organized capital market should be increased. This will attract the savings both from the country and out of the country. It will also create equilibrium between the demand for loan able funds and supply of loan able funds.
2. There should be free access on equal terms to capital funds by modern and traditional sector. This will reduce misallocation of resources between the two sectors.

To sum up, dualism states the co-existence of two separate worlds. There is a chronic difference between the two worlds which tends to increase over time if developed nations do not help the developing counterparts. It is also a major characteristic of developing countries. Hence, the term was used to refer to various asymmetries of production and organisation that exist in developing countries.

There is both production asymmetry and organisational asymmetry in dual economies. The former implies that capital is not used at all in agriculture and land is not used at all in industry. The latter implies that even when returns to labour are equalised across the sectors by labour mobility, it is not the marginal products of labour in the two sectors which are so equalised.

19

Science, Technology and Innovations

Technology has been called as the game changer for human civilization ever since the industrial revolution which started in Europe in the middle of the 18th century. Be it grocery shopping or talking to friends or reading and commenting on news items, we turn to our smart phones. Technology has changed our day-to-day lives.

19.1 Importance of Science and Technology

The per capita income and quality of life that a nation enjoys is, in the final analysis, dependent largely on the technology it adopts, and which in turn has to be appropriate to its endowments, resources and skills.

The foundations of industrial and agricultural advance lie ultimately in the availability and effective use of human skills. Human skills are a formidable asset since they last not merely during one working life but because they are transmitted for generations. If these assets are used effectively, they may well turn out to be one of the most fruitful results of planning.

The pace of economic development depends on a variety of factors which constitute the psychological and sociological setting within which the economy operates. A major element in this setting is the community's will to progress and its readiness to develop and adopt new and more efficient methods and processes of production. Basically, development involves securing higher productivity all round and this is a function of the degree of technological advance the community is able to make. The problem is not one merely of adopting and applying the processes and techniques developed elsewhere, but of developing new techniques specially suited to local conditions.

Modern technology is changing rapidly and no country can hope to maintain a steady pace of advance unless it keeps abreast of current developments. Techniques in turn affect and are affected by economic and social organisation. Certain forms of economic and social organisation are unsuited to or incapable of absorbing new techniques and utilising them to the best advantage. To some extent techniques must of course be adapted to economic and social organisation, but the latter has also to change in order to accommodate new techniques which need to be applied not merely in one or two isolated lines but in several lines of economic activity.

The vital role of science in modern life is now generally recognised. Apart from the vast changes it has brought about, the development of a scientific temper in the people is considered important. Improvements in techniques evolved as a result of scientific research bring about great increases in production in the different sectors of the economy. National resources are augmented by the substitution of cheap and abundant materials for those in scarce supply and by finding uses for materials which have remained unutilised. A balanced programme of research covering every sector of the economy is essential therefore for the development of a country.

High standards of living in the more advanced countries are the direct result of progress in science and technology and the rapid pace of development associated with it. The flow of new scientific knowledge is continuous and ever expanding and covers both pure and applied research. Pure research leads to new knowledge and understanding of nature and its laws, and creates the scientific capital from which practical applications of knowledge are drawn. New products and processes are based on new principles and concepts. The advance of technology presents new problems to science and also provides new tools with which to resolve them.

19.2 Need for Technology Upgradation in Underdeveloped Countries

The level of technology and the concomitant levels of skills directly determine productivity of labour. Improvement of skill enhances labour productivity even with the existing technology. Labour productivity determines the potential relative shares of both labour and capital. Rise in labour productivity is a necessary condition for raising living standards of both wage and non-wage earners.

Potential for better wages of workers and remuneration of the self-employed and the living standards of the working poor increase *parri passu* with increased productivity of labour. Moreover, higher incomes and wages of the working poor would contribute to increased aggregate effective demand for goods and services produced, both in informal and formal sectors, stimulating investment and growth in both the sectors. Thus, a multiplier effect may result leading to faster growth all across.

The immediate challenge before less developed countries (LDCs) is development of appropriate technologies for various manufacturing processes which will lead to substantial reduction in cost of manufacturing by enhancing labour productivity, reducing material wastage and minimising energy consumption. Such technologies could be developed by close interaction of research and development (R&D) institutions with industries and through innovative projects of technopreneurs. Accordingly, a multi-tier support system may be required for inducing technology-based competitiveness of the sector with the collaboration of government, industry clusters, industry associations and private R&D institutions. Liberal government policies and assistance are pre-requisites for nurturing innovative ideas both by academic institutions and technopreneurs.

The issue may be addressed by developing collaborations of public/private R&D institutions with the cluster/industry associations to take up R&D in focused areas of manufacturing with clear objectives, and project budget. This will ensure industry acceptability of the technology developed and delivery of the technology within the specified time frame. Government assistance may vary depending upon the level of the technology and the transaction cost involved and may be kept at an attractive level, especially for the projects taken up for technology development for nano-technology, aerospace, defence sector etc. to incentivize these sectors.

Competitive manufacturing technologies are available in the international market for various industries. To facilitate absorption of such globally competitive technologies, government can subsidise the industry. Extent of support may again vary with the type of industry and the level of technology being adopted.

Unregulated or haphazard application of modem techniques in all spheres of production is apt to create or aggravate technological unemployment. There is need for regulation here. This is not to suggest freezing of existing techniques. It only means that conditions have to be created in which modern techniques can be adopted in these lines of production and that the transition is orderly.

19.3 Applications of Technological Advancement

Science and technology plays a crucial role in catalysing and accelerating economic and social development. It has an overarching impact in almost all sectors of the economy. It plays a lead role in contributing to sustainable development and self-reliance. It is now becoming increasingly clear that while the investments in physical infrastructure are important, it is the intellectual infrastructure derived through innovative initiatives that will give LDCs a comparative advantage.

Science is an endless frontier, a unique human activity without limits. Massive support should be provided to basic research, especially in universities, so that LDCs can contribute significantly towards advancing that frontier. While building on the comparative advantage that India possess in the emerging areas of information technology (IT) and biotechnology, special attention should be given to agriculture and agro-based industries and infrastructure sectors like energy, transportation, communication and housing.

19.3.1 Small Industries: The establishment of national laboratories and research institutes has a special importance in a country where medium and small-scale producers contribute a considerable proportion of industrial production. These industries cannot afford to have research facilities of their own, as the larger producers can. The research institutions will bring the fruits of research within their reach and enable them to reduce costs and improve the quality of their products. The establishment of these laboratories and institutes is thus complementary to the objective of promoting the development of small enterprises. In addition to these major research institutes, it is desirable to direct particular attention to the improvement of techniques in cottage industries. Such improvement may ultimately produce a far greater result all over the country than a limited number of large-scale industries.

19.3.2 Technology and Rural Development: Rural technology should not be taken to mean primitive technology or technology of yesterday. A determined effort is needed to take modern science and technology to the rural areas so that it is brought well within the material, financial and skill resources of rural people. Therefore, while searching for and improving upon such technologies which increase employment opportunities for the people, it will be simplistic and dangerous to confine indigenous efforts to relatively simple technology for rural needs and depend on import of technology in the high technology areas.

19.3.3 Technology and Human Resources Development: Technology can play a significant role in the promotion of human welfare. In the coming years, the benefits of technology must percolate more effectively to the vulnerable sections of the community and backward areas of the country.

In promoting the applications of science and technology for the benefit of the weaker sections, special programmes should be devised. A more coordinated and vigorous effort than in the past is needed to equip suitable persons from socially backward groups and weaker sections of the society to play a purposeful role in the area of technology.

High priority should be given to technologies that are oriented towards human welfare. These include technologies that provide creative and cost-effective solutions in health services, population management, mitigating the effects of natural hazards, conservation of land, water and energy resources and their integrated management for sustainable development.

Human resource development in science and technology is an area of concern today. The declining popularity of science and the unwillingness among the youth to take up science as a career would jeopardise the future of LDCs. Imaginative and innovative programmes need to be undertaken to attract the students to science and technology and enhance the number of young scientists.

19.4 Challenges for the Future

Developing countries have unique challenges and large unmet needs across diverse areas such as health, education, skills, agriculture, urban and rural development, energy and so on. They also have significant challenges of exclusion and inequitable access due to multiple deprivations of class, caste and gender—all of which require innovative approaches and solutions, and looking beyond the conventional way of doing things. Innovation is going to be central to providing answers to the most pressing challenges and for creating opportunity structures for sharing the benefits of the emerging knowledge economy. Affordable solutions, innovative business models or processes which ease delivery of services to citizens can enable more people to join the development process.

19.4.1 Upgrading Institutions of Higher Learning: The higher education institutions with their research facilities are a unique base for the training of competent scientists and technologists. However, with the rapid expansion of the number of institutions and students, without the corresponding inputs by way of facilities, the role of universities as advanced centres of teaching and research has been eroded, leading not only to the weakening of science teaching and research but also adversely affecting the climate so essential for higher learning. The need today is, therefore, to restore to the universities their proper image as centres of higher learning. Although it would be unrealistic to expect all the members of the academic community to take up research in addition to teaching, there is an urgent need to integrate teaching and research so that universities present a different image and are restored to their recognised position.

Facilities available in universities are not adequate. That they should be increased cannot be overemphasised. It is in the general interest of not only the universities, but also scientific agencies, public enterprises and technical departments, that the resources in the education sector are considerably augmented, since the manpower that they need comes from the university sector.

There is widespread concern regarding the quality and extent of the technology base in LDCs. Engineering education and research need significant support. It would be necessary to establish a mechanism which will enable funds from research stations regionally distributed, or created for sectors of industry in cooperation with industry. The mechanical and electronic engineering areas require immediate attention. There is need to establish a mechanism which will enable funds from government as well as from industry, including the public and private sectors, to be received and used for engineering research.

Unless a true enthusiasm for science is generated during school and college stages, even the very intelligent and scientifically minded, who would achieve much in science, would turn to safer and more lucrative professions, as is already happening. Government has to be particularly sensitive in spotting talent and creativity, wherever it exists and providing opportunities for its emergence.

19.4.2 Selecting Thrust Areas: There are major new areas in science and technology emerging on the world scene as, for example micro-electronics, informatics and telematics, robotics, biotechnologies, material sciences, oceanography, instrumentation, several areas in chemistry, modern biology and earth sciences and space technologies. These should be reorganised as thrust areas and should receive significant support.

With the present constraints of fiscal and human resources, it would not be possible to deal with all the problems or all areas of science and technology at the same time. Therefore, there has to be a degree of selectivity and allocation of priorities. There is need to not only define areas of strength for consolidation and development, but also areas of weakness that require corrective action, together with identification of gaps, particularly in newly emerging areas of great promise.

19.4.3 Percolation of Technology to Grassroots: There has been a tendency to regard science and technology as a separate and compartmentalised activity, to be carried out in universities, in research laboratories and in large specialised scientific institutions. It is not generally realised that science and technology should be an integral and essential part of all sectors of the national activity. The results of science and technology are yet to be felt in terms of a major impact on the economic development, improvement in the quality of life of the people and in the availability of better goods and services. It should be ensured that the efforts in science and technology are not confined in laboratories and academic institutions but percolate to the grassroots levels so that science, technology and innovations increasingly become part of the life of the people. For this, appropriate mechanisms and management practices would need to be introduced.

19.4.4 Indigenous Development of Technology: Issues of natural resource conservation and agricultural growth cannot be effectively tackled in the absence of an appropriate technological base. In addition, technology is essential for increasing the competitiveness of any economy in international markets. Indigenous development of technology is therefore of the highest importance and deliberate planned steps need to be taken to increase technological self-sufficiency of the country.

Rapid technical progress is altering fundamentally the skills, knowledge, infrastructure and institutions needed for the efficient production and delivery of goods and services. So broad and far-reaching are current technological developments that many see the emergence of another industrial revolution driven by a new technological paradigm. This paradigm involves not only new technologies and skills in the traditional sense, but also different work methods, management techniques and organisational relations within firms. As new transport and communications technologies shrink international economic space, it also implies a significant reordering of comparative advantage, and trade and investment relations, between countries.

Experience of many developing and industrialised countries suggests that a rapid acceleration of industrial technology development calls for a deliberate strategy, in the sense that it requires the government to coordinate and guide an essentially market-driven process.

19.4.5 Technology Information and Dissemination Services: Technology upgrading requires that enterprises of all types have information on relevant technologies in international markets and also within the country. Many countries have well-developed systems of computerised on-line technology information and dissemination services, often backed up with consultancy and financial assistance for small and medium enterprises to enable them to know about, test, and implement new technologies. The availability of similar facilities is weak in LDCs. Note needs to be taken of the emerging trends of restrictions on access to technology through stringent intellectual property restrictions and on dual use technologies by certain groups of industrially advanced countries. Special efforts have to be made both at national as well as at international levels, to ensure that such restrictions do not inhibit progress in high technology sectors.

Technology development generally requires the setting up of clusters of industries that can share information and skills, as in *science parks* or dedicated industrial estates. Some such facilities exist in LDCs, but their efficacy and functioning need to be strengthened.

19.4.6 Funding Pattern: Governments in have so far been the main source of funding science and technology activities in LDCs. This needs to be significantly supplemented by the industry. The challenge is how to create a vibrant landscape of public-private-partnership (PPP) and an enabling framework for attracting investment from the industrial sector into R&D system and incentivize the same for linking development with deployment in the innovation and technology sector. The corporate sector, in particular, must play a much larger role in building research capability as happens in other countries.

The pace of scientific and technological research in more advanced countries has .greatly increased. In the economy of these countries, scientific research has an important and honoured place and receives every encouragement. As the field of enquiry and investigation widens, larger funds are invested and there is intense search for scientific talent. One of the results of this activity in the more advanced countries, however, has been that the gap between the advanced and less advanced countries tends to become ever larger. The task before LDCs is to cover this distance by putting in the utmost effort in the development of scientific and technological research, and in the application of science in the furtherance of their development programmes. Investment in scientific research will make a large and enduring contribution to the prosperity of LDCs.

In short, science and technology is widely recognised as an important tool for fostering and strengthening the economic and social development of a country. Given the rapid pace of globalisation, fast-depleting material resources, increasing competition among nations and the growing need to protect intellectual property, the importance of strengthening the knowledge base is an important issue that needs to be recognised.

It must be borne in mind that scientific explorations and widening the frontiers of knowledge are important activities of all civilised societies. A competitive knowledge economy must be built on the pillars of: (a) an educational system that produces human resources which are employable and globally benchmarked, (b) science and technology pursued on an enormous scale to generate knowledge for long-term use, and (c) strategic translational research inspired by national needs and global opportunities.

It is necessary to establish linkages between the different sectors of education, scientific research, technology development, productive activities in agriculture, industry etc. and government decision-making structures.

19.5 Innovations

Scientific research utilizes money to generate knowledge and, by providing solutions, innovation converts knowledge into wealth and/or value. Innovation thus implies solutions based on science and technology that are successfully deployed in the economy or the society. It has assumed centre stage in the developmental goals of nations. Paradigms of innovation have become country and context specific.

Science has played a key role in enhancing the growth and development of society and generating access to new and improved goods and services. Science underpins most breakthrough initiatives, but beyond the domain of science, innovations play a critical role in enhancing delivery of services and enabling access to improved goods. In view of this, emerging economies need to stimulate and strengthen its entire formal scientific and industrial system as well as the innovation system to develop solutions for the country's agenda of faster, sustainable and more inclusive growth.

19.5.1 Innovation Defined: Innovation is a process whereby people or groups of people with an entrepreneurial mindset (organizations, enterprises) develop new ideas or absorb and adapt existing ones. Together with institutions and policies that affect their behaviour and performance, they create new products, processes, and forms of organization. Innovation is not only about scientists in laboratories, theoretical science, or new discoveries. It is about building the capacity to find solutions to practical everyday development problems. So, an innovative economy is marked by ideas for new products or new ways of doing things and transforming them into profitable products or activities.

Joseph Schumpeter (1883-1950), an American economist, was one of the first academicians to study the idea of innovation. He developed a theory of economic and social change which focused on the importance of innovation and the factors influencing it. He suggested an important distinction between invention and innovation. According to him, invention is the first occurrence of the idea for a new product or process while innovation occurs when the idea is put into practice. Thus, refrigerator was an invention; but double-door refrigerator was an innovation. Similarly, the use of smart phones to conduct banking transactions (mobile banking) is an example of adapting the technology to non-traditional use.

19.5.2 Importance of Innovations: Bringing about innovation has never been as important as today, as the global economy shifts away from the industrial economy towards the innovation economy. Traditional manufacturing is becoming increasingly commoditized while intellectual property is the need of the hour. What is heartening is that recent economic theory suggests that government investment in R&D, knowledge-creation, and technological progress does have a role to play in fuelling innovation, productivity, capital creation, and therefore growth. This thinking highlights the scope for appropriate government policy and investment to enable entrepreneurship and innovation.

Innovation can play a very important role in the development discourse, because it can offer a new approach to a system that is currently over-burdened by the multiple demands and has limited resources at its disposal. Enhanced focus on innovation can have an impact in diverse areas such as health and education delivery, governance, enterprise development and much more. Collectively, this can herald a generational change in the country and can lay out a chart for a more sustainable and inclusive growth paradigm.

For countries to make the next big move—from developing the right skills demanded by the market to dynamically improving the quality and quantity of that demand—developing an innovation system is critical.

19.5.3 Skills Required for Innovations: Innovations can come in various forms. They encompass the products, processes, and services that meet market needs. They may be developed and marketed in the manufacturing sector, but they may also apply to new ways of doing things in all sectors, including commerce and service delivery. And the innovative idea needs to be widely tested and applied by those who have the skills and financing to bring it to scale. This calls for engaging those with marketing and managerial skills and venture capital.

Research is important—but not always central—to innovation, which may also be realized through less technical experimentation and discovery.

Innovation—and thus growth—can be encouraged by three human development–related factors, and the accompanying policies that facilitate them. First, individuals need a range of skills. Second, these skills and the ideas flowing from them have to be connected to others. Third, productivity increases when innovative small business owners can grow with the aid of risk management tools or as innovative skilled workers enter the labour market. This three-part process is relevant to all individuals despite their starting points.

Three types of skills are necessary to unlock creative potential and take it to market.

1. The general skills are necessary to adapt existing technologies, compete in an innovation-driven economy, and manage the increasingly networked innovation process.

These skills include basic literacy and numeracy, problem-solving, and social and interpersonal skills.

2. Creativity produces new ideas. Innovative thinkers are curious and persevering and have *divergent thinking*—imagining several responses to a single problem rather than converging to a single, right answer.
3. Entrepreneurial skills range from managerial skills in running a business to motivation. These are the skills to sort out good ideas from bad ones, find the resources and means to create a prototype, and take the idea through its growth phases. Education and training systems can teach individuals to be cognitively developed, creative, and entrepreneurial.

Both creativity and entrepreneurial skills can be incorporated into teaching methodologies at all points of the skill formation process. And education systems can encourage innovation-related specialties, such as math, science, and business and managerial skills. But these strategies will be successful only if education systems improve the quality of the basic mathematics and science skills for the majority of students. Without such a basis, efforts to instil risk-taking and entrepreneurial skills will be wasted.

Innovation cannot realize its full potential if innovators are isolated. The innovator needs other creative and skilled individuals to share ideas with and bring those ideas to market, capital to finance the realization of the idea, and an enabling environment that accepts new ideas.

In the knowledge economy, universities as a source of knowledge have become far more important than in the past. In recent years, they have acquired a crucial *third mission*, of contributing to economic development after teaching and research. Among the developed countries, the United States is feted for offering entrepreneurs many structural advantages, among them close linkages with universities. Many universities have incubators, technology parks, and venture funds within their sprawling campuses. Similarly, in Cambridge, UK, engagement of the faculty with industry has spawned many *millionaire dons.* The private sector can be tapped to fund research and development at universities.

Effective mechanisms of collaboration need to be created for universities and industry bodies so that research output and innovations can effectively be commercialized and transformed into marketable products and services for last mile benefits. A cluster-based approach to spur innovations at universities could be adopted wherein a minimum critical mass of universities is identified and efforts are made to create or strengthen the innovation system around them. The innovation universities could also provide a platform for experimenting with new models of universities where the above mentioned integration could be realized.

Collaborations can play a crucial role in stimulating innovations and fostering knowledge transfers which would foster interconnections that link intellectual, financial, human, and creative capital as well as unleash underutilized capital. Such enterprises could take the shape of physical or virtual clusters, which bring together research, business, risk capital, and creativity to turn ideas into products, processes, and services.

19.5.4 Innovations Need Incentives: Innovations are risky. New ideas need time and experimentation to develop, and if the idea fails, the individual has a negative return on his or her investment. So, in societies with few safety nets, innovation may be constrained. Policy can give a push to individual innovators by providing fall-back options. Risk management instruments, for example, can provide security to innovators so that they may expend resources on their new activities.

The poorest innovators need social safety nets to ensure that their families survive if the innovations fail. Since the greatest cost to these innovators is the time they spend on developing an innovation, general social safety nets insure against this income loss.

Those farther from the poverty line may need incentives to invest in innovation rather than more secure income generation activities. Innovation funds that provide grants to individuals to develop creative ideas are becoming more common. And for innovators across the poverty spectrum, policies that ensure a monopoly of returns from marketable innovations—patents, copyright laws—lower the income risk associated with developing non-rival ideas. While such legislation is outside the human development arena, its fair implementation and monitoring is crucial as individuals move through the process of implementing their ideas.

Incentives have long been used as a tool to encourage innovation in the developed world. Grand Challenges for instance, have a long history, dating all the way back to the 1700s, when the British Crown announced a *Grand Prize* for finding a way to measure longitude. In recent times, Grand Challenges have been on the rise after the Ansari X-Prize, which called for innovation in spaceflight, was introduced in the US in 1996. In 2014, the British Government announced Grand Challenges—to promote innovation in science and technology. More recently, in China, state-backed groups and institutes use the challenge-approach to widen the debate on innovation and find solutions to problems. China Association of Construction Enterprise Management, for instance, gives over 100 awards annually for innovation in construction. China's Ministry of Education oversees several national competitions in areas ranging from advertising to electric design to cloud computing. The US also has several reality TV shows that focus on business plan competitions.

Innovators need financial support at an early stage to develop and test their ideas in the marketplace. Venture funds are recognised globally as the most suitable form of providing risk capital for the growth of innovative technology and breakthrough ideas. While India is amongst the top recipients in Asia for venture funds and private equity funds, these investments are so far focused on relatively large and *safer* investments. Thus, despite the growth in the venture capital industry in India and some government schemes for supporting entrepreneurs, the seed funding stage in the innovation pipeline, where amounts required may be small but risks high, is severely constricted.

An extensive innovation ecosystem requires many lateral connections, often at local levels, between producers, sellers and financiers, and the facilitating government machinery. To induce a culture of innovation in the country, there is a need to offer encouragement through awards and challenges which mobilise people to engage and respond creatively and bring focus on neglected societal challenges.

To sum up, innovations can play a very important role in the development discourse, because they can offer a new approach to a system that is currently over-burdened by the multiple demands and has limited resources at its disposal. Enhanced focus on innovations can have an impact much beyond the realm of S&T in diverse areas such as health and education delivery, governance, enterprise development and much more. Collectively, this can herald a generational change in the country and can lay out a chart for a more sustainable and inclusive growth paradigm.

Innovation requires a financial system which is supportive and inclusive and which provides the necessary risk capital to spur innovations and enterprises. Venture funds are recognized globally as the most suitable form of providing risk capital for the growth of innovative technology and breakthrough ideas.

Presently, innovation is no longer a mere appendage to science and technology but has assumed centre stage in the developmental goals of countries around the world. New paradigms of innovation have emerged and systems that foster innovation are not universal. They have become country and context specific.

20

Entrepreneurship and Start-ups

Entrepreneurship has been considered the backbone of economic development. It has been well-established that the level of economic growth of a country, to a large extent, depends on the level of entrepreneurial activities. The myth that entrepreneurs are born, no more holds good. Rather, it is well-recognised now that the entrepreneurs can be created and nurtured through appropriate interventions in the form of entrepreneurship development programmes.

20.1 Entrepreneurship Defined

In political economics, entrepreneurship is the quality of being an entrepreneur, i.e. one who *undertakes an enterprise*. The term puts emphasis on the risk and effort taken by individuals who both own and manage a business, and on the innovations resulting from their pursuit of economic success.

Entrepreneurship in this sense may result in new organizations or may be part of revitalizing mature organizations in response to a perceived opportunity. The most obvious form of entrepreneurship is that of starting new businesses (referred as a start-up company). In recent years, the term has been extended to include social and political forms of entrepreneurial activity. When entrepreneurship is describing activities within a firm or large organization it is referred to as intra-preneurship and may include corporate venturing, when large entities spin-off organizations.

Entrepreneurial activities are substantially different depending on the type of organization and creativity involved. Entrepreneurship ranges in scale from solo projects (even involving the entrepreneur only part-time) to major undertakings creating many job opportunities. Many high value entrepreneurial ventures seek venture capital or angel funding (seed money) in order to raise capital to build the business. Many kinds of organizations now exist to support would-be entrepreneurs including specialized government agencies, business incubators, science parks, and some NGOs. In more recent times, the term entrepreneurship has been extended to include elements not related necessarily to business formation activity such as conceptualizations of entrepreneurship as a specific mindset resulting in entrepreneurial initiatives e.g. in the form of social entrepreneurship, political entrepreneurship, or knowledge entrepreneurship have emerged.

The supposition that entrepreneurship leads to economic growth is an interpretation of the residual in endogenous growth theory and as such is hotly debated in academic economics. An alternate description suggests that the majority of innovations may be much more incremental improvements such as the replacement of paper with plastic in the construction of a drinking straw.

Entrepreneurship is about taking risk. The behaviour of the entrepreneur reflects a kind of person willing to put his or her career and financial security on the line and take risks in the name of an idea, spending much time as well as capital on an uncertain venture. The acts of entrepreneurship are often associated with true uncertainty, particularly when it involves bringing something really novel to the world, whose market never exists.

20.2 Who is an Entrepreneur?

An entrepreneur is an individual who organizes and operates a business or businesses, taking on financial risk to do so. The entrepreneur is commonly seen as an innovator of new ideas, and business processes. Management skill and strong team building abilities are often perceived as essential leadership attributes for successful entrepreneurs. Leadership, management ability, and team-building are considered to be the essential qualities of an entrepreneur.

Psychological studies show that the psychological propensities for male and female entrepreneurs are more similar than different. A growing body of work shows that entrepreneurial behaviour is dependent on social and economic factors. For example, countries with healthy and diversified labour markets or stronger safety nets show a more favourable ratio of opportunity-driven rather than necessity-driven women entrepreneurs. Empirical studies suggest that male entrepreneurs possess strong negotiating skills and consensus-forming abilities.

Research studies that explore the characteristics and personality traits of, and influences on, the entrepreneur have come to differing conclusions. Most, however, agree on certain consistent entrepreneurial traits and environmental influences. Although certain entrepreneurial traits are required, entrepreneurial behaviours are also dynamic and influenced by environmental factors. The entrepreneur is solely concerned with opportunity recognition and exploitation, although the opportunity that is recognised depends on the type of entrepreneur.

Some of the most significant influences on an individual's decision to become an entrepreneur are workplace peers and the social composition of the workplace.

The ability of entrepreneurs to innovate is thought to relate to innate traits such as extroversion and a proclivity for risk-taking. The capabilities of innovating, introducing new technologies, increasing efficiency and productivity, or generating new products or services. are characteristic qualities of entrepreneurs. Entrepreneurs are catalysts for economic change, and researchers argue that entrepreneurs are highly creative individuals with a tendency to imagine new solutions by finding opportunities for profit or reward. It is widely maintained that entrepreneurs are unusual individuals. In line with this view, there is an emerging research tradition investigating the genetic factors that are perceived to make entrepreneurs so distinctive.

However, there are also critical perspectives that attribute these research attitudes to oversimplified methodological and/or philosophical assumptions. For example, it has been argued that entrepreneurs are not that distinctive, but that it is in essence unrealistic preconceptions about *non-entrepreneurs* that maintain laudatory portraits of *entrepreneurs*.

20.3 Role and Importance of Entrepreneurs

Entrepreneurs play an important role in the economic development of a country. Successful entrepreneurs innovate, bring new products and concepts to the market, improve market efficiency, build wealth, create jobs, and enhance economic growth.

De novo firms that unleash creative destruction shift surpluses from rent-seeking large producers to consumers and broader society. Joseph Schumpeter, eminent American economist, put innovation at the heart of economic theory and capitalism. He proposed that innovation was the process by which economies were able to break out of their static mode and enter a path of dynamism. It was his theory of *creative destruction* that first highlighted the importance of innovators in revolutionizing the economic structure, leading to the creation of new products, services, and markets, and the decay of the old. Just as boosting entrepreneurship can lead to growth and job creation, failing to promote entrepreneurship can lead to stagnation, and social and economic inertia.

The growth and prosperity of all economies remains highly dependent on entrepreneurial activity. Entrepreneurs are the essence of economic growth as they provide a source of income and employment for themselves, create employment for others, produce new and innovative products or services, and drive greater upstream and downstream value-chain activities. Supportive environments are increasingly essential to successful entrepreneurship and these are evolving across the world. The ideal entrepreneurial environment has 5 pillars:

1. Access to funding.
2. Entrepreneurial culture.
3. Supportive regulatory and tax regimes.
4. Educational systems that support entrepreneurial mindsets.
5. A co-ordinated approach that links the public, private and voluntary sectors.

The face of entrepreneurship is also changing. Across the world, entrepreneurs are increasingly young and/or female due to increasing unemployment. The public and private sector each have an important role to play in creating entrepreneurial ecosystems that, in addition to funding, are essential to promoting entrepreneurial success.

Highlighting the diversity of the country, four kinds of entrepreneurial activities exist: (a) factor-driven entrepreneurship, (b) efficiency-driven entrepreneurship, (c) innovation-driven entrepreneurship, and (d) necessity-driven entrepreneurship.

Developed economies generate entrepreneurial opportunities as a result of their wealth and innovation capacity, yet they also offer more wage employment options to attract those that might otherwise become independent entrepreneurs. If these opportunities for entrepreneurship and innovation are to be captured, it is essential to create an enabling eco-system for entrepreneurship to thrive and instil a mind-set and culture of opportunity and innovation-based motives and entrepreneurial incentives.

In the era of liberalisation, privatisation and globalization along with ongoing IT revolution, capable entrepreneurs are making use of the opportunities emerging from the evolving scenario. However, a large segment of the population, particularly in the industrially backward regions/rural areas generally lags behind in taking advantage of these opportunities. Therefore, there is a need to provide skill development and entrepreneurship development training to such people in order to bring them to mainstream of economic growth.

20.4 Obstacles to Entrepreneurship in Developing Countries

Following can be listed as factors responsible for limited entrepreneurship in underdeveloped countries:

1. Lack of incentives for innovation at the national level.
2. Lack of efficient business incubators.
3. Insufficient access to capital.
4. Archaic education system.
5. Lack of work-related skills amongst the youth.
6. Disabling business environment.
7. General sense of apathy and untimeliness in law enforcement.
8. Aversion to change within the bureaucracy.
9. Culture of rent-seeking at several layers of governance.
10. General, pervasive and deeply corrosive sense of mistrust between the government and the private sector.

20.4.1 Culture and Mindset: The biggest cultural obstacle to unleashing entrepreneurial potential in less developed countries (LDCs) is scepticism about entrepreneurship. Young creative individuals are often held back from starting new ventures due to inherent scepticism amongst family members. Given this cultural context, any blueprint that intends to effectively encourage entrepreneurship must promote and embrace a risk-taking and creative mindset. A related cultural obstacle to innovation is the limited tolerance for failure. Experimentation and failure are integral parts of creating and building new ventures. Therefore, a societal tolerance for failure as part and parcel of the learning process needs to be inculcated.

Apart from the overarching theme of a generalized aversion toward risk-taking and failure, other more subtle cultural impediments also present a challenge to entrepreneurship and innovation. These include general de-prioritization of soft skills in favour of hard technical knowledge, and a bias by employers against graduates hailing from non-elite institutions or non-engineering backgrounds, amongst others.

20.5 Women Entrepreneurship

Women entrepreneurs may be defined as the women or a group of women who initiate, organize and operate a business enterprise. A sense of independent decision-making is the motivational factor behind this urge. Saddled with household chores and domestic responsibilities, women want to get independence. Under the influence of these factors the women entrepreneurs choose a profession as a challenge and as an urge to do something new. Such a situation is described as pull factors. Push factors pertain to women engaged in business activities due to family compulsions and/or family responsibilities.

Women owned businesses are increasing in the economies of almost all countries.

The hidden entrepreneurial potentials of women have gradually been changing with the growing sensitivity to the role and economic status in the society.

In spite of all these, women still find themselves at the receiving end in the labour market. Women are dependant on informal sector more heavily than men, and as a result, their share in this sector is higher than their share in total labour force. Even within the informal sector most of the women are own account workers or home-based workers. However, this traditional setting is changing, albeit slowly, and the share of women in wage employment is increasing along with intrusion of more and more women into hitherto male bastions.

The concept of women entrepreneurship is multi-disciplinary in nature embodying economic, psychological, social, cultural and political as well as environmental characteristics. The types of responses women are generating in certain circumstances highlight women as special type of entrepreneurs, away from men with distinction. The need for bringing women to the main stream of economic development is because of their proven success in all fields, wherever they got the opportunity. Traditionally, women, be it mother, wife or sister, used to be in-charge of the household management. Although, over the last few decades women have come forward to establish their own enterprises, their number remains small in male-dominated world. Women's work, however innovative it might be, goes unrecognized.

Several factors influence women to take up entrepreneurial ventures. The economic role is largely determined by the traditional division of labour by sex where women tend to undertake and specialize in work near the home such as food processing, household maintenance, horticulture and handicrafts etc. There are various factors that motivate a woman to take on entrepreneurial activities. Prominently, it is not always easy for a woman to find a job that is compatible with her family responsibilities and household chores. This encourages women towards self-employment in enterprises adjoining their places of residence with flexible working hours, which allows them to take care of both home and business.

Entrepreneurship development is a very crucial factor for the acceleration of economic growth of any country and the role of women is essential in this regard. Women have started showing more interest in entrepreneurship because it provides them an opportunity to be their own boss.

20.6 What is a Start-up?

A start-up company (or simply a start-up) is an entrepreneurial venture which is typically a newly emerged, fast-growing business that aims to meet a marketplace need by developing a viable business model around an innovative product, service, process or a platform. A start-up is usually a company designed to effectively develop and validate a scalable business model. Start-ups have high rates of failure, but the minority of successes includes companies that have become large and influential.

Although there are start-ups created in all types of businesses, and all over the world, some locations and business sectors are particularly associated with start-up companies.

The internet bubble of the late 1990s was associated with huge numbers of internet start-up companies, some selling the technology to provide internet access, others using the internet to provide services. Most of this start-up activity was located in the most well-known start-up ecosystem—Silicon Valley, an area of northern California renowned for the high level of start-up company activity.

20.6.1 Unicorn Start-ups: In business, a unicorn is a privately-held start-up company valued at over US$ 1 billion. The term was coined in 2013 by venture capitalist Aileen Lee, choosing the mythical animal to represent such successful ventures which are limited in number.

20.7 Start-up Ecosystem

The size and maturity of the start-up ecosystem where the start-up is launched and where it grows have an effect on the volume and success of the start-ups. The start-up ecosystem consists of the following:

1. Individuals, i.e. entrepreneurs, venture capitalists, angel investors, mentors.
2. Institutions and organizations, i.e. top research universities and institutes, business schools and entrepreneurship programmes operated by universities and colleges.
3. Non-profit entrepreneurship support organizations.
4. Government entrepreneurship programmes and services.
5. Chambers of commerce.
6. Business incubators and business accelerators.

A region with all of these elements is considered to be a *strong* start-up ecosystem. The most famous start-up ecosystem is Silicon Valley in California, where major computer and internet firms and top universities such as Stanford University have created a stimulating start-up environment. Boston [where Massachusetts Institute of Technology (MIT) is located) and Berlin, home of WISTA (a top research area) are other examples of start-up ecosystem.

Large or well-established companies often try to promote innovation by setting up internal start-ups, i.e. new business divisions that operate at arm's length from the rest of the company. Then, there are re-starters, i.e. failed entrepreneurs who after some time restart in the same sector with more or less the same activities.

20.8 Characteristics of a Start-up

Start-ups can come in all forms and sizes. Some of the critical tasks are to build a co-founder team to secure key skills, know-how, financial resources, and other elements to conduct research on the target market. Co-founders are people involved in the initial launch of start-up companies.

1. Anyone can be a co-founder, and an existing company can also be a co-founder, but frequently co-founders are entrepreneurs, engineers, hackers, web developers, web designers and others involved in the ground level of a new, often high-tech, venture.
2. Typically, a start-up will begin by building a first minimum viable product (MVP), a prototype, to validate, assess and develop the new ideas or business concepts. In addition, start-ups founders do research to deepen their understanding of the ideas,

technologies or business concepts and their commercial potential.

3. A shareholders' agreement (SHA) is often agreed early on to confirm the commitment, ownership and contributions of the founders and investors and to deal with the intellectual properties and assets that may be generated by the start-up.
4. Beyond founders' own contributions, some start-ups raise additional investment at some or several stages of their growth (called investing rounds). The first round is called *seed round*. The seed round generally is when the start-up is still in the very early phase of execution when their product is still in the prototype phase. At this level angel investors will be the ones participating. The next round is called Series A. At this point the company already has traction and may be making revenue. In Series A rounds venture capital firms will be participating alongside angels or super angel investors. The next rounds are Series B, C, and D. These three rounds are the ones leading towards initial public offer (IPO). Venture capital firms and private equity firms will be participating. Not all start-ups trying to raise investments are successful in their fundraising.
5. Business models for start-ups are generally found via a *bottom-up* or *top-down* approach. A company may cease to be a start-up as it passes various milestones, such as becoming publicly traded on the stock market in an IPO, or ceasing to exist as an independent entity via a merger or acquisition.
6. Companies may also fail and cease to operate altogether, an outcome that is very likely for start-ups, given that they are developing disruptive innovations which may not function as expected and for which there may not be market demand, even when the product or service is finally developed. Given that start-ups operate in high-risk sectors, it can also be hard to attract investors to support the product/service development or attract buyers.
7. Investors are attracted to start-ups because of the latter's strong co-founding team, a balanced *risk/reward* profile—in which high risk due to the untested, disruptive innovations is balanced out by high potential returns—and *scalability*, i.e. the likelihood that a start-up can expand its operations by serving more markets or more customers.
8. Attractive start-ups generally have lower *bootstrapping* (self-funding of start-ups by the founders) costs, higher risk, and higher potential return on investment.
9. Successful start-ups are typically more scalable than an established business, in the sense that the start-up has the potential to grow rapidly with a limited investment of capital, labour or land.
10. Start-ups have several options for funding. Venture capital firms and angel investors may help start-up companies begin operations, exchanging seed money for an equity stake in the firm. Venture capitalists and angel investors provide financing to a range of start-ups, with the expectation that a very small number of the start-ups will become viable and make money. In practice though, many start-ups are initially funded by the founders themselves using *bootstrapping*, in which loans or monetary gifts from friends and family are combined with savings and credit card debt to finance the venture.

11. Start-ups usually need to form partnerships with other firms to enable their business model to operate. To become attractive to other businesses, start-ups need to align their internal features, such as management style and products with the market situation.
12. Start-up founders often have a more casual or offbeat attitude in their dress, office space and marketing, as compared to traditional corporations. Thus, instead of *tie culture,* start-up founders may wear bermudas, hoodies, sneakers and other casual clothes to business meetings. Their offices may have recreational facilities in them, such as pool tables, ping pong tables and pinball machines, which are used to create a fun work environment, stimulate team development and team spirit, and encourage creativity. Some start-ups do not use a strict command and control hierarchical structure, with executives, managers, supervisors and employees.

21

Micro Finance and Self-help Groups (SHGs)

Micro finance is a movement whose objective is a world in which as many poor and near-poor households as possible have permanent access to an appropriate range of high quality financial services, including not just credit but also savings, insurance, and fund transfers. Many of those who promote micro finance believe that such access will help poor people get out of poverty. For others, micro finance is a way to promote economic development, employment and growth through the support of micro entrepreneurs and small businesses.

21.1 History of Micro Finance

Modern micro finance emerged in the 1970s with a strong orientation towards private sector solutions. This resulted from evidence that state-owned agricultural development banks in developing countries had been a monumental failure, actually undermining the development goals they were intended to serve. Nevertheless, public officials in many countries hold a different view, and continue to intervene in micro finance markets.

Micro finance sector has grown rapidly over the past few decades. Nobel Laureate Muhammad Yunus is credited with laying the foundation of the modern micro finance institutions (MFIs) with establishment of Grameen Bank, Bangladesh in 1976. Today, micro finance has evolved into a vibrant industry exhibiting a variety of business models. In India, National Bank for Agriculture and Rural Development (NABARD) took up this idea and started micro finance operations in the early 1990s.

Loans to poor people by banks have many limitations including lack of security and high operating cost and so micro finance was developed as an alternative to provide loans to poor people with the goal of creating financial inclusion and equality.

21.1.1 UN Report on the Role of Micro Credit: The objective of the First United Nations Decade for the Eradication of Poverty (1997-2006), proclaimed by the General Assembly in its resolution of December 20, 1995, was to achieve the goal of eradicating absolute poverty through national action and international co-operation.

The General Assembly, in its resolution of December 18, 1997, noted that in many countries micro credit programmes have proved to be an effective tool in freeing people from poverty and have helped to increase their participation in the economic and political processes of society. Among other provisions, the Assembly called upon the relevant organs, organizations and bodies of the United Nations system to explore the micro credit approach in their programmes as a tool for the eradication of poverty. The Assembly requested the Secretary General—in collaboration with relevant organizations of the United Nations system, including funds and programmes and the World Bank—to submit to it at its Fifty-third session a report on the role of micro credit in the eradication of poverty.

The World Summit for Social Development, held in Copenhagen in March 1995, also underlined the importance of improving access to credit for small rural or urban producers, landless farmers and other people with low or no income, with special attention to the needs of women and disadvantaged and vulnerable groups. Governments were called upon to:

1. Review national legal, regulatory and institutional frameworks that restrict the access of people living in poverty, especially women, to credit on reasonable terms.
2. Promote realistic targets for access to affordable credit.
3. Provide incentives for improving access to and strengthening the capacity of organized credit systems to deliver credit and related services to people living in poverty and vulnerable groups.
4. Expand financial networks, building on existing networks, promoting attractive opportunities for savings and ensuring equitable access to credit at the local level.

21.2 Meaning and Salient Features of Micro Finance

Micro finance is the provision of a diverse range of financial services and products including small loans (micro credit), savings accounts, insurance, pensions and money transfers. These are designed to assist people living in poverty who are not able to access financial services in the mainstream banking sector because they have no collateral, formal identification or steady income.

Poor people borrow from informal moneylenders and save with informal collectors. They receive loans and grants from charities. They buy insurance from state-owned companies. They receive funds transfers through formal or informal remittance networks. It is not easy to distinguish micro finance from similar activities. It could be claimed that a government that orders state banks to open deposit accounts for poor consumers, or a moneylender that engages in usury, or a charity that runs a heifer pool are engaged in micro finance. Ensuring financial services to poor people is best done by expanding the number of financial institutions available to them, as well as by strengthening the capacity of those institutions. In recent years there has also been increasing emphasis on expanding the diversity of institutions, since different institutions serve different needs.

21.2.1 Salient Features of Micro Finance: These are as under:

1. Borrowers are from the low-income group.
2. Loans are of small amount.
3. Loans are for short duration.
4. Loans are offered without collaterals.
5. Loans are generally given for income generation purpose.
6. Repayment frequency is high.
7. Terms of loan vary, but once repaid, the money is recycled and lent out to someone else.

21.2.2 Micro Finance and Micro Credit Distinguished: Micro finance is different from micro credit. Micro finance is a broad category of services, which includes micro credit. Micro credit is provision of credit services to poor clients. Micro credit is one of the aspects of micro finance and the two are often confused. Under micro credit, small amounts of loans are given to the borrower but under micro finance besides loans many other financial services are provided such as savings account, insurance etc. Therefore micro finance is a wider concept as compared to micro credit.

Micro credit is the provision of small, collateral-free loans to people living in poverty to use as business capital. Loans are used to start or grow micro enterprises that help give them a regular income—whether it is a small farm, food stall, jewellery-making business or taxi. They may use loans to buy stock or equipment, creating a sustainable livelihood for themselves and their families. Through the profits they earn, they are able to provide for their children and repay the loans over time.

21.3 Micro Finance and Allied Services

Apart from providing small loans, micro finance also includes a range of financial services to the poor. Some of these are as follows:

21.3.1 Savings Accounts: These are meant to help provide a safety net in times of need and help to plan for the future. Without an alternative, people living in poverty hide their money in boxes under their beds or in holes in the ground. They also put their money into assets (such as livestock or pieces of jewellery) which offer little real security and can be stolen or destroyed by natural disasters.

Micro savings are deposit services offered by financial institutions that allow people living in poverty to securely store small amounts of money. Micro finance institutions offer savings facilities—some even make them compulsory, encouraging families to plan for unexpected expenses so they can have the freedom to invest in healthcare, education, housing and their businesses when the need arises. In many cases, banking regulations do not allow micro finance institutions to directly offer micro savings services. Agency arrangements with banks can help overcome this problem.

21.3.2 Micro Insurance: This is meant to protect against emergencies and disasters. Micro insurance is insurance for low-income households that protects against unforeseen events so that savings and working capital can be maintained rather than eroded. Like savings, it helps provide security against the many risks faced by those living in poverty. Innovative products offered by micro finance institutions cover policyholders with crop, loan, health, life and property insurance, offering families a safety net when an unexpected hardship occurs so they are not forced back into poverty.

21.3.3 Micro Pensions: Micro pensions are accumulation superannuation accounts. They are funded by an individual's contribution and, in some cases, a matched contribution from the government. They are meant to help provide an income in old age.

21.3.4 Fund Transfers and Remittance Products: These are meant to help families, living far apart, access their incomes. Money transfers are domestic and international electronic transfers of money. They are used for a variety of purposes, including regular bill payment, one-time-only money needs, delivering money from people working in urban areas to their family members in rural areas, and sending money from migrants to family members in their country of origin (remittances).

Many developing countries lack any viable money transfer services, and substantial volumes of global remittances continue to flow through informal and sometimes dangerous underground channels which are outside government supervision and regulation. Micro finance institutions are increasingly trying to seek alliances with banks and money transfer companies to offer safe, convenient and lower-cost transfers to their clients, many utilising mobile phone technologies.

21.4 Relevance of Micro Finance

All economies rely upon the financial intermediary function to transfer resources from savers to investors. In market economies, this function is performed by commercial banks and the capital markets. More widespread financial intermediation is a hallmark of modern economy. However, in many developing countries, capital markets are still at a rudimentary stage, and commercial banks are reluctant to lend to the poor largely because of the lack of collateral and high transaction costs. The poor would borrow relatively small amounts, and the processing and supervision of lending to them would consume administrative costs that would be disproportionate to the amount of lending. Complicated loan procedures and paperwork, combined with a lack of accounting experience, limit poor people's access to formal sources of credit. Commercial lenders in rural areas prefer to deal mainly with large-scale farmers.

It is in this context that micro credit has recently assumed a certain degree of prominence. It is based on the recognition that the latent capacity of the poor for entrepreneurship would be encouraged with the availability of small-scale loans and would introduce them to the small enterprise sector. This could allow them to be more self-reliant, create employment opportunities, and engage women in economically productive activities. Several factors have led to increased interest in micro credit in promoting growth with greater equity. There has been a growth in the recognition of the importance of empowering all people by increasing their access to all the factors of production, including credit. In addition, the value of the role of non-governmental organizations in development is receiving more attention.

With financial inclusion emerging as a major policy objective in the country, micro finance has occupied centre stage as a promising conduit for extending financial services to unbanked sections of population. Micro finance is the provision of financial services to low-income clients or solidarity lending groups including consumers and the self-employed, who traditionally lack access to banking and related services.

Micro finance is not just about giving micro credit to the poor rather it is an economic development tool whose objective is to assist poor to work their way out of poverty. It covers a wide range of services like credit, savings, insurance, remittance and also non-financial services like training, counselling etc. In the past few decades it has helped out remarkably in eradicating poverty. People who have taken micro finance have been able to increase their income and hence the standard of living. Poor also need financial services to fulfil their needs like consumption, building of assets and protection against risk.

Micro credit targets people who are often unemployed or otherwise excluded from the traditional banking system and who wish to start their own business. Studies show that micro credit significantly contributes to self-employment and job creation. The fiscal cost per job created is usually below that of alternative labour market instruments and jobs created through micro credit positively contribute to income and self-esteem of entrepreneurs. In fact, micro finance and the impact it produces goes beyond just business loans. The poor use financial services not only for business investment in their micro enterprises but also to invest in health and education, to manage household emergencies, and to meet a wide variety of other cash needs. The range of financial services includes loans, savings facilities, insurance, transfer payments, and even micro pensions. Access to financial services enables poor people to increase their household incomes, build assets and reduce their vulnerability to the crises that are so much a part of their daily lives.

21.5 Sector/Group-wise Role of Micro Finance

21.5.1 Micro Finance and Individuals/Households: Micro finance is the provision of financial services to people who would not usually qualify for traditional banking services because they have no form of collateral or formal identification. Even a small loan of ₹ 5,000 can help someone living in poverty to start or grow his own small business. This enables them to earn an income so they no longer have to struggle to afford food, clean water, healthcare and an education for their children.

By helping a mother buy a sewing machine to start a tailoring business or a father buy seeds to plant a vegetable garden, small loans enable people in poverty to earn an income and provide for their families. As each business grows, loans are paid back and lent out again. With loans repaid, the cycle continues, year after year. Each successful business can feed a family, employ more people and eventually help empower a whole community.

Various studies of the impact of micro finance have been carried out over the past 20 years, including large-scale studies by the World Bank. These studies have established that micro finance can improve the living standards of poor households and the communities in which they live. The benefits of micro finance include:

1. Higher and more reliable income and savings.
2. Improved access to healthcare and better nutrition.
3. Greater female empowerment.
4. Better housing.
5. More children being placed in school.

These studies provide good evidence that micro finance projects can indeed be effective. Experience shows that micro finance can help people living in poverty to increase their income, build viable businesses and reduce their vulnerability to external shocks. It can also be a powerful instrument for self-empowerment by enabling the poor, especially women, to become agents of change, not just economically, but also socially as they emerge as influential leaders in their community. Income generation from a business helps not only the business activity expand, but also contributes to household income, resulting in better food, shelter, education, sanitation, healthcare and so on.

Families living in poverty are often vulnerable to shocks such as the illness of a wage earner, extreme weather, theft or other such events. These shocks place a huge burden on the limited financial resources of a family, and can drive a family deeper into poverty if they do not have access to financial services like credit, insurance and savings.

It should be noted that although a large number of studies undertaken so far on the impact of micro credit programmes on household income show that participants of such programmes usually have higher and more stable incomes than they did before they joined the programmes, some practitioners still have reservations about the findings of these studies. Moreover, not many micro credit programmes can afford to undertake impact assessments because they are generally expensive and time-consuming. There are serious disagreements among experts on the validity of methodologies used in some of the published studies. In some cases, even the more rigorous studies have produced inconclusive results. Some studies show that there are limits to the use of credit as an instrument for poverty eradication, including difficulties in identifying the poor and targeting credit to reach the poorest of the poor. Added to this is the fact that many people, especially the poorest of the poor, are usually not in a position to undertake an economic activity, partly because they lack business skills and even the motivation for business.

21.5.2 Micro Finance and Women: Micro finance experts generally agree that women should be the primary focus of service delivery. Evidence shows that they are less likely to default on their loans than men. Because operating margins become tighter the smaller the loans delivered, many MFIs consider the risk of lending to men to be too high. Women are typically poorer than men and have fewer options for earning a livelihood to provide adequate food, housing and education for their children. They are also the *change agents* of the family. Women are more likely to invest their earnings into improving the lives of the families. By encouraging women to take charge of their futures, MFIs can impact families and whole communities.

In developing countries, more women are involved in the informal labour sector. Men are more likely to be employed in contract work as labourers or overseas workers. Women are often left to support their families or supplement their husband's income by using any skills they possess. With limited resources to start or expand a small business, micro finance is attractive to women who are prepared to work hard to give their children a brighter future. Micro finance generally targets poor women because they have proven to be reliable credit risks and when they have the financial means, they invest that money back into their families, resulting in better health and education and stronger local economies.

21.5.3 Micro Finance and Social Interventions: There are currently a few social interventions that have been combined with micro finance to increase awareness of HIV/AIDS, and gender equity. Such interventions educate on different gender roles, gender-based violence, and HIV/AIDS infections to strengthen the communication skills and leadership of women. Micro finance has also been combined with business education and with other packages of health interventions.

Micro finance programmes have been instrumental in generating employment, income and enhancing living standards of poor in underdeveloped and developing countries. They have good potential for uplifting the economic conditions of assetless poor people through group approach. Micro finance through self-help groups ensures active participation and involvement of the beneficiaries in effective implementation of the programmes for socio-economic development.

In India, micro finance programme has a crucial role to play in uplifting people living below poverty line. Poor people have less access to financial services because of their inability to provide collateral security which is demanded by the banks.

21.5.4 Micro Finance and the Economy: Micro finance is a form of financial services for entrepreneurs and small businesses lacking access to banking and related services. The two main mechanisms for the delivery of financial services to such clients are: (a) relationship-based banking for individual entrepreneurs and small businesses, and (b) group-based models, where several entrepreneurs come together to apply for loans and other services as a group. There is a rich variety of financial institutions in India which serve micro entrepreneurs and small businesses.

A significant proportion of the working population in many developing countries survives through involvement in the informal sector. By offering people a means to grow their small businesses to the point where many employ other people, micro finance has flow-on effects for local economies, decreasing unemployment and providing incomes for other poor families in the community.

With an increased income and therefore more money spent on items such as food, clothing and transport, micro finance clients become active participants in their local economies, also benefiting the providers of those products and services. By boosting local economies, micro finance benefits the developing world.

21.6 Micro Finance and Self-help Groups (SHGs)

Micro finance is routed through SHGs. The target groups broadly comprise small and marginal farmers, agricultural and non-agricultural labourers, artisans and craftsmen and other poor engaged in small businesses like vending, and hawking. The programme has been providing the rural poor access to the formal banking system and has achieved several milestones in terms of gender sensitisation, empowerment and poverty alleviation. The programme provides thrift linked credit support to the members of SHGs. While the programme directly benefits the members, it also helps banks in reducing their transaction costs as well as risk in delivering small loans. The programme has now assumed the form of a micro finance movement in many parts of the world.

21.6.1 Meaning of Self-help Group (SHG): A SHG is a small voluntary association of 10-20 poor people from the same socio-economic background who come together for the purpose of addressing their common socio-economic problems through self-help and mutual-help. They collect small savings (thrift) on regular basis. Out of the pooled money, small interest bearing loans are given to the members and some amount is deposited with a bank regularly. The bank lends money for economic activities of the group without collateral security and at market rates. The savings of poor members are pooled resources saved with great difficulty. This hard-earned money is termed as *warm money.* The money obtained by the group from outsiders, i.e. banks, MFIs is termed as *cold money.*

Members make small regular contributions over a few months until there is enough capital with the group to begin lending. Funds may then be lent back to the members or to others in the village for any purpose. In India, many SHGs are *linked* to banks for the delivery of micro credit.

SHGs are started by non-governmental organizations (NGOs) that generally have broad anti-poverty agendas. SHGs are seen as instruments for a variety of goals including empowering women, developing leadership abilities among poor people, increasing school enrolments, and improving nutrition and the use of birth control. Financial intermediation is generally seen more as an entry point to these other goals, rather than as a primary objective.

21.7 Role of SHGs in Socio-economic Upliftment of the Poor

SHGs have been instrumental in initiating micro entrepreneurial activities among those poor people who have been neglected so far and far away from the process of social as well economic development. Self-help groups-bank linkage programme is responsible for developing banking habits among the poorest of the poor people.

The basic objective of a SHG is upliftment of poor people by means of micro economic activities so that the members get job opportunities, sustainable income and some assets for generation of regular income. There is tremendous enthusiasm in formation of the groups but care is not taken for their proper growth and survival.

The most significant contribution of SHGs is that they have been instrumental in building up enough confidence among the poor people and now they are ready to participate in the process of development. Many of these have been running fair price shops very successfully. A sizable number of the groups in India are working as caterers for the government-sponsored Mid-Day Meal Scheme. It is noteworthy that a good number of the SHGs have been marketing successfully the products of domestic as well as multinational corporations in remote rural areas.

The banking system, with its larger overheads, is perhaps not best suited to deal with small credits. This is where SHGs and similar collective guarantee credit schemes have a big role to play.

21.7.1 Savings Promotion: SHGs provide savings mechanism, which suits the needs of SHGs members. It also provides a cost-effective delivery mechanism for small credit to its members. It plays a very significant role in connecting the poor people to the banking system by encouraging and mobilising the savings which results in collective economic development of the country. It also contributes to improving the social and economic life of SHG members.

21.7.2 Income Generating Activities: The major objective of SHGs is removal of poverty. SHGs provide credit which, in turn, accords opportunities for investment to generate income for the poor people, especially in rural areas. This enhances the living standards of its members, which belong to low income groups. SHG members take up different income generating activities. The following is an illustrative list of such activities:

1. Hosiery items.
2. Candle making.
3. Poultry farming.
4. Sheep rearing.
5. Embroidery and tailoring.
6. Carpets weaving.
7. Basket weaving.
8. Sale of fruits and vegetables.
9. Small grocery shops.

21.7.3 Skill Development: Many poor people are uneducated, especially in rural areas. SHGs enable its members to learn to co-operate and work in a group environment. As a SHG member, an individual develops certain skills which he can utilize to earn more. By providing training to its members, a SGH develops entrepreneurial capabilities among its members, leading to social and economic development of the poor in urban and rural areas.

21.7.4 Utilisation of Resources: Members of a SHG make regular, though small, contributions over a few months until there is enough money in the group to begin lending. Funds so collected are lent back to its members for productive purposes. Hence, SHGs play a very important role in utilising local resources for the betterment of the members of the group and betterment of the society as well.

21.7.5 Awareness and Empowerment: SHGs are at the forefront in creating awareness about the rights of the poor so that they are not exploited by money lenders, landlords, local politicians, creditors etc. SHGs are also contributing in empowering a number of rural women economically, socially and politically.

21.7.6 Solving Social and Personal Problems: Majority of the rural people belong to low income group. SHGs help to overcome the problem of poverty, especially in rural areas. SHGs also help the group members to understand each other's problems in a better way. The members come together for the purpose of mutual help and co-operation for peaceful coexistence.

21.8 Alternative Models of SHGs

A self-help group may be registered or unregistered. It typically comprises a group of micro entrepreneurs having homogenous social and economic backgrounds, all voluntarily coming together to save small sums of money regularly, and mutually agreeing to contribute to a common fund and to meet their emergency needs on the basis of mutual help. They pool their resources to become financially stable, taking loans from the money collected by that group and by making everybody in that group self-employed. The group members use collective wisdom and peer pressure to ensure proper end-use of credit and timely repayment. This system eliminates the need for collateral and is closely related to that of solidarity lending, widely used by micro finance institutions. To make the book-keeping simple enough to be handled by the members, flat interest rates are used for most loan calculations.

Generally, the SHGs need self-help promoting institutions (SHPIs) to promote and nurture them. These SHPIs include various NGOs, banks, farmers' clubs, government agencies, self-employed individuals and federations of SHGs. However, some SHGs have also been formed without any assistance from such SHPIs. Three distinct linkage models of micro credit are currently being followed in India.

Under Model-I, banks themselves take up the work of forming and nurturing the groups, opening their saving accounts and providing them bank loans.

Under Model-II, SHGs are formed by NGOs and formal agencies but are directly financed by banks.

Under Model-III, SHGs are financed by banks using NGOs and other agencies as financial intermediaries. In areas where formal banking system faces constraints, the NGOs are encouraged to approach suitable bank for bulk loan assistance.

India has adopted a multi-agency approach for the development of its micro finance programme. All the major credit institutions, *viz.* commercial banks, co-operative banks, regional rural banks (RRBs) along with non-governmental organisations (NGOs) have been associated with the micro finance programme. The role of the delivering agents and their interface has led to alternative models of micro finance.

21.9 Problems of SHGs

SHG programme is not without difficulties and challenges. Some of these are mentioned below.

1. **Lack of Support from Family Members:** Lack of support from family members discourages woman to join the SHG. In case of mixed groups, male members do not extend support to female members. Thus, the essential objective of SHGs programme is defeated.
2. **Low Income Generating Activities:** Economic activities undertaken by the members are traditional. Obviously, the activities generate lower income. Therefore, the micro finance movement is losing its main objective of empowering poor people.
3. **Political Interference:** Political affiliations of group members disturb group activities. Actually, the concept of self-help group is based on the principle of co-operation, i.e. equality, mutual help, democracy and thrift. It has been observed that political leaders are taking interest in the formation of SHGs to add to their vote bank. Political interference might have adverse impact on the progress of self-help group movement.

SHGs are for holistic development of the poor and building the social capital on the pillars of affinity, trust and mutual support. Therefore, practices and the procedures which undermine the group approach are to be guarded against.

22

Financial Inclusion and Financial Literacy

Financial inclusion is increasingly being recognized as a key driver of economic growth and poverty alleviation the world over. Access to formal finance can boost job creation, reduce vulnerability to economic shocks and increase investments in human capital. Without adequate access to formal financial services, individuals and firms need to rely on their own limited resources or rely on costly informal sources of finance to meet their financial needs and pursue growth opportunities. At a macro level, greater financial inclusion can support sustainable and inclusive socio-economic growth for all.

There has been growing evidence on how financial inclusion has a multiplier effect in boosting overall economic output, reducing poverty and income inequality at the national level. Financial inclusion of women is particularly important for gender equality and women's economic empowerment. With greater control over their financial lives, women can help themselves and their families to come out of poverty; reduce their risk of falling into poverty; eliminate their exploitation from the informal sector; and increase their ability to fully engage in measurable and productive economic activities. An inclusive financial system supports stability, integrity and equitable growth. Converse holds when there is financial exclusion of disadvantaged sections of society.

22.1 Financial Exclusion

Financial exclusion is the inability of individuals, households or groups to access financial services in an appropriate form. Financial exclusion is either a cause or a consequence of social exclusion, or both. Access to financial services is essential for citizens to be economically and socially integrated in today's society. It is also a requirement for employment, economic growth, poverty reduction and social inclusion.

In most developing countries, a large segment of society, particularly low-income people, has very little access to financial services, both formal and semi-formai. As a consequence, many of them have to necessarily depend either on their own or high cost informal sources of finance such as moneylenders. This is particularly true for the sporadic financing requirements of low income households for non-productive consumption purposes and other emergency requirements such as medical expenditure. Benefits of growth, therefore, tend to concentrate in the hands of those already served by the formal financial system.

Despite the rapid spread of banking over the years, a significant segment of the population, predominantly in the rural areas, is excluded from the formal financial system. It is well-known that poor people, potential entrepreneurs, small enterprises and others are excluded from the financial sector, which leads to their marginalisation and denial of opportunity for them to grow and prosper. Therefore, access to a greater proportion of the population to the organised financial system should be high on the agenda of a government. The key issue, however, is how to mainstream the institutional sources so as to achieve wider coverage in terms of extending credit. There are also a large number of households with low income and small savings, which need to be mobilised.

Apart from the rural areas, there is significant degree of financial exclusion in urban areas as well. The cost of financial exclusion is recognised to be enormous for the society as well as for individuals, particularly in terms of inability to realise full potential due to financial constraints.

The recent developments in banking technology have transformed banking from the traditional brick-and-mortar infrastructure like staffed branches to a system supplemented by other channels like automated teller machines (ATMs), credit/debit cards, internet banking, online money transfers etc. However, the access to such technology is restricted only to certain segments of the society. Indeed, some trends, such as increasingly sophisticated customer segmentation technology—allowing, for example, more accurate targeting of sections of the market—have led to restricted access to financial services for some groups. There is a growing divide, with an increased range of personal finance options for a segment of high and upper middle income population and a significantly large section of the population who lack access to even the most basic banking services. This is termed *financial exclusion*. These people, particularly, those living on low incomes, cannot access mainstream financial products such as bank accounts, credit, remittances and payment services, financial advisory services, insurance facilities etc.

Merely having a bank account may not be a good indicator of financial inclusion. The ideal definition should look at people who want to access financial services but are denied the same. If genuine claimants for credit and financial services are denied the same, then that is a case of exclusion. As this aspect would raise the issue of credit worthiness or bankability, it is also necessary to dwell upon what could be done to make the claimants of institutional credit bankable or creditworthy. This would require re-engineering of existing financial products or delivery systems and making them more in tune with the expectations and absorptive capacity of the intended clientele.

In short, financial exclusion is mainly concentrated among those suffering from poverty and social marginalization.

22.2 Financial Inclusion

Financial inclusion may be defined as the process of ensuring access to financial services and timely and adequate credit where needed by vulnerable groups such as weaker sections and low income groups at an affordable cost.

The essence of financial inclusion is in trying to ensure that a range of appropriate financial services is available to every individual and enabling them to understand and access those services. Apart from the regular form of financial intermediation, it may include a basic no-frills banking account for making and receiving payments, a savings product suited to the pattern of cash flows of a poor household, money transfer facilities, small loans and overdrafts for productive, personal and other purposes, insurance (life and non-life) etc.

While financial inclusion, in the narrow sense, may be achieved to some extent by offering any one of these services, the objective of *comprehensive financial inclusion* would be to provide a holistic set of services encompassing all of the above.

The nexus between economic growth, financial deepening and financial inclusion has been well-recognized in development strategy. The concept of financial inclusion has a special significance for a fast-emerging economy such as India, as it encompasses a large segment of the productive sectors of the economy under formal financial network to unleash their creative capacities.

22.2.1 Digital Financial Inclusion: It refers broadly to the use of digital financial services to advance financial inclusion. These include payments, transfers, savings, credit, insurance, securities, financial planning and account statements. They are delivered via digital/electronic technology such as e-money (initiated either online or on a mobile phone), payment cards and regular bank accounts. Beyond the income dimension, digital financial inclusion includes users who are shut out of the financial system based on gender, language spoken, disabilities, and even lack of a mobile phone.

Digital financial inclusion brings in many users into the digital financial system. Many of these users are new to digital, and others are new to finance as well. While the new users may have lower awareness, this is also a time of great change, with new products, services, providers and channels coming in. This increases the risks to users.

On the other hand, customer confidence increases with each good experience the user has with the payment system, and even more with early resolution of problems encountered. When customers see their refunds come in on time, it will be an additional boost for their confidence. User education also plays a role in improving customer confidence, and it must be a part of the strategy to manage risk.

22.3 Origins of the Current Approach to Financial Inclusion

The present concern for financial inclusion can be traced to the United Nations Capital Development Fund (UNCDF) initiatives [1], which broadly underlined the main goals as also the broad frameworks and parameters of inclusive finance, as access to a range of financial services, including savings, credit, insurance, remittance and other banking/payment services to all *bankable* households and enterprises at a reasonable cost.

According to UNCDF the main goals of inclusive finance are as under:

1. Access at a reasonable cost of all households and enterprises to the range of financial services for which they are 'bankable', including savings, short and long-term credit, leasing and factoring, mortgages, insurance, pensions, payments, local money transfers and international remittances.
2. Sound institutions, guided by appropriate internal management systems, industry performance standards, and performance monitoring by the market, as well as by sound prudential regulation where required.
3. Financial and institutional sustainability as a means of providing access to financial services over time.
4. Multiple providers of financial services, wherever feasible, so as to bring cost-effective

and a wide variety of alternatives to customers (which could include any number of combinations of sound private, non-profit and public providers).

The Report of the Centre for Global Development (CGD) Task-Force on Access to Financial Services further laid down the broad policy principles for expanding financial access, including the implicit institutional mechanisms, with particular emphasis on the need for ensuring data collection, monitoring and evaluation. [2]

G-20 Toronto Summit [3] had also outlined the "Principles for Innovative Financial Inclusion", which serves as a guide for policy and regulatory approaches aimed at fostering safe and sound adoption of innovative, adequate, low-cost financial delivery models, helping provide conditions for fair competition and a framework of incentives for the various bank, insurance, and non-bank actors involved in the delivery of a full-range of affordable and quality financial services. The G-20's highest priority, as declaration goes, is to safeguard and strengthen the recovery and lay the foundation for strong, sustainable and balanced growth, and strengthen our financial systems against risks.

The problem of financial exclusion is not exclusive to the developing world. The developed countries too have been affected by it and many poor and disadvantaged people in the world still lack access to financial services. However, the type, degree and magnitude differ between the two worlds. Therefore, emphasis has been on empowerment of the disadvantaged groups for access to public goods and services including banking services in the developed countries. The UN General Assembly had designated the year 2005 as the International Year of Micro Credit stating that the year will be an important opportunity to give impetus to micro finance programmes throughout the world. Thus, the International Year of Micro Credit 2005 aimed at "Building Inclusive Financial Sectors to Achieve the Millennium Development Goals".

22.4 Advantages of Financial Inclusion

The objective of financial inclusion is to extend financial services to the large hitherto unserved population of the country to unlock its growth potential. In addition, it strives towards a more inclusive growth by making financing available to the poor in particular. Access to safe, easy and affordable credit and other financial services by the poor and vulnerable groups, disadvantaged areas and lagging sectors is recognised as a pre-condition for accelerating growth and reducing income disparities and poverty. A developing country can benefit from financial inclusion in the following ways:

1. Access to a well-functioning financial system—by creating equal opportunities—enables economically and socially excluded people to integrate effectively into the economy and contribute to development and protect themselves against economic shocks.
2. Availability of external finance to potential entrepreneurs and small firms enables new entrants, leading to increased competition to incumbents. This, in turn, encourages entrepreneurship and productivity.
3. Inclusive finance—including safe savings, appropriately designed loans for poor and low-income households and for micro, small and medium-sized enterprises, and appropriate insurance and payments services—can help people to enhance incomes,

acquire capital, manage risk, and come out of poverty.

4. Access to financial services contributes to higher production and social protection, as the financial sector—through stored savings, credit and insurance—serves as a measure of crisis mitigation.
5. Financial inclusion can improve the efficiency of the process of intermediation between savings and investments while facilitating change in the composition of the financial system with regard to the transactions that take placc the clients that use the various services, the new risks created, and possibly the institutions that operate in newly created or expanded markets. As the balance sheet of the financial sector grows more diversified and encompasses a broader spectrum of economic agents, its contribution to a more resilient economy is commensurately higher.
6. For financial institutions, especially banks, financial inclusion helps provide a more stable retail base of deposits. As the recent global crisis also demonstrated, stable retail sources of funding, as against reliance on borrowed funds, can greatly enhance the soundness and resilience of financial institutions and can reduce volatility in earnings. It has been well-recognised that access to financial services facilitates making and receiving financial payments and reduces transaction costs. Financial inclusion enables to finance activities or firms or individuals that are at the margin, thereby promoting their growth-inducing productive activities.
7. Financial inclusion facilitates greater participation by different segments of the economy in the formal financial system. The presence of a large informal sector can impair the transmission of monetary policy as a significant segment of financially excluded households and small businesses make financial decisions independent of and un-influenced by, the monetary policy actions of the central bank. As the share of the formal financial sector increases through greater financial inclusion, it yields an important positive externality by making monetary policy transmission more effective.
8. To the extent that financial inclusion helps people move from the cash economy to bank accounts which can be monitored, it helps facilitate implementation of anti-money laundering and combating the financing of terrorism.
9. Financial inclusion can contribute to enhanced financial stability through contributing to the improved health of the household sector, of small businesses and, to some extent, that of the corporate sector. The health of the household sector is improved through improved economic linkages, reducing reliance on the costly informal sector and through improved ability to make and receive payments.
10. Financial inclusion can improve the access to finance and the social quality (including gender equality) and cost of the service that small businesses receive from banks. These factors are a key to the profitability and prosperity of these businesses and that are the backbones of the growing economy. Therefore, achieving greater financial inclusion and maintaining financial stability are now complementary policy compulsions in so far as India is concerned.

In majority of the developing countries, access to finance is now being perceived as a public good, such as access to safe drinking water, primary healthcare, or primary education. One of the important effects of financial inclusion is that the entire national financial system benefits by greater inclusion (and lesser exclusion), especially when promoted in the wider context of economic inclusion. Financial inclusion efforts do have multiplier effect on the economy as a whole through higher savings pooled from the vast segment of the *bottom of the pyramid population* by providing access to formal savings arrangement resulting in expansion in credit-base and investment by banks. Deeper engagements of the under-banked population in the economy through the formal financial system could lead to improvement of their financial conditions and living standards, particularly the poorer segments of the society, enabling them to create financial assets, generate income and build resilience to meet macro-economic and viable income-generating livelihood support systems. In this endeavour, the Government also immensely benefits from financial inclusion drives by way of efficient and leakage-proof transfer of vast amounts of social welfare benefits to the targeted and largely disadvantaged groups of population.

22.5 Strategies for Financial Inclusion

Financial inclusion strategies can be defined as road maps of actions, agreed and defined at the national or sub-national level that stakeholders follow to achieve financial inclusion objectives. Successful strategies coordinate efforts with the main stakeholders, define responsibilities among them, and state a clear planning of resources by, for example, prioritizing targets. A strategy can promote a more effective and efficient process to achieve significant improvements in financial inclusion, and is ideally prepared with the private sector in order to establish and achieve shared, achievable goals for financial inclusion. Strategies can integrate public and private sector actions to address different barriers to financial inclusion, and can also focus on high-impact, high-priority areas, such as finance for small enterprises or financial education action plans. Financial inclusion is interlinked with financial stability, financial integrity, market conduct, and the financial capability of consumers, and should be prepared with reference to analysis and objectives for those areas, irrespective of whether the financial inclusion strategy is a standalone document or a component of a broader financial sector development strategy.

Bringing the larger population within the structured and organised financial system has to be an important item on the development agenda of a government. While several central banks focus solely on inflation, many in developed and emerging economies alike also focus on growth. In a fast growing economy, an important issue is how to sustain and diversify growth so that the risk to growth process is diversified across sectors. It is in this context that the search for potential sources of incremental growth, i.e. sectors that have difficulty in accessing financial services, assumes importance. Therefore, including such segments or sectors would, on the one hand, unleash their productive capacities, and on the other, would augment domestic demand on a sustainable basis driven by income and consumption growth from such sectors. This would also have strong inter-sectoral linkages.

22.6 Barriers to Financial Inclusion

Access to financial products is constrained by several factors which include lack of awareness about the financial products, high transaction costs and products which are inconvenient, inflexible, not customized and of low quality. However, we need to understand here that apart from the supply side factors, demand side factors such as lower income and/or asset holdings, financial literacy/awareness issues, etc. also have a significant bearing on inclusive growth. Owing to difficulties in accessing formal sources of credit, poor individuals and small and micro enterprises usually rely on their personal savings and internal sources or take recourse to informal sources of finance to invest in health, education, housing and entrepreneurial activities. The mainstream financial institutions like banks have an important role to play in helping overcome this constraint, not as a social obligation, but as a business proposition.

The major barriers that are to be seen to be potential constraints in extension of appropriate services to poor by financial service providers are the lack of reach, higher cost of transactions and time taken in providing those services, apart from attitudinal issues. In this regard, major barriers to financial inclusion require to be identified are as under:

22.6.1 Demand Side Barriers: These are as under:

1. Low literacy levels.
2. Lack of awareness and/or knowledge/understanding of financial products.
3. Irregular income.
4. Frequent micro transactions.
5. Lack of trust in formal banking institutions.
6. Cultural obstacles (e.g., gender and cultural values).

22.6.2 Supply Side Barriers: These are as follows:

1. Outreach (low density areas and low income populations are not attractive for the provision of financial services and are not financially sustainable under traditional banking business models).
2. Regulation (frameworks are not always adapted to local contexts).
3. Business models (mostly with high fixed costs); service providers (limited number and types of financial service providers).
4. Services (non-adapted products and services for low income populations and the informal economy).
5. Age factor (financial service providers usually target the middle of the economically active population, often overlooking the design of appropriate products for older or younger potential customers. There are hardly any policies or schemes for the younger lot or the old people who have retired, as the banks do not see any business from them).
6. Bank charges (in most of the countries, transaction is free as long as the account has sufficient funds to cover the cost of transactions made. However, there is a range of other charges that have a disproportionate effect on people with low income).

22.7 Financial Literacy

Economic theories have been formulated with the belief that human beings take rational decisions and always want to maximize or optimise benefits. However, most of the people do not take rational decisions when it comes to money and finance. Behavioural finance has created a huge body of evidence to support the idea that the so-called rational man is anything but rational. Many a time, our financial decisions are driven by greed, herd behaviour and emotions.

Financial literacy has assumed greater significance in 21st century due to complex financial products, prevalence of fraudulent schemes, deregulation policies of regulators and government. Financial literacy enables one to manage one's personal finance in a prudent manner and achieve financial wellbeing. The objective of any financial literacy programme is to improve knowledge, skills and behaviour of individuals which will lead to awareness and action towards better management of their and family finances.

Financial literacy is the possession of a set of skills and knowledge which allow an individual to make informed and effective decisions with all of his financial resources. Understanding basic financial concepts allows people to know how to navigate in the financial system. Lack of awareness of digital financial literacy, especially among the rural population, is a major challenge in developing countries. There is an urgent need to create awareness among the citizens, especially in rural and semi-urban areas regarding digital finance services and also enable/support in access to digital finance services options.

22.7.1 Importance of Financial Literacy: People with appropriate financial literacy training make better financial decisions and manage money better that those without such training. Financial literacy focuses on the ability to manage personal finance matters in an efficient manner, and it includes the knowledge of making appropriate decisions about personal finance such as investing, insurance, real estate, budgeting, retirement and tax planning. Financial literacy also involves the proficiency of financial principles and concepts such as financial planning, compound interest, managing debt, profitable savings techniques and the time value of money.

The main steps to achieving financial literacy include learning the skills to create a budget, the ability to track spending, learning the techniques to pay off debt and effectively planning for retirement. These steps can also include counselling from a financial expert. Education about the topic involves understanding how money works, creating and achieving financial goals and managing internal and external financial challenges.

There are many advantages of financial literacy. Financial literacy helps individuals to become self-sufficient so that they can achieve financial stability. Those who understand the subject should be able to answer several questions about purchases, such as whether an item is required, whether it is affordable, and whether it an asset or a liability. This skill can help a person develop a financial road map to identify what he earns, what he spends and what he owes. This topic also affects small business owners, who greatly contribute to economic growth and stability.

The lack of financial literacy can lead to owing large amounts of debt and making poor financial decisions. Similarly, financial illiteracy may lead to making poor financial choices that can have negative consequences on the financial well-being of an individual. Financial illiteracy affects all ages and all socio-economic levels. Financial illiteracy causes many people to become victims of predatory lending, sub-prime mortgages, and fraud and high interest rates, potentially resulting in bad credit, bankruptcy or foreclosure.

Since the business environment is fiercely competitive, many businesses adopt malpractices and cut corners for growth and profitability. Poor customer services and malpractices such as mis-selling are often the result of such behaviour. Particularly in financial services, where the products are intangible and complex, customers can be duped easily. Hence, there is a need for careful decision-making on the part of the layman.

Endnotes

1. United Nations Capital Development Fund (UNCDF), *Building Inclusive Financial Sectors for Development*, UNCDF, May 2006. UNCDF is the UN's capital investment agency for the world's 48 least developed countries. It creates new opportunities for poor people and their communities by increasing access to micro finance and investment capital.
2. Report of the Taskforce set up by the Centre for Global Development, October 2009.
3. G-20 Toronto Summit Declaration, June 26-27, 2010.

23

Inclusive Growth and Social Justice

Inclusive growth is the new paradigm that is related essentially to equality and opportunity to all and sundry for productive and meaningful life with freedom and equality. There is a lot of talk on growth and equity but there is no operational plan. An immediate plan for achieving equitable development is urgently needed. The challenge before the governments is to evolve a system in which reforms and globalization can proceed on one track, and the poor can be protected from the ill effects of it, on the other. Local communities and markets should be reinforced to take advantage of finance, trade and investment changes flowing from the national and global levels. Investing to improve productivity in agriculture is essential for sustainable poverty reduction. There is no globalization without successful localization.

23.1 Meaning and Dimensions of Inclusive Growth

Inclusive growth may be defined as growth that promotes equal opportunities and increases access to these opportunities, i.e. growth that allows all members of society to participate in and contribute equally to development efforts, regardless of individual circumstances. This concept appears in Asian Development Bank's (ADB) *Strategy 2020* that examines the extent of inequality of opportunities and to what extent it can be overcome by different types of growth process. The main idea in the ADB's approach is to focus on productive employment as an important element of inclusive growth.

Inclusive growth, defined in a broader sense has three dimensions:

1. Equity among all sections of the society.
2. Equity among all sectors of the economy.
3. Equity among all regions in the country.

Thus, inclusive growth means inter-group, inter-sector as well as inter-regional equity. Growth is inclusive when it creates economic opportunities along with ensuring equal access to them.

Inclusive growth is different from poverty reduction, where the focus is on re-distributing wealth and making transfers through public expenditure activities. In poverty reduction, the poor are primarily passive recipients of donation. In inclusive growth, the objective is to enable the poor with the opportunities to empower them in a better way.

Inclusive growth is the new mantra of national and international agencies like United Nation Development Programme (UNDP) and the World Bank. UNDP defines inclusive growth—by laying emphasis on the production and income side of the GDP—as "the process and the outcome where all group of people have participated in the organization of growth and have benefited equitably from it. Thus, inclusive growth represents an equation with organization on the left hand side and benefits on the right hand side".

Inclusiveness means many different things and each aspect of inclusiveness poses its own challenges for policy.

23.1.1 Inclusiveness as Poverty Reduction: Distributional concerns have traditionally been viewed as ensuring an adequate flow of benefits to the poor and the most marginalised. This must remain an important policy focus. It is worth noting that the record in this dimension of inclusiveness is encouraging. The percentage of the population below the official poverty line has been falling but even as that happens, the numbers below the poverty line remain large.

23.1.2 Inclusiveness as Group Equality: Inclusiveness is not just about bringing those below an official fixed poverty line to a level above it. It is also about a growth process which is seen to be *fair* by different socio-economic groups that constitute our society. The poor are certainly one target group, but inclusiveness must also embrace the concern of other groups such as destitute women, differently-abled persons, and other marginalised groups. These distinct *identity groups* are sometimes correlated with income slabs and all poverty alleviation strategies help them directly.

23.1.3 Inclusiveness as Regional Balance: Another aspect of inclusiveness relates to whether all regions, are seen to benefit from the growth process. The regional dimension has grown in importance in recent years. An important constraint on the growth of backward regions in a country is the poor state of infrastructure, especially road connectivity, schools and health facilities and the availability of electricity, all of which combine to hold back development. Improvement in infrastructure must therefore be an important component of any regionally inclusive development strategy.

23.1.4 Inclusiveness and Inequality: Inclusiveness also means greater attention to income inequality. Perfect equality is not found anywhere and there are many reasons why it may not even be a feasible objective. However, there can be no two opinions on the fact that inequality must be kept within tolerable limits. Some increase in inequality in a developing country during a period of rapid growth and transformation may be unavoidable and it may even be tolerated if it is accompanied by sufficiently rapid improvement in the living standards of the poor. However, an increase in inequality with little or no improvement in the living standards of the poor is a recipe for social tensions. Static measures of inequality do not capture the phenomenon of equality of opportunity which needs special attention. Any given level of inequality of outcomes is much more socially acceptable if it results from a system which provides greater equality of opportunity. As a society, we therefore need to move as rapidly as possible to the ideal of giving every child in a country a fair opportunity in life, which means assuring every child access to good health and quality education.

23.1.5 Inclusiveness as Empowerment: Inclusiveness is not just about ensuring a broad-based flow of benefits or economic opportunities, it is also about empowerment and participation. It is a measure of the success achieved in building a participatory democracy that people are no longer prepared to be passive recipients of benefits doled out by the Government. They are slowly beginning to demand these benefits and opportunities as rights and they also want a say in how they are administered. This brings to the fore issues of governance, accountability and peoples' participation to much greater extent than before. This also covers areas like access to information about government schemes, knowledge of the relevant laws and how to access justice. The growing concern with governance has also focused attention on corruption.

Each of the dimensions of inclusiveness discussed above is relevant, and public attention often focuses on one or the other at different times. The aim should be to achieve steady progress in each of these dimensions. Accelerated growth in recent years has yielded distinct benefits to many and the prosperity which this has generated is visible to all, raising the expectations of all sections of the population, and creating a demand for a fair share of the benefits of growth. Policymaking has to be watchful of developments in each dimension of fairness and be quick to take corrective steps as soon as the need arises.

23.2 Need for Inclusive Growth

Although high overall economic growth rates have been recorded in many Asian countries in recent years, increasing concern has been voiced that this growth has been too uneven and often accompanied by rising income inequality. Disadvantaged groups in the remote rural area, women, members of ethnic minorities etc. have not benefited proportionately from rapid economic growth. These disparities, if left unchecked, could threaten the fragile political consensus for economic reforms or even political stability.

Inclusive growth entails responsible and sustainable creation as well as just distribution of both wealth and welfare. Social cohesion and human dignity lie at its core. It requires extending access to opportunities more widely. It is a key response to the rising inequalities undermining the sustainability of the global market economy, growth and development. Inclusive growth seeks to redirect and broaden the flows of globalization towards its intended beneficiaries, i.e. the excluded ones. It has two mutually reinforcing strategic pillars: sustainable growth and diffusion of opportunities. Good governance is fundamental to advancing each of these pillars.

Inclusive growth is an absolute imperative for global market economy to be sustainable and indeed one could say for peace to reign. If globalization is to be sustained, with all the benefits it can bring to humanity, growth must be inclusive. It has to be seen to benefit the greatest numbers, and good and transparent governance has a key strategic role to play.

Apart from addressing the issue of inequality, inclusive growth may also make the poverty reduction efforts more effective by explicitly creating productive economic opportunities for the poor and vulnerable sections of the society. Inclusive growth by encompassing the hitherto excluded population, sectors and regions, can bring in several other benefits as well to the economy. The concept *inclusion* should be seen as a process of including the excluded as agents whose participation is essential in the very design of the development process, and not simply as welfare targets of development programmes. Policy makers are sometimes criticised for focusing too much on gross domestic product (GDP) growth, when the real objective should be to achieve an improved quality of life of the people across both economic and non-economic dimensions. It should be fully recognized that the objective of development is broad-based improvement in the economic and social conditions of the people. However, rapid growth of GDP is an essential requirement for achieving this objective.

There are two reasons why GDP growth is important for the inclusiveness objective. First, rapid growth of GDP produces a larger expansion in total income and production which, if the growth process is sufficiently inclusive, will directly raise living standards of a large section of people by providing them with employment and other income enhancing activities. The focus should not be just on GDP growth itself, but on achieving a growth process that is as inclusive as possible. For example, rapid growth which involves faster growth in agriculture, and especially in rain-fed areas where most of the poor live, will be much more inclusive than a GDP growth that is driven entirely by mining or extraction of minerals for exports. Similarly, rapid growth which is based on faster growth for the manufacturing sector as a whole, including small enterprises, will generate a much broader spread of employment and income earning opportunities and is therefore more inclusive than a growth which is largely driven by extractive industries.

The second reason why rapid growth is important for inclusiveness is that it generates higher revenues, which help to finance critical programmes of inclusiveness. There can be many such programmes which either deliver benefits directly to the poor and the excluded groups, or increase their ability to access employment and income opportunities generated by the growth process.

23.3 Essential Components of Inclusive Growth

The inclusive growth as a strategy of economic development received attention owing to a rising concern that the benefits of economic growth have not been equitably shared. Inclusive growth focuses on economic growth which is a necessary and crucial condition for poverty reduction. The concept of inclusive growth encompasses the following:

1. Inclusive growth is a broader concept covering economic, social, and cultural aspects of development.
2. It focuses on both the pace and pattern of growth. How growth is generated is critical for accelerating poverty reduction, and any inclusive growth strategies must be tailored to country-specific circumstances.
3. Inclusive growth adopts a long-term perspective and is concerned with sustained growth. For growth to be sustained in the long-run, it should be broad-based across sectors. Issues of structural transformation for economic diversification therefore take a front stage.
4. It should also be inclusive of the large part of the country's labour force, where inclusiveness refers to equality of opportunity in terms of access to markets, resources and unbiased regulatory environment for businesses and individuals.
5. Inclusive growth focuses on productive employment rather than income redistribution. Hence, the focus is not only on employment growth but also on productivity growth.
6. Inclusive growth is not defined in terms of specific targets such as employment

generation or income distribution. These are potential outcomes, not specific goals.

7. Inclusive growth is typically fuelled by market-driven sources of growth with the government playing a facilitating role.

23.4 Strategy for Inclusive Growth

The strategy for achieving faster growth with greater inclusiveness involves several interrelated components. These are as under:

1. Continuation of the policies of economic reform which have created a buoyant and competitive private sector capable of benefiting from the opportunities provided by globalization of world economy.
2. Revival in agricultural growth which is the most important single factor affecting rural prosperity.
3. Improved access to essential services in health and education especially for the poor, which is essential to ensure inclusiveness and also to support rapid growth.
4. Special thrust on infrastructure development which is a critical area for accelerating growth.
5. Environmental sustainability which is becoming increasingly important.
6. Special attention to the needs of disadvantaged groups.
7. Good governance at all levels.

Financial inclusion of all individuals and all sections of population is very vital from the point of view of ensuring inclusive growth of the national economy. Adoption and implementation of inclusive practices by all banks and financial institutions and also by insurance companies and mutual funds will go a long way in bringing about financial inclusion of all those who presently stand financially excluded. Financial inclusion refers to the process of bringing into the financial and banking fold all those who are outside and giving them opportunities to utilize various banking and financial services at affordable cost.

Inclusive growth calls for higher degree of attitudinal transformation of individuals, institutions, administrative and governing agencies towards concern and commitment for work coupled with ethical and social values of development. Good governance is the key to achieving inclusive growth by translating outlay into outcome.

23.5 Target Groups for Inclusive Growth

These include the following:

1. Isolated communities (away from habitations).
2. Households of bonded labourers.
3. Women headed/managed households (single, divorced, deserted, widows).
4. Households with person/persons with disability.
5. Households with elderly but with no persons in the age group of 16-59 years.
6. Destitute households.
7. Shelterless households.
8. Households involved in daily wage labour.

9. Households with migrant labour.
10. Households with people working in hazardous occupations.
11. Households having persons living with HIV and AIDS.
12. Communities affected by/displaced by natural calamities/development projects.

23.6 Enabling Role of the State for Inclusive Growth

For achieving inclusive growth there is critical need to rethink the role of the state. The early debate among economists about the size of the government can be misleading. The need of the hour is to have an *enabling* government. Asking the government to produce all the essential goods, create all the necessary jobs, and keep a curb on the prices of all goods is to court failure, and lead to a large, cumbersome bureaucracy and widespread corruption. The aim must be to take a more modern view of what the state can realistically deliver. This is what leads to the idea of an enabling state—a government that does not try to directly deliver to the citizens everything that they need. Instead, it creates an enabling environment for the market so that individual enterprise can flourish and citizens can provide for the needs of one another.

Besides, government steps in to help those who do not manage to do well for themselves, because there will always be individuals, irrespective of the system, who need support and help. Therefore, the need is for a government which, when it comes to the market, sets effective, incentive-compatible rules and remains on the sidelines with minimal interference. At the same time, it plays an important role in directly helping the poor by ensuring that they get basic education and health services and receive adequate nutrition and food.

Progress towards inclusiveness is more difficult to assess because inclusiveness is a multi-dimensional concept. Inclusive growth should result in lower incidence of poverty, broad-based and significant improvement in health outcomes, universal access for children to school, increased access to higher education and improved standards of education. It should also be reflected in better opportunities for both wage employment and livelihoods and in improvement in provision of basic amenities like water, electricity, roads, sanitation and housing.

24

Urbanization Policies and Issues

Urbanization has gathered considerable momentum in recent times and this has put urban infrastructure and services under severe strain. Smaller cities, because of inadequate financial resources, have found it particularly difficult to cope with the increasing demands on services. Urbanization is a natural process associated with economic growth. It is well-known that agglomeration and densification of economic activities in urban areas stimulate economic efficiency and provide more opportunities for earning livelihoods. Possibilities for entrepreneurship and employment increase when urban concentration takes place, in contrast to the dispersed and less diverse economic possibilities in rural areas.

24.1 Urbanization and Economic Development

Urbanization is directly associated with economic development. In fact, a shift of population from rural to urban areas is an indicator of economic development. Urbanization has become an important and irreversible process, and an important determinant of national economic growth and poverty reduction. The process of urbanization is characterized by a dramatic increase in the number of large cities and a transition from a predominantly rural to a quasi-urban society. It is acknowledged that this transition to urbanization has not been accompanied by a commensurate increase in the supply of basic urban services like water supply, sewerage and drainage network, garbage disposal facilities, roads, public transport, and public safety systems like street lighting and pedestrian pathways. The supply of land and housing has not kept pace with the increase in urban population.

Urban population in most less developed countries (LDCs) is concentrated in large cities. This pattern of population concentration in large cities reflects spatial polarisation of the employment opportunities. While it is expected that gains from an agglomeration economy would lead to some polarisation of economic activities, there is a need for developing an optimal portfolio of cities by drawing regional development plans and promoting growth centres that are employment intensive and consistent with the economic potential including the natural endowment of cities and regions. The availability of water to provide for the needs of a large urban population must be a critical factor in plans for urban development.

Though the proportion of urban population concentrated in larger cities continues to remain high, there is some evidence that other urban growth nodes are emerging underscoring the need for adequate policy attention to smaller cities and peri-urban areas as against the narrow focus of concentrating on large cities.

An accelerated pace of urbanization would imply significant spill over of existing cities into peri-urban areas which are centres of intense economic activities. Jobs and people are flowing from metropolitan cores to nearby settlements—regardless of whether they are classified as urban or rural, often giving rise to haphazard urbanization in the peri-urban areas. The challenge is to ensure that new cities and existing metropolises are connected and land use change is co-ordinated with infrastructure development to accommodate urban redevelopment and urban spatial expansion.

Since a significant part of national income originates in urban areas, efforts must be made to maintain and enhance urban productivity which, in turn, depends on the level and quality of urban infrastructure. The demand for urban infrastructure services has increased, and is likely to accelerate further, due to rising personal incomes, rapid growth of population, and general increase in economic activities. Inability of municipal governments to meet the rising demand would adversely affect growth prospects of the economy.

Urbanization should be central to any strategy of achieving faster and more inclusive growth because agglomeration and densification of economic activities in urban conglomerations stimulates economic efficiencies and provides more opportunities for earning livelihoods. Thus, urbanization increases avenues for entrepreneurship and employment compared to what is possible in dispersed rural areas. It, thereby, enables faster inclusion of more people in the process of economic growth.

Cities hold tremendous potential as engines of economic and social development, creating jobs and generating wealth through economies of scale. They need to be sustained and augmented through the high urban productivity for country's economic growth. National economic growth and poverty reduction efforts will be increasingly determined by the productivity of these cities and towns. For cities to become growth-oriented and productive, it is essential to achieve a world class urban system. This, in turn, depends on attaining efficiency and equity in the delivery and financing of urban infrastructure.

Attitudes to urban growth within the country tend to swing between two extremes. Cities are seen either as an unavoidable evil or in a more positive way as *engines of growth*. The former view is held by those who focus on the growth of slums and squatter colonies, the congestion on the roads and environmental degradation. The others, in contrast, focus on the bustling formal and informal sectors in urban areas and their contribution to the economy, the diversification of occupations away from traditional land-based ones to newer forms of production and services, and the lower levels of poverty as compared to rural areas. From this point of view, the moderate pace of urbanization in the country has been a cause of disappointment. There is, however, no rural versus urban conflict either in terms of national growth, or in development priorities.

24.2 Effects of Urbanization

As in the case of many other demographic changes, urbanization has also both positive and negative effects.

24.2.1 Positive Effects of Urbanization: Urbanization is a key indicator of economic development and should be seen as a positive factor for overall development. As an economy grows, its towns and cities expand in size and volume. Urbanization is a natural consequence of economic changes that take place as a country develops. At the same time, urbanization helps to contribute to the growth process at large. This is manifest in the increasing contribution of urban sector to national income.

Cities and towns have become the engines of social change and rapid economic development. Urbanization is associated with improved access to education, employment, and healthcare, resulting in increase in the age at marriage, reduction in family size and improvement in health indices. As people have moved towards and into cities, information has flowed outward.

Better communication and transportation now link urban and rural areas both economically and socially, creating an urban-rural continuum of communities with improvement in some aspects of lifestyle of both. The ever increasing reach of mass media communicates new ideas, points of reference, and available options are becoming more widely recognized, appreciated and sought. This phenomenon has affected health care, including reproductive health, in many ways. For instance, radio and television programmes that discuss gender equity, family size preference and family planning options are now reaching formerly isolated rural populations. This can create demand for services for mothers and children, higher contraceptive use, and fewer unwanted pregnancies, smaller healthier families and lead to more rapid population stabilisation.

The positive role of urbanization is often over shadowed by the evident deterioration in the physical environment and quality of life in the urban areas caused by widening gap between demand and supply of essential services and infrastructure. This results from increasing population, pressure on urban centres, most of which are financially and organisationally ill-equipped to respond to infrastructural needs. Public investment in urban infrastructure has also been less than adequate. The challenge of reorienting the urbanization process, thus, lies in overcoming the infrastructural deficiencies and taking the best advantage of economic momentum inherent in urbanization.

In short, advantages of urbanization can be summarized as follows:

1. Protection of the countryside, green spaces and biodiversity.
2. Reduction of travel distance.
3. Reduction in the use of material for construction of infrastructure.
4. Economies of scale in providing social and institutional services like hospitals, schools and banks.
5. Better interactive community life.

24.2.2 Negative Effects of Urbanization: The rapid growth of urban population also poses some serious challenges. Urban population growth has outpaced the development of basic minimum services. Housing, water supply, sewerage and solid waste disposal are far from adequate. Increasing waste generation at home, offices and industries, coupled with poor waste disposal facilities result in rapid environmental deterioration. Increasing automobiles add to air pollution. All these have adverse effect on ecology and health. Poverty persists in urban and peri-urban areas. Awareness about the glaring inequities in close urban setting may lead to social unrest. As a consequence cities are facing problem of expanding urban slums.

In short, the disadvantages of urbanization are as follows:

1. Overcrowding and traffic congestion.

2. Health problems, criminal activities, and pollution.
3. High energy demand in compact high rise buildings.

24.3 Features of Urban Infrastructure Services

Urban infrastructure services have the following features:

1. Most urban infrastructure services are natural monopolies and their marginal cost declines over a very large range of output. As such, it is feared that the private sector might exploit the monopolistic situation. Such services include electricity and water supply, waste water management, and transport and communication services.
2. Many services like sanitation and solid waste disposal (SWD) have significant external economies. As a consequence, market-based systems may fail to provide the service in adequate quantity and quality.
3. It is difficult to exclude anyone from using certain public services like roads or street lighting. The consumer may refuse to pay for the service since he may be able to use it free of charge legally or otherwise.
4. Certain infrastructure services being necessities (like water) have almost inelastic demand. Private provision of these could result in exploitative pricing unless prices are regulated.
5. Requirement of heavy investment in capital equipment discourages private sector entry into certain infrastructure segments.

The above mentioned characteristics have for long been used as valid arguments for blocking entry of private sector into infrastructure. The arguments, however, are slowly losing their validity due to many technological and organizational innovations. Unbundling of services has been a major mechanism through which the misconception about the economies of scale argument has been overcome. Technological innovations in the areas of sanitation and sewerage have permitted low-cost supply options. Increasing range and quality of service has reduced the cost of providing the service, making the operation commercially viable and also opening up areas for private sector operations. The recognition of the demand aspect has made remunerative pricing possible in some segments.

By and large, governments have not been very effective suppliers of many services. The cost of government failures has been much higher than the possible cost of market failure. Commercialisation of infrastructure projects basically means efficient provision of services to the satisfaction of consumers on cost-recovery basis. Since the public sector in most cases is an inefficient provider due to its inherent characteristics, promotion of privatisation itself becomes an instrument for commercialisation.

24.4 Urbanization and Local Bodies

Functional responsibilities of local bodies in urban areas vary from country to country and within a country. Still some common patterns are discernible. Broadly speaking, the functions of a local body (e.g. a municipality) can be divided into the following three categories.

24.4.1 Essential Civic Functions: The main function of a municipality is to provide and maintain core (or essential) civic services. These include refuse collection, street lighting, water supply, sewage disposal, fire protection, abattoirs, and primary health services. These are services for which decision-making rests with the municipalities.

24.4.2 Regulatory Functions: These functions pertain to regulation of industry, trade and construction activities. Municipalities issue licences, permits and levy fees of various kinds, and also impose fines for violation of rules and regulations. Charges for regulatory functions should be so fixed as to cover at least the cost of administration and surveillance. If these services are subsidised it would put strain on resources.

24.4.3 Agency Functions: These are functions (e.g., protection of environment) which are funded out of state revenues by specific transfers.

Rising urbanization has increased the functional responsibilities of municipalities. To meet the scale and challenge of urbanization, municipal governments are always looking for additional funds from various sources.

24.5 Financing of Local Bodies

Managing rising urbanization would place huge requirements on financial as well as human resources in a country. Given the scarcity of resources, innovation will have a significant role to play. It is critical to promote innovation and research in several ways.

It is both fair and efficient that projects with long-term benefits are financed through long-term borrowings. If long-term capital projects are financed out of current revenues and/or short-term borrowings, the future generations would enjoy free-riding. Since the benefits of a capital project are reaped over a long period of time, i.e. by more than one generation of tax payers, the financing of such projects should place the repayment burden on the present as well as future generations.

In the public finance literature, the following general rules are mentioned as regards the financing of local bodies.

1. Where the benefits of a local public service are measurable and accrue to readily identifiable individuals/households within a jurisdiction, user charges are the most appropriate method of financing the service.
2. Local public services—which are services to general public in the sense that identification of beneficiaries and measurement of benefits to individuals/households is difficult—should be financed by taxes on local residents. Such services include traffic control, street lighting, security, and general administration.
3. Services the benefits of which spill over to neighbouring jurisdictions should be financed by inter-governmental transfers. These services include health, education, anti-pollution measures, and other social welfare activities.
4. Long-term borrowings are the appropriate source to finance capital projects with long gestation period as, for example, flyovers, sport stadiums, and metro rail services.

Higher level governments generally assign certain taxes to local bodies to augment their resources. Tax literature suggests the following principles regarding assignment of taxes to local bodies.

1. Municipal governments should be assigned those taxes that are leviable on bases which are *immobile* or *location-specific* and those whose burden cannot be exported outside the municipal jurisdiction. Property tax is a case in point.
2. Local tax base should be easily identifiable and its incidence transparent.
3. Tax yield should be stable, predictable, and buoyant.
4. Rate schedule of the tax should possess a reasonable degree of progressivity.
5. Tax should be easy to administer.

Based on the foregoing considerations, the following taxes are generally assigned to local bodies: (a) property tax, (b) entertainment tax, (c) tax on professions, (d) tax on advertisements, and (e) octroi/tolls.

The fact that infrastructure services do not pay for themselves, and the government does not have the financial capacity to continue to subsidise the beneficiaries, has resulted in low availability of funds. With increasing requirements, this has meant deficiency in volumes as well as quality of service. Consequently, a parallel unorganised sector for provision of many of these services has developed, resulting in high prices and qualitatively deficient services. From a societal point of view, these are expensive solutions. It is high time that a commercial approach is adopted.

In terms of financing patterns, the foundation of urban infrastructure has to be user charges. It is possible for urban institutions to access funds from the capital markets to finance a large portion of capital expenditure on urban infrastructure, which can be serviced by user charges in the future. While municipal bond issues have indeed taken place, the magnitude of resources raised is as yet insignificant. The user charge financed approach can facilitate a massive increase in capital expenditure on urban infrastructure without worsening the fiscal problem. In addition, the tariff restructuring or subsidy design allows for more efficient and targeted impact on the poor.

24.5.1 Cost Effectiveness: The major demands of the strategy to minimise cost should be technological appropriateness, proper attention to maintenance, curbing misuse of services and efficient institutional arrangements for providing services. To promote cost effectiveness, different infrastructure projects may be packaged together like water supply and drainage projects. Coordination between different departments providing different services will also reduce overall cost of production. Given the huge requirement of funds, it is critical to incentivise cost reducing innovations in the fields of materials and processes. The support can be in the form of incubation assistance and low cost funds. Incentives could be in the form of recognition and rewards.

24.6 Privatisation of Municipal Services

The scope for privatisation of some municipal services in order to reduce costs is another issue. Municipalities alone cannot handle huge infrastructural projects like water supply, sewage disposal, and urban transport. Involvement of public authorities, and private sector is required to meet the scale of investment needed in these areas. Similarly, greater participation of private sector is desirable in the provision of civic services, particularly those the consumption of which can be attributed to individuals and households. There are many types of arrangement in respect of public-private-partnership (PPP) depending on situation. However, care should be taken not to dilute current social commitments while embarking on PPP projects.

The historical and ideological resistance to private sector participation persists in most countries. Consequently, few local bodies have tried out private sector participation in civic services on any significant scale. Wherever it has happened, the experiment has remained limited to disposal of solid wastes, maintenance of parks, and electricity supply. The disenchantment with utility enterprises of municipalities is not conceptual but borne out of their inefficient and sometimes corrupt management. The merits of privatisation are seen in terms of improvement in efficiency and reduction in the budgetary burden of state-owned enterprises.

Though the need for private sector participation is widely felt, it is not openly expressed. Very rarely political parties have spoken publicly against the public sector. Contrarily, there is a stiff opposition by political parties to any move to undermine the importance of public sector. The strong unions of public sector enterprises come in handy for politicians to prevent the erosion of state and municipal activities.

Since overall government resources are limited and must be applied to other priority sectors such as health and education, it is necessary that cities, especially the larger ones, and progressively even the smaller ones, are encouraged and enabled to draw resources from the market and the private sector. For this, they must improve their governance and ability to implement projects. They will also have to manage their land resources more strategically, both to ensure better land use and to secure what will be a principal resource for their future financial needs. They must become able to recover adequate service charges, and equitably, from their inhabitants, which will require them to demonstrate an ability to deliver better and more reliable services.

24.7 Urban Planning

As more people in LDCs will inevitably live within urbanized conglomerations, with densification of villages, sprouting of peri-urban centres around large towns, and also migration of people into towns, the quality of their lives and livelihoods will be affected by the infrastructure of urban conglomerations, which presently is poor. Sewage, water, sanitation, roads and housing are woefully inadequate for their inhabitants. The worst affected are the poor in the towns. As more urban conglomerations form and grow without adequate infrastructure, the problems will only become worse. Therefore, urban agenda must get much more attention.

Absence of any long-term plan prevents development of smart cities in which all the parts of the system—urban services, transportation, housing, commercial activities—fit together harmoniously. Planning must be holistic before it is detailed, e.g. urban housing and urban poverty issues cannot be separated from other aspects of urban planning. Holistic planning, even if not detailed, is required at the local urban level, at the metropolitan level and at state and national levels too. City governments should be made accountable for greenhouse gas emissions caused by poorly planned sub-urban sprawl. Low rise and higher density is a way to improve the overall energy efficiency of urban areas. General urban consolidation and more intensive mixed use of local activity centres close to public transport nodes provide opportunities to lower carbon emissions. The planning of housing areas can significantly affect living comfort during heat waves. Innovative cooling systems contribute to limitation of emissions.

Planting trees around buildings to shade urban surfaces and green roofs to reduce their temperature lead to substantial reductions in energy consumption for air conditioning and sequester carbon while growing. Trees to shade roads and parking lots reduce evaporative emissions from gasoline, which contribute to increased levels of urban ozone. Biomass from trees and shrubs can be used as wood energy to replace fossil fuels, thus contributing to climate adaptation.

Planners should take into account specific effects of climate change while planning for a district/region. Some issues which need to be tackled at the regional level include flexible management of resources, including allocation of water, and preservation of threatened areas. High population density improves accessibility of services, reduces per capita domestic energy consumption and also promotes infrastructure efficiency and use of public transport. However, it may aggravate negative externalities like air pollution, noise and loss of green space.

Information technology (IT) can play an important role in improving governance. With municipal administration becoming increasingly complex, the benefits of IT adoption are becoming more visible across several municipalities. E-governance must be a mandatory reform and its implementation should be required in all cities.

Good urban governance calls for adequate policy and legal frameworks, the existence of regulatory and planning authorities, human skills, a sound revenue base, accounting and accountability. A large part of civic amenities in developing countries, particularly water supply, sanitation and sewerage, are managed with assets that have outlived their operational efficiency. The required massive upgradation and renovation of these assets, is constrained by high population density and concentrated commercial activities at the locations where these service assets are installed. The lack of comprehensive urban planning in the past to promote regular upgradation and renewal has resulted in a large backlog of development activities.

24.8 Urban-Rural Co-ordination

Attention needs to be focussed not only on the growing challenges of urbanization but on the relationship between urban and rural development. Rapid transformation in urban scenario must be taken into account and provided for, in order that urban growth becomes compatible with healthy socio-economic development of the country. It will be necessary to take note of the prevailing dichotomy in rural and urban development and evolve a mechanism for bringing about rural-urban cohesion in the management of growth. This can be achieved through the process of spatial planning, which is an integrating concept that makes it possible to achieve the composite development of human settlements while stimulating economic growth.

The rural hinterland has played a critical role in sustaining urbanization. This is reflected in the indicators of sources of primary inputs, competitively priced labour for urban economic activities, primary funds as reflected in comparative urban and rural credit-deposit ratios and market for urban products. However, the unending migration of the rural poor to urban areas may have a destabilising effect on urbanization and its sustainability. Income and employment opportunities will have to rise in the rural areas, through both the farm and non-farm sectors and habitats and basic services have to be improved so that with rural development and congenial habitats, rural areas emerge as sustainable centres of economic activities and human settlements.

In a country still largely rural and agricultural in character, it is natural that programmes for agricultural and rural development should receive the greatest emphasis, in particular those for rural employment creation and assistance to the rural poor. Urban development should, however, be seen as complementary to rural development and policies affecting the process of urbanization should be such as to strengthen the links between towns and cities and their hinterland. Urban areas of all sizes operate as market centres for agricultural output and provide a variety of service functions in addition to operating as centres of manufacturing activity. These functions should be strengthened such that towns and cities serve the rural areas more effectively.

The process of urbanization should then be seen as aiding employment and income generation in rural areas rather than as a competitive process. Larger towns serve as distribution centres for seed, fertilisers and credit for farmers as well as serving as organised markets for their produce. The bigger cities provide services and facilities to both the smaller towns as well as rural areas in their hinterland. Thus, national policy on urban development should view the whole range of urban settlements as having a role to play in the national development process.

It is also important to view the provision of services in rural areas in an integrated manner. Availability of shelter, safe water supply and facilities for hygienic sanitation are as necessary in the rural areas as in the urban. Owing to different residential densities, different technologies can be used in different sizes of settlements in providing these services.

It is only through purposive public programmes providing essential services like water and sewerage along with low cost shelter programmes like sites and services that the urban landscape of the country can be improved to enable the urban population to function more efficiently. Particular attention must be paid to the functioning of the small, medium and intermediate cities in order to aid them in their role as market centres and as suppliers of goods and services for agriculture. The environmental and infrastructural conditions in some of these towns and cities have been neglected so long that their efficient functioning is beginning to be hampered.

Although the theme of a *rural-urban divide* still colours some policy discourse in LDCs, there is a growing recognition that urbanization is necessary to realise growth potential of the country, and that rural-urban linkages must be strengthened. Indeed this will accelerate growth of the rural sector also.

The fortunes of the agricultural sector are crucially linked to the manner in which growth in the industry and services sectors unfolds. People living in rural areas typically tap the opportunities that cities provide for employment, entrepreneurial avenues, and education. As urbanization grows, demand for food items other than foodgrains, i.e. vegetables, lentils, milk, eggs and so on, also grows. This leads to investments in infrastructure, logistics, processing and packaging in rural and peri-urban areas. Such investments and other economic inter-linkages connect and build synergy between rural and urban centres. Thus, the rural sector also benefits from good management of neighbouring urban conglomerations.

The rural-urban continuum should be strengthened so that gaps between rural and urban lifestyles are reduced. Effective urban strategies and programmes cannot be developed in isolation of those in the rural areas.

There is no doubt that the condition of the poor in rural areas must continue to get major attention but the urban sector development should not be viewed as negating such attention or weakening it in any way. On the contrary, it must be acknowledged that there is a synergistic relationship between rural prosperity and the continuum of urban development from small towns through larger cities to metros. A holistic approach to spatial development is needed in LDCs if they wish to achieve more inclusive growth.

To sum up, cities and towns are emerging as centres of domestic and international investments where most of the commercial activities take place. The higher productivity of any urban area depends on the availability and quality of infrastructure services. Urban economic activities are dependent upon urban infrastructure like roads, water supply, power, telecommunication, mass transportation and other civic infrastructure like sanitation and solid waste management. Massive urban growth has led to complex problems of inadequacy of basic urban services. Rapid economic growth will inevitably lead to an increase in urbanization as cities provide large economies of agglomeration for individual activity. Poor urban infrastructure inflicts a severe hardship on people. Congested roads, poor public transport, inadequate availability of water, improper treatment of sewage, uncollected solid waste and above all grossly inadequate housing, all these severely decrease the quality of life and lower the well-being of urban population.

Rising urbanization in LDCs has led to tremendous pressure on civic infrastructure systems, water supply, sewerage and drainage, uncollected solid waste, parks and open spaces, transport etc. It has also led to deterioration in the quality of city environments. In several cities, the problems of traffic congestion, pollution, poverty, inadequate housing, crime, and social unrest are assuming alarming proportions. Further, growing urbanization is characterized by incomplete devolution of functions to the elected bodies, lack of financial resources, and hesitation in levy of user charges.

As the proportion of the urban population continues to grow, investments in urban infrastructure for the provision of services such as roads, water supply and sewerage, transportation and the like will need to be much higher than they have been in the past. There will be heavy demand for better quality infrastructure in urban areas, especially water, sewerage, public transport and low cost housing. Since it takes time to create urban infrastructure, it is necessary to have a sufficiently long-term focus on urban planning.

25

Foreign Trade and Economic Development

Trade, internal and external, is as old as human civilization. Countries have been trading with each other since times immemorial. Although importance of foreign trade differs from country to country, it is an important element of world economy.

25.1 Why Does Trade Take Place?

Trade takes place because the facilities for the production of various goods are unequally distributed over the world. These facilities include: (a) mineral deposits (b) soil and climatic conditions, and (c) labour skills etc. Based on these differences in factor endowments, different regions of the world and different regions within a country specialise in the production of goods for which they are best suited.

In fact, the basis for international trade is the same as for trade within a country, viz. geographical specialisation. In other words, both international trade and inter-regional trade have their root in territorial specialisation. As Swedish economist Bertil Ohlin observed, "International trade is but a special case of inter-local or inter-regional trade".

Why should then one study international trade separately? The study of international trade as a separate subject from inter-regional trade is necessitated because the former poses certain peculiar problems. These include the following:

1. Exchange rate determination because of different currencies involved in international transactions.
2. Balance of payments problem.
3. Barriers to international trade in the form of tariffs and quotas.

25.2 Benefits of Foreign Trade

How does trade contribute to economic development? There are many ways in which trade can contribute to the economic growth of countries. Following are some of the important beneficial effects that international trade can have on economic development:

1. Trade can lead to the full utilization of otherwise underemployed domestic resources. Through trade, a country can move from an inefficient production point, with unutilized resources because of insufficient internal demand, to a point of optimum production. For such a country, trade would represent a vent for surplus, or an outlet for its potential surplus of commodities and raw materials. This has indeed occurred in many developing nations, particularly those in Southeast Asia.
2. By expanding the size of the market, trade makes possible division of labour and economies of scale. This is especially important in the production of light manufactures in small economies in the early stages of development.
3. International trade is the vehicle for the transmission of new ideas, new technology,

and new managerial and other skills.

4. Trade also stimulates and facilitates the international flow of capital from developed to developing nations. In the case of foreign direct investments, where the foreign firm retains managerial control over its investment, the foreign capital is likely to be accompanied by foreign skilled personnel to operate it.
5. In several large developing nations, such as Brazil and India, the importation of new manufactured products stimulated domestic demand until efficient domestic production of these goods became feasible.
6. Foreign trade is an excellent anti-monopoly weapon because it stimulates greater efficiency by domestic producers to meet foreign competition. This is particularly important to keep low the cost and price of intermediate or semi-finished products used as inputs in the domestic production of other commodities.
7. For developing countries, exports provide employment opportunities and earnings to pay for the many products that they cannot now produce at home and for the advanced technology that they need.

25.3 Trade and Developing Countries

Most countries of the world are classified as less developed or, to put it more positively, as developing countries. In relation to developed countries, developing nations are characterized in general by low average real per capita income, a high proportion of the labour force in agriculture and other primary activities (such as mineral extraction), low life expectancies, high rates of illiteracy, and high rates of population growth.

In the past, economic relationship between developed and developing countries was characterized by developing countries exporting primarily food and raw materials in exchange for manufactured goods from developed nations. This is still the case for the poorest developing nations, but not for the more advanced ones.

Although the level and rate of economic development depend primarily on internal conditions in developing nations, most economists today believe that international trade can contribute significantly to the development process. This was not always the case. Until the 1980s, it was strongly believed that international trade and the functioning of international economic system hindered rather than facilitated development through secularly declining terms of trade and widely fluctuating export earnings for developing countries. It was contended that standard international trade theory based on comparative advantage was completely irrelevant for developing countries and the development process. Therefore, they advocated industrialization through import substitution (i.e. domestic production of manufactured goods previously imported) and generally placing less reliance on international trade by developing countries. Moreover, reform of the international economic system was advocated to make it more responsive to the special needs of developing countries.

According to traditional trade theory, if each nation specializes in the production of the commodity of its comparative advantage, world output will be greater and, through trade, each nation will share in the gain. With the present distribution of factor endowments and technology between developed and developing nations, the theory of comparative advantage thus prescribes that developing nations should continue to specialize primarily in the production and export of raw materials, fuels, minerals, and food to developed countries in exchange for manufactured products. While this may maximize welfare in the short-run, developing countries believe that this pattern of specialization and trade relegates them to a subordinate position vis-à-vis developed countries and keeps them from reaping the dynamic benefits of industry and maximizing their welfare in the long-run.

China, which for security and ideological reasons strove for self-sufficiency during most of the post-War period, came to appreciate during the 1990s the potential contribution of trade to its growth and development and is indeed now reaping major benefits from international trade.

25.4 Import Substitution versus Export Orientation

Most developing countries chose import substitution as their strategy for industrialization and development during the 1950s, 1960s, and 1970s.

Industrialization was relied on to provide for the following:

1. Faster technological progress.
2. Creation of high-paying jobs to relieve the serious unemployment and underemployment problems faced by most developing nations.
3. Higher multipliers and accelerators through greater backward and forward linkages in the production process.
4. Rising terms of trade and more stable export prices and earnings.
5. Relief from balance-of-payments difficulties that result because the demand of developing nations for manufactured products rises faster than their export earnings.

The desire of developing nations to industrialize is natural in view of the fact that all rich nations are industrial while most poor nations are primarily agricultural. Having decided to industrialize, developing nations had to choose between industrialization through import substitution or export-oriented industrialization. Both policies have advantages and disadvantages.

An import-substitution industrialization (ISI) strategy has three main advantages:

1. The market for the industrial product already exists, as evidenced by imports of the commodity, so that risks are reduced in setting up an industry to replace imports.
2. It is easier for developing nations to protect their domestic market against foreign competition than to force developed nations to lower trade barriers against their manufactured exports.
3. Foreign firms are induced to establish so-called tariff factories to overcome the tariff wall of developing nations.

Against these advantages are the following disadvantages:

1. Domestic industries can grow accustomed to protection from foreign competition and have no incentive to become more efficient.
2. Import substitution can lead to inefficient industries because the smallness of the

domestic market in many developing nations does not allow them to take advantage of economies of scale.

3. After the simpler manufactured imports are replaced by domestic production, import substitution becomes more and more difficult and costly (in terms of the higher protection and inefficiency) as more capital-intensive and technologically advanced imports have to be replaced by domestic production.

Export-oriented industrialization also has advantages and disadvantages. Advantages include the following:

1. It overcomes the smallness of the domestic market and allows a developing nation to take advantage of economies of scale. This is particularly important for the many developing countries that are both very poor and small.
2. Production of manufactured goods for export requires and stimulates efficiency throughout the economy. This is especially important when the output of an industry is used as an input of another domestic industry.
3. The expansion of manufactured exports is not limited (as in the case of import substitution) by the growth of the domestic market.

On the other hand, there are two serious disadvantages:

1. It may be very difficult for developing nations to set up export industries because of the competition from the more established and efficient industries in developed nations.
2. Developed nations often provide a high level of effective protection for their industries producing simple labour-intensive commodities in which developing nations already have or can soon acquire a comparative advantage.

During the 1950s, 1960s, and 1970s, most developing nations, particularly the larger ones, strongly opted for a policy of import substitution to industrialize. They protected their infant industries or stimulated their birth with effective tariff rates that rose sharply with the degree of processing. This was done at first to encourage the relatively simple step of assembling foreign parts, in the hope that subsequently more of these parts and intermediary products could be produced domestically (backward linkage). Heavy protection of domestic industries also stimulated the establishment of tariff factories in developing nations.

25.5 Effects of Trade

Trade affects world economies in a variety of ways:

1. Trade tends to equalise commodity prices in different countries of the world. However, perfect equalisation is not possible due to: (a) cost of transportation, and (b) tariffs.
2. Another effect of trade is the tendency toward equalisation of factor prices.
3. Trade raises the real incomes of participating countries through gains of specialisation.

25.5.1 Effects of Trade on Factor Prices (or Factor Price Equalisation): It is assumed that there are no impediments to trade. Now if trade takes place, commodity prices will be the same in both countries. But what about factor prices? What effects will trade have on factor prices?

The basic assumption of the theory of international trade is that factors of production are completely immobile between countries. Let us drop this assumption and instead assume full mobility internationally for factors of production. In other words, capital and labour can move freely between countries without cost. Then it is quite obvious that factor prices would be the same in all countries.

In a world where factors of production cannot move between countries but where goods can move freely, trade in goods can be viewed as a substitution for factor mobility. Free trade leads toward equalisation of factor prices. The demand for scarce factors in a country will be reduced because the goods produced by them (scarce factors) are now imported and hence the prices of scarce factors will fall. Conversely, the demand for abundant factors in a country will increase because the goods produced by them are exported. This will push up their rewards. Although there will be a tendency toward factor price equalisation, a complete factor price equalisation is ruled out.

25.5.2 Factor Prices and Divergences of Incomes: Under certain strict assumptions, trade will equalise factor prices. However, we live in a world where wide divergences in incomes are observed. Why is the situation in the real world different from the results of the factor price equalisation theorem?

To be sure, factor-price equalisation theorem does not say that trade will equalise incomes. It says that factor reward (wages, interest) will be equal. Nevertheless, wages are not the only source of income. Someone must own the capital, and capital also commands its factor reward. Therefore, the more capital a country has for a given amount of labour, the higher the average income will be. So even if factor rewards were completely equalised, as long as the capital stocks differ, incomes will also differ.

Furthermore, the factor-price equalisation theorem is a completely static type of theory. It only studies some characteristics of a given equilibrium situation at a given point in time. It says only what the effects of trade will be with a given technique, with given factor endowments, and so on. However, the real world is not in a given equilibrium forever, and all sorts of changes occur.

25.5.3 Factor Reversals and Factor Prices: The factor-price equalisation is based on the following critical assumption: There is a one-to-one relationship between factor intensities and factor prices, so that regardless of factor prices one good is always labour-intensive and the other good capital-intensive.

If this condition is not fulfilled, it becomes a case of factor reversal. The meaning of factor reversals is that at a certain set of factor prices one good is labour-intensive, whereas at another set of factor prices the same good is capital-intensive. One never knows a priori whether industry A is labour-intensive or capital-intensive. It depends on factor prices. Once the total factor endowments are specified, the set of factor prices compatible with economic equilibrium will be restricted. At this restricted set of factor prices one good will always be labour-intensive and the other will always be capital-intensive.

25.6 Changing Pattern of World Trade

Post-Second World War period has witnessed fundamental changes in the pattern of international trade. The period 1950-80 witnessed a revival of world trade, especially among the industrialised countries. This was facilitated by the economic reconstruction following the two World Wars and reduction in transportation costs.

Another phase of trade integration started during the late 1970s when a number of East Asian economies embarked on the path of export-led growth. This was reinforced further during the 1980s and the 1990s wherein a large number of developing countries gradually increased their degree of openness. During this period, outward- oriented policies were undertaken on the grounds of efficient resource allocation, infusion of modern technologies, promotion of economies of scale, retention of consumer surplus, and reduction of rent-seeking and unproductive profit-seeking activities. For Latin America, the necessity to regain access to the international capital markets to refinance outstanding debt was an important consideration in their opening up during the 1970s.

In India, while the signs of liberalised trade policy were clearly discernible in the latter half of 1980s, it was only in the 1990s that the country embarked on a truly liberalised trade regime.

Increasing trade openness by developed countries and later by developing economies resulted in significant changes in the pattern of world trade. In contrast to earlier periods, world economic integration in the 1990s was much more widespread and was primarily driven by liberalisation of trade and capital controls. The technological revolution witnessed in recent years and the emergence of the new economies further aided this integration process. As the process of opening up of economies unfolded during the 1990s, world trade witnessed its strongest revival in terms of volume growth.

Along with growth in overall volume, the pattern of world trade also underwent changes following structural shifts in production caused by new technologies, demand patterns and new international trade rules under WTO. Primary products and resource-based manufactures have been gradually losing importance with world trade witnessing a shift towards non-resource-based products of increasing technology intensity. In keeping with this trend, there has also been a rapid change in the composition of exports of developing countries from being primary commodity exports to exports of manufactures.

US, East Asian countries and China played a crucial role in expanding world trade in the 1980s. Buoyancy in world trade in the 1990s was sustained despite the lacklustre economic performance of several industrialised countries especially those in Europe and Japan. Although the Asian crisis did cause a major disruption in international trade, the crisis-affected countries have rebounded in recent years with growing trade volumes. Moreover, trade among developing countries has increased significantly in recent years.

25.7 Foreign Trade: A Critique

Open economies tend to grow faster and more steadily than closed economies. Trade can be a catalyst for greater efficiency and productivity. This is because domestic producers can have access to a wider range of high-quality, affordable inputs. They also have access to technology and know-how they could not obtain in a closed economy. Access to technology and quality inputs can boost innovation and creativity in the workplace. Moreover, competition in the marketplace can be a powerful stimulus to domestic companies seeking new ways of making things better and more cheaply. An infusion of new ideas from other countries can make companies more productive. So can enhanced access to export markets.

Critics of international trade can match the impressive list of benefits with an equally impressive list of the allegedly harmful effects of trade. However, since a country can refuse to trade if it gains nothing or loses, the presumption is that it must also gain from trade. It is true that when most of the gains from trade accrue to developed countries, there is a great deal of dissatisfaction and justification for demands to rectify the situation, but this should not be construed to mean that trade is actually harmful.

One can, of course, always find cases where, on balance, international trade may actually have hampered economic development. However, in most cases it can be expected to provide invaluable assistance to the development process. This has been confirmed empirically by many researchers.

With developing countries specializing in primary commodities and developed nations specializing in manufactured products, most of the benefits of trade accrue to developed nations, leaving developing nations poor, undeveloped, and dependent. This belief is reinforced by the observation that all developed countries are primarily industrial, whereas most developing nations are, for the most part, primarily agricultural or engaged in mineral extraction or the production of simple manufactured goods. Thus, traditional trade theory is attacked for being static and irrelevant to the development process.

26

Foreign Investment, Foreign Borrowing and Foreign Aid

26.1 Foreign Investment

Foreign investment is a subject of topical interest. Countries of the world, particularly developing economies, are vying with each other to attract foreign capital to boost their domestic rates of investment and also to acquire new technology and managerial skills. Intense competition is taking place among the fund-starved less developed countries to lure foreign investors by offering repatriation facilities, tax concessions and other incentives. However, foreign investment is not an unmixed blessing. Governments in developing countries have to be very careful while deciding the magnitude, pattern and conditions of private foreign investment.

The world economy has witnessed a dramatic flow of foreign investment into developing economies, indicating that encouragement of foreign investment has become an integral part of the economic reforms process of these economies. Foreign investment is seen as an instrument of technology transfer, managerial skills, augmentation of foreign exchange reserves, export competitiveness and globalisation of the economy.

Recent years have witnessed a dramatic world-wide increase in foreign investment, accompanied by a marked change in the attitude of most developing countries towards inward foreign investment. As against a highly suspicious attitude of these countries towards foreign investment in the past, most countries now regard it as beneficial for their development efforts and compete with each other to attract it. The explanation for this shift in attitude lies in the changes in political and economic systems that have occurred during the closing years of the 20th century. Many countries, particularly in Eastern Europe, have abandoned socialism in its various forms and embraced the market economy. In many of these countries, mass privatisation has taken place mainly with funds from abroad. The success of East Asian economies is attributable chiefly to a high level of foreign investment and export promotion.

Foreign investment is a zero-sum game in which a country can attract investment only at the expense of another country. Additional investment is likely to take place when new investment opportunities emerge in countries opening up to the world. All countries have the chance to become attractive to foreign investors, not only large and advanced countries.

In the 1980s, foreign investment was concentrated within the Triad (EU, Japan and the US). However, in the 1990s, investment flows to developed countries declined while those to developing countries increased in response to rapid economic growth and fewer restrictions. The global trends in investment and the attitude of the developing world towards it have shown marked changes over the last few decades.

During the period 1950-1980, developing countries of the world relied on restricting imports, promoting exports and adopting import substitution along with pegged exchange rate regime. They relied heavily on debt and grants for external capital. The countries which followed these policies faced structural balance of payments problem and consequently had to open their economies by inviting foreign investments and liberalising their trade regime. Over the recent past, there has been a marked change in the relative significance of foreign investments vis-à-vis debt and grants.

The growth of investment flows to developing countries is unevenly distributed among regions and groups of developing countries. Most investment flows continue to be concentrated overwhelmingly in Asia and Latin America. China is now the largest host country in the developing world. However, countries with poor infrastructure, high indebtedness, slow progress in market-oriented reforms and low technological capabilities are not attractive to foreign investors. The rapid increase in foreign investment has been accompanied by significant changes in the sectoral composition, from the primary sector and resource-based manufacturing towards services and technology-intensive industries.

26.1.1 Direct versus Portfolio Investment: There are two main types of foreign investments: direct investments and portfolio investments. Direct investments are real investments in factories, capital goods, land, and inventories where both capital and management are involved and the investor retains control over use of the invested capital. Direct investment usually takes the form of a firm starting a subsidiary or taking control of another firm (for example, by purchasing a majority of the stock). In the international context, direct investments are usually undertaken by multinational corporations engaged in manufacturing, resource extraction, or services.

Portfolio investments, on the other hand, are purely financial assets, such as bonds, denominated in a national currency. With bonds, the investor simply lends capital to get fixed payouts or a return at regular intervals and then receives the face value of the bond at a pre-specified date. Portfolio or financial investments take place primarily through financial institutions such as banks and investment funds.

26.2 Foreign Direct Investment (FDI)

Investment in a country by individuals and organisations from other countries is an important aspect of international finance. This flow of international finance may take the form of direct investment (creation of productive facilities) or portfolio investment (acquisition of securities).

FDI is the outcome of the mutual interests of multinational firms and host countries. According to the International Monetary Fund (IMF), FDI is defined as "investment that is made to acquire a lasting interest in an enterprise operating in an economy other than that of the investor. The investor's purpose being to have an effective voice in the management of the enterprise". [1] The essence of FDI is the transmission to the host country of a package of capital, managerial, skill and technical knowledge. FDI is generally a form of long-term international capital movement, made for the purpose of productive activity and accompanied by the intention of managerial control or participation in the management of a foreign firm.

26.2.1 Advantages of FDI for the Host Country: FDI can make up not only for deficiencies in the availability of savings and foreign exchange—which is true of all external flows—but also for weaknesses in domestic entrepreneurial capacity. In other words, the role of FDI in directly stimulating investment activity in the country can be of great significance. This is particularly important for India since there is a likelihood that corporate investment activity may not be dynamic enough to absorb the available resources, particularly in those areas which are being vacated by the public sector. In such a situation, the entrepreneurial function played by FDI can have the effect not only of bringing in additional resources, but also leading to better absorption of domestic savings.

Foreign investment takes place for private gain but it has the following potential benefits for less developed countries (LDCs).

A. Raising the Level of Investment: Foreign investment can fill the gap between desired investment and locally mobilised savings. Local capital markets are often not well developed. Thus, they cannot meet the capital requirements for large investment projects. Besides, access to the hard currency needed to purchase investment goods not available locally can be difficult. FDI solves both these problems because it is a direct source of external capital. It can fill the gap between desired foreign exchange requirements and those derived from net export earnings. Foreign investment can stimulate domestic investment through forward and backward linkages. For example, output of a foreign firm can be an input of domestic industries. Similarly, output of the domestic industries can be inputs for the foreign firms. If this is so, foreign firms create demand for industries producing goods purchased by them.

B. Upgradation of Technology: Production units in developing countries use out-dated equipment and techniques that can reduce the productivity of workers and lead to the production of goods of a lower standard. The ability of domestic producers to compete abroad for export market is reduced which, in turn, contributes to the difficulties of the developing countries to earn hard currencies. Foreign investment can supply a package of needed resources such as management experience, entrepreneurial abilities, organisational and technological skills. Foreign investment brings with it technological knowledge while transferring machinery and equipment to developing countries.

Similarly, as the foreign-owned enterprise comes into competition with the local firms, the latter category of enterprises are forced to improve their technology and standards of product quality. Further, the foreign-owned enterprises pressurise and assist the local support industries to improve the quality of their products and ensure greater reliability of delivery, both of which make it necessary for the support industries to upgrade their technology.

The indirect effects of FDI on development which arise from the diffusion of technology and other know-how are sometimes more important than the direct effects of FDI. Therefore, one should consider not only the actual transfer of technology but also the spread of better managerial practices and the contribution of FDI to enhancing competition in host country markets. The emphasis on the technology-related spill over effects of FDI is warranted in the light of the fact that most FDI originates from a small number of developed countries which play a dominant role in the development of new technology and that multinational enterprises from these countries dominate the demand and use of new technology. The overall positive effect of FDI in respect of technology is undeniable, whether these effects occur through actual transfers, licensing or through spill over. With reference to the positive effects of FDI through technology spill over, it has been argued that it varies depending upon the characteristics and policies of host countries, and that the existence of a competitive environment and local technological capabilities is especially important in this regard.

C. Improvement in Export Competitiveness: FDI can help the host country improve its export performance. By raising the level of efficiency and the standards of product quality, FDI makes a positive impact on the host country's export competitiveness. Further, because of the international linkages of MNCs, FDI provides to the host country better access to foreign markets. Also, where the foreign investment has been made with the specific intention of sourcing parts/components (or even final products) from the host country to take advantage of low cost conditions, FDI contributes to exports directly. Enhanced export possibility contributes to the growth of the host economies by relaxing demand side constraints on growth. This is especially important for those countries which have a small domestic market and must increase exports vigorously to maintain their tempo of economic growth.

D. Resilience of FDI during Financial Crises: FDI is considered less prone to crisis because direct investors typically have a longer-term perspective when engaging in a host country. For instance, in East Asian countries, such investment was remarkably stable during the global financial crisis of 1997-98. In sharp contrast, other forms of private capital flows like portfolio equity and debt flows were subject to large reversals during the same crisis. The resilience of FDI during financial crisis was also evident during the Mexican crisis of 1994-95 and the Latin American debt crisis of the 1980s. This resilience has led many developing countries to favour FDI over other forms of capital flows to supplement national savings by capital inflows and promote economic development. In addition to the risk-sharing properties of FDI, it is widely believed that FDI provides a stronger stimulus to economic growth in host countries than other types of capital inflows. FDI is more than just capital, as it offers access to internationally available technologies and management know-how.

E. Other Benefits: Foreign investment can create employment in the modern sectors of developing countries. Recipients of FDI gain training of employees in the course of operating new enterprises, which contributes to human capital formation in the host country. Consumers in developing countries stand to gain from FDI through new products, and improved quality of goods at competitive prices. Profits generated by FDI contribute to corporate tax revenues in the host country.

26.2.2 Disadvantages of FDI for the Host Country: FDI is not an unmixed blessing. Governments in developing countries have to be very careful while deciding the magnitude, pattern and conditions of private foreign investment. Possible adverse implications of foreign investment are the following:

1. When foreign investment is competitive with home investment, profits in domestic industries fall, leading to fall in domestic savings.
2. Contribution of foreign firms to public revenue through corporate taxes is comparatively less because of liberal tax concessions, investment allowances, disguised public subsidies and tariff protection provided by the host government.
3. Foreign firms reinforce dualistic socio-economic structure and increase income inequalities. They create a small number of highly paid modern sector executives. They divert resources away from priority sectors to the manufacture of sophisticated products for the consumption of the local elite. As they are located in urban areas, they create imbalances between rural and urban opportunities, accelerating flow of rural population to urban areas.
4. Foreign firms stimulate inappropriate consumption patterns through excessive advertising and monopolistic/oligopolistic market power. The products made by multinationals for the domestic market are not necessarily low in price and high in quality. Their technology is generally capital-intensive which does not suit the needs of a labour-surplus economy.
5. Foreign firms are able to extract sizeable economic and political concessions from competing governments of developing countries. Consequently, private profits of these companies may exceed social benefits.
6. Continual outflow of profits is too large in many cases, putting pressure on foreign exchange reserves. Foreign investors are very particular about profit repatriation facilities.
7. Foreign firms may influence political decisions in developing countries. In view of their large size and power, national sovereignty and control over economic policies may be jeopardised. In extreme cases, they (foreign firms) may bribe public officials at the highest levels to secure undue favours. Similarly, they may contribute to friendly political parties and subvert the political process of the host country.

Key question, therefore, is how host countries can minimise possible negative effects and maximise positive effects of FDI through appropriate policies.

26.2.3 Tax Incentives to Attract (FDI): Governments seeking to attract FDI through tax inducements have a number of available options to make their economies as fiscally attractive as their competitors. Some of the commonly employed forms of tax incentives are described below.

A. Tax Holidays: Tax holidays have been the most popular form of tax incentives used by countries, especially developing economies. With a tax holiday, firms are allowed a period of time free from the burden of income taxation. Further, this initial period is sometimes extended to a subsequent period of taxation at a reduced rate of tax. Tax holidays have been popular in emerging economies where authorities have favoured a discretionary approach. For example, several African Investment Codes have included tax holidays, with differentiated rebates and periods of abatement, depending on the government's objectives. China offers long tax holidays to foreign firms with long-term operating periods. India offers 10 year tax holidays to firms operating in free trade zones and to 100 percent export-oriented undertakings.

B. Investment Allowances and Tax Credits: Many countries, especially in the industrial world, provide investment allowances or tax credits, which are forms of tax relief based upon the value of expenditures on qualifying investments. These tax benefits are over and above the depreciation allowed for the asset, with the result that the investor is effectively able to write off an amount greater than the cost of the investment. This form of tax incentive can take the following two forms: (a) an investment expenditure allowance that lets companies write off a percentage of qualifying investment expenditures from their taxable income, and (b) an investment tax credit that allows companies to reduce taxes paid by a percentage of investment expenditures. While a tax allowance is used to reduce the taxable income of the firm, a tax credit is used to directly reduce the amount of taxes to be paid.

C. General Tax Rate Reductions/Exemptions: Reduced rates of corporate income tax/profits tax can be granted to income from certain sources or to firms satisfying certain criteria. These reductions differ from tax holidays in that the tax liability of firms is not entirely eliminated. The benefit is extended beyond new enterprises to include income from existing operations and the benefit is not time-limited. Some countries provide a reduced rate of tax for manufacturing, agriculture or other activities. Reduced rates are also provided for investment in particular locations or regions. The standard corporate income tax rate of 30 percent in China is reduced to 15 percent or 24 percent in special economic zones and other designated regions. Foreign investment enterprises engaged in infrastructure projects including energy, transportation and port development are also taxed at the reduced rate of 15 percent in China.

D. Accelerated Depreciation: The most common form of accelerated deduction is accelerated depreciation where the cost of an asset acquired may be written off at a rate greater than the economic rate of depreciation. This can either be in the form of a shorter period of depreciation or a special deduction in the first year. This has an impact similar to that of an investment allowance in the first year, but differs since the amount written off reduces the depreciation base for future years and so the total amount written off does not exceed the actual cost of the investment. It only allows the deduction to occur sooner than otherwise.

E. Reinvestment Incentives: Some countries such as China, Malaysia, and Vietnam provide incentives for the reinvestment of profits. One way of doing so is by allowing deduction of the amount reinvested, or a proportion thereof, from the profits otherwise taxable. An alternative approach is to give the parent company a refund of the tax paid by the local enterprise up to a stated proportion of the amount reinvested.

The effectiveness of reinvestment incentives is, however, doubtful. Once an enterprise has made its initial investment, it will normally base its additional investment decisions on actual business needs, so that the incentive may reward the enterprise for doing what it would have done in any event. Further, the international tax system provides built-in incentives to reinvest profits where they are made, by allowing freedom from withholding tax in the host country.

F. Indirect Tax Incentives: Indirect tax incentives such as exemptions of raw materials and capital goods from value added tax (VAT) are sometimes provided as an inducement to foreign investors. Generally, such incentives are of doubtful validity as indirect taxes are of little concern to investors since these are borne by the consumers rather than businesses. In the case of market-oriented FDI, the same taxes are borne by competitors.

Exempting raw materials and capital goods used to produce exports from import tariffs is a more justifiable approach. In developing countries, customs duties are often one of the most important sources of government revenue and are imposed at relatively high rates. While taxes on raw materials are passed on to domestic consumers, or remitted on export, the taxes on capital goods may be less easily recovered and can add substantially to the initial cost of an investment. Thus, exemption from customs duties and import taxes can be an important factor in investment decisions. The difficulty with this exemption lies in ensuring that the exempted purchases are, in fact, used as intended by the incentive. Further, there is a risk that goods imported free of duty will subsequently be sold in the domestic market. Thus, it may be prudent to exclude such readily saleable articles (e.g., automobiles) from the exemption.

26.3 Foreign Portfolio Investment

One of the major forces changing the face and structure of international capital markets since 1990s has been the flow of cross-border portfolio investments. Portfolio investment occurs when individual investors, and more significantly foreign institutional investors (FIIs), invest in stocks of companies in foreign lands in search of profit opportunities.

26.3.1 Advantages of Portfolio Investment Inflows: Following are the chief advantages of having portfolio investments by foreigners.

A. Improvement in Corporate Capital Structure: FIIs are well-known for a greater appetite for equity than debt in their asset structure. Thus, opening up the economy to FIIs is in line with the accepted preference for non-debt creating foreign inflows over foreign debt. Furthermore, because of this preference for equities over bonds, portfolio inflows can help in compressing the yield-differential between equity and bonds and improve corporate capital structure.

B. Competition in Financial Markets: Institutional investors promote financial innovation and development of hedging instruments. Institutions, for example, because of their interest in hedging risks, are known to have contributed to the development of zero-coupon bonds and index futures. FIIs, as professional bodies of asset managers and financial analysts, not only enhance competition in financial markets, but also improve the alignment of asset prices to fundamentals.

Institutions in general and FIIs in particular are known to have good information and low transaction costs. By aligning asset prices closer to fundamentals, they stabilize markets. Fundamentals are known to be sluggish in their movements. Thus, if prices are aligned to fundamentals, they should be as stable as the fundamentals themselves. Furthermore, FIIs with a variety of risk-return preferences also help in dampening volatility.

C. Enhanced Efficiency in Capital Markets: FIIs as professional bodies of asset managers and financial analysts enhance competition and efficiency of financial markets. Equity market development aids economic development. By increasing the availability of riskier long-term capital for projects, FIIs can help in the process of economic development.

D. Improvement in Corporate Governance: Good corporate governance is essential to overcome the principal-agent problem between shareholders and management. Information asymmetries and incomplete contracts between share-holders and management are at the root of the agency costs. Bad corporate governance makes equity finance a costly option. FIIs contribute to better understanding of operations and improve corporate governance of firms. Institutions are known for challenging excessive executive compensation, and removing under performing managers. There is some evidence that institutionalization increases dividend payouts, and enhances productivity growth.

26.3.2 Disadvantages of Portfolio Investment Inflows: Among others, the two common apprehensions about FIIs inflows are the fear of management takeovers and potential capital outflows.

A. Management Control: FIIs act as agents on behalf of their principals as financial investors maximising returns. There are domestic laws that effectively prohibit institutional investors from taking management control. For example, in India all takeovers are governed by Substantial Acquisition of Shares and Takeovers Regulations, 1997, framed by Securities and Exchange Board of India (SEBI). In the absence of such laws, management takeover by foreigners is possible.

B. Volatility of Portfolio Flows: FIIs inflows are popularly described as *hot money* because of the herd behaviour and potential for large capital outflows. Herd behaviour means FIIs trying to either only buy or only sell at the same time, particularly at times of market stress. Value at risk models followed by FIIs may destabilise markets by leading to simultaneous sale by various FIIs. Extrapolative expectations or trend chasing, rather than focusing on fundamentals, can lead to destabilization.

It has been argued that under the process of globalisation, highly diversified investors participate in cross-border movement of capital. Such investors pay little attention to economic fundamentals and in the presence of asymmetric information they resort to herd behaviour, which results in volatility of international capital flows. Such a view has, however, been challenged and it has been argued that there is high level of substitutability between various forms of foreign capital.

Countries with modest growth potentials and semi-developed financial market infrastructure are most vulnerable to reversal of portfolio investment flows. Existence of large asymmetry of information in such countries can lead to sharp changes in portfolio and private debt flows in the face of even a slight change in investor perception about the health of the recipient economy. This type of volatility is, however, not limited to portfolio flows. Even external commercial borrowings, in the form of bank borrowing or bond financing, show similar patterns.

C. Pro-cyclical: The most important disadvantage of portfolio inflows is that it tends to be pro-cyclical, in the sense that it comes in when the balance of payments (BOP) position is seen to be strong and goes out when the BOP position is expected to weaken. Thus, it accentuates the direction of movement of the BOP, which can cause serious problems in macroeconomic management. In the case of countries where the foreign exchange markets are very thin as compared to the international financial market, a free FII regime carries the danger of speculative movements, which can lead to serious disruption in the economy.

D. Hedge Funds: Hedge funds are another source of concern which (unlike pension funds, life insurance companies and mutual funds) engage in short-term trading, take short positions and borrow more aggressively. There are also downside risks of portfolio inflows. The downside risks include political risk, currency risk, problems associated with low liquidity and volatility on returns. Cross-country studies indicate that reversal of portfolio flows could be disorderly and result in substantial economic hardship for developing countries.

E. Foreign Portfolio Investors are Fair-weather Friends: In rapidly growing economies, high real gross domestic product (GDP) growth needs concomitant growth in monetary aggregates, which also needs expansion of base money. To this extent, the accretion of foreign exchange reserves to the central bank's balance sheet is helpful in expanding base money at the required rate. However, net capital flows and accretion to foreign exchange reserves in excess of such requirements necessitate sterilisation and more active monetary and macroeconomic management. Thus, large inflows of capital, well in excess of the current financing needs, can lead to high domestic credit and monetary growth, boom in stock market and other asset prices, leading to macroeconomic and financial instability. Abrupt reversals in capital flows also lead to significant difficulties in monetary and macroeconomic management.

Reversals of capital flows are quick, necessitating a painful adjustment in bank credit, and collapse of stock prices. Such reversals also result in the contraction of the central bank's balance sheet, which may be difficult to compensate with accretion of domestic assets as fast as the reserves depletion. These developments can then lead to banking and currency crises, large employment and output losses and huge fiscal costs. Thus, the boom and bust pattern of capital inflows can, unless managed proactively, result in macroeconomic and financial instability. Hence, the monetary authorities in developing countries need to watch closely and continuously financial and economic developments in the advanced economies and also manage their capital account actively.

26.4 Foreign Borrowing

A government or a non-government entity may raise loans either internally or externally. Loans raised within the country are called internal loans. Internal loans are in terms of the domestic currency. Thus, domestic loans raised by the Government of India or some private entity are in terms of Indian rupee. In contrast, borrowings from other countries are referred as external debt. External loans are in terms of foreign currencies (generally USA dollar). External loans are uncertain and conditioned by a country's relations with foreign governments. External loans increase the foreign exchange resources of the borrowing country. However, when there is repayment of such loans, foreign exchange reserves are depleted.

Gross foreign debt is a stock variable and is measured at a point in time. Foreign debt is defined as the outstanding amount of those actual current, and not contingent, liabilities that require payment of principal and/or interest by the debtor at some point in the future and that are owed to non-residents by residents of an economy.

26.4.1 Classification of Foreign Borrowings: Such borrowings are classified as under:

A. Government and Non-Government Debt: The borrower classification of external debt provides break-up into government (sovereign) and non-government debt. The latter is further categorized into financial, public and private sectors. Financial sector represents borrowings by banks and financial institutions. Public sector debt represents borrowings of non-financial public sector enterprises and private sector debt represents borrowings of non-financial private sector enterprises.

B. Concessional and Non-concessional Debt: Softer terms of a loan in relation to prevailing market conditions indicate concessionality. Concessionality could be reflected in terms of lower rate of interest, elongation of maturity or repayment periods etc. and is measured by the difference between the face value of a credit and the sum of the discounted future debt service payments. Different multilateral institutions follow different norms for classifying credits into concessional and non-concessional. Generally, a loan is defined as concessional when the grant portion of the loan exceeds 25 percent. In India, loans from multilateral [e.g., International Development Association (IDA)] and bilateral sources are categorized as concessional, based on their terms of long maturity and less than market rate of interest charged on them.

Non-concessional debt is as per prevailing market conditions as, for example, external commercial borrowings (ECBs). ECBs include loans from commercial banks, other commercial financial institutions, money raised through issue of securitized instruments like bonds. ECBs include commercial bank loans, buyers' credit, suppliers' credit, and commercial borrowings from the private sector window of multilateral financial institutions such as International Financial Corporation (IFC) and Asian Development Bank (ADB). ECBs provide an additional source of funds for corporates to finance the expansion of existing capacity as well as new investment, taking cognisance of interest rate differentials between domestic and international markets and the associated market risks.

C. Original and Residual Maturity: Original maturity is defined as the period encompassing the precise time of creation of the financial liability to its date of final maturity. Debt by residual maturity (or remaining maturity) includes short term debt by original maturity of up to one year, combined with medium to long term debt repayment by original maturity but falling due within the twelve-month period from a reference date. External debt is commonly expressed in terms of original maturity.

D. Long-term and Short-term Debt: One way of classifying external debt is the two-way scheme based on maturity: long-term and short-term. Long-term debt is defined as debt with an original maturity of more than one year, while short-term debt is defined as debt repayments on demand or with an original maturity of one year or less.

E. Multilateral and Bilateral Debt: Multilateral creditors are primarily multilateral institutions such as the International Development Association (IDA), International Bank for Reconstruction and Development (IBRD), Asian Development bank (ADB) etc. Bilateral creditors are sovereign countries with whom sovereign and non-sovereign entities enter into one-to-one loan arrangements. For example, some of India's bilateral creditors who extend loans to both sovereign and non-sovereign debtors include Japan, Germany, United States, France, and Netherlands

F. Suppliers' Credit and Buyers' Credit: Suppliers' credit is extended by the overseas supplier of goods in the form of deferred payments. Buyers' credit is provided by a bank or financial institution and carries insurance from export credit agency of the concerned country. Trade credit/export credit refers to loans and credit extended for imports directly by overseas supplier, bank and financial institution to sovereign and non-sovereign entities. Depending on the source of finance, such credit can be either suppliers' credit or buyers' credit.

26.4.2 Indicators of Sustainable Level of Foreign Borrowings: While indebtedness is useful as an indicator of the level of debt burden of a country, it is the debt servicing capacity of the country that is critical. It determines not only the country's ability to meet its debt obligations, but also its chance of default. Difficulties in servicing of debt may arise from liquidity as well as insolvency problems. Accordingly, the sustainable level for a country's foreign debt is determined in terms of a set of solvency and liquidity indicators.

A. Solvency Factor: From a national perspective, solvency can be defined as the country's ability to discharge its external obligations on a continuing basis. In order to remain solvent, the debtor country's economy in the first place must be able to do without an amount of domestic income and savings equivalent to the debt service. Second, the debtor country must be in a position to convert such segregated savings into the required foreign exchange. If the debt servicing is increasing, there must be an increase in both the capacity to save and the capacity to transfer savings. The analysis of debt servicing capacity of a country over time, therefore, requires an examination of the performance of debtor countries in generating income and savings and increasing foreign trade. Not surprisingly, ratio of foreign debt to exports, foreign debt to national income, debt service ratio and interest service ratio have evolved as some of the most common solvency indicators.

Debt to exports ratio can be measured as an indicator of solvency, since an increasing debt to exports ratio indicates that the country may have problems meeting its debt obligations in future. Furthermore, the debt to national income ratio provides some indication of the potential to service external debt by switching resources from production of domestic goods to the production of exports.

In terms of other solvency indicators, the ratio of debt-service payments to exports of goods and services indicates how much of a country's export revenue will be used up in servicing its debt. Furthermore, the ratio of average interest payments to export earnings indicates terms of external indebtedness and thus the debt burden.

B. Liquidity Factor: Apart from the solvency factor, the other factor that has acquired greater bearing on debt servicing capacity of a country is the liquidity position of the country. Liquidity problems arise when there is a shortage of liquid assets to discharge immediate external obligations and could be independent of solvency problem. Liquidity problems can be triggered by a sharp drop in export earnings or an increase in interest rates or an increase in prices for imports. The currency and interest rate composition of debt, the maturity structure of debt, and the availability of assets to pay debts are all important determinants of the vulnerability of the economy to external liquidity crisis. The ratio of short-term debt to total outstanding debt and the ratio of international reserves to short-term debt are the two most common indicators of liquidity.

C. Monitoring System: There is the need for monitoring the level of private non-guaranteed (PNG) debt. Accurate data on PNG debt burden is important as it includes various financial instruments including inter-company loans, bonds, debentures and notes, money market instruments, financial derivatives, trade credits, loans for projects, financial leases, repurchase agreements, and foreign currency deposits held by non-residents. It has been argued that high levels of short-term debt owed by private financial institutions and non-financial corporations can be directed into speculative activities. There is, thus, an imperative need for monitoring various components of short-term debt.

26.5 Foreign Aid

Economists usually consider aid as international flow of resources in the form of public development assistance. If this assistance is from individual national governments, it is called *bilateral aid*. If it is from international donor agencies like UN and other global bodies, regional development banks and aid consortia, it is called *multilateral aid*. Thus, foreign aid is any international transfer made on concessional terms (rather than at market/commercial terms) for promoting economic development. International financial transfers can take two forms: (a) grants, and (b) loans. Grants are unilateral transfers which are not to be repaid. Loans carry relatively lower rate of interest and longer period of repayment. Foreign aid may take a variety of physical forms such as capital goods, commodities (especially food), technical assistance and military equipment. Normally, military aid is not considered as part of foreign aid.

26.5.1 Justification for Foreign Aid: Many believe that foreign aid from rich countries is indispensable for the development of less developed countries (LDCs). If LDCs wish to emerge from poverty, they must save and invest. Foreign aid can help them fill the gap between low level of domestic savings and desired level of investment. Foreign aid may bring with it managerial skills and technical know-how. This will help LDCs to discard their outdated methods of production. Better technology is the key to increased productivity. It is also argued that aid is an international redistributive mechanism. The widening gap between developed and underdeveloped countries can be reduced through foreign aid. It is the moral duty of the rich nations to help the starving people of Africa and Asia. The present poverty of LDCs is partly attributed to their economic exploitation by the developed countries of Europe and America.

A number of studies have shown that foreign aid can facilitate economic and social transformation by overcoming temporary shortages in specific human and material resources, promoting strategic activities, inducing and facilitating critical government policies and providing certain amount of working capital for carrying out programmes involving a transformation of the structure of the economy. A time series analysis of several countries in Asia, including India, Pakistan and China, suggests that aid contributed to growth both in poor and middle income countries. There is no evidence to suggest that countries that received a large amount of external aid have performed poorly, apart from countries suffering from civil or external conflicts.

It is often argued that governments of the aid-receiving countries divert foreign aid from intended purposes to various unproductive uses and/or to support general government expenditure. In view of this, it has been argued that rather than targeting aid to specific sectors or activities, it is more efficient to link aid to overall public expenditure programme in the recipient country. As effectiveness of aid depends on the policy framework of the recipient economy, it is argued that such flows should be concentrated in countries with sound policy frameworks.

External assistance with high element of concessionality played a significant role in the development process in India till the early 1980s. During the 1980s, however, the share of external assistance in the capital account declined as the widening current account deficit necessitated recourse to additional sources of foreign savings such as commercial borrowings and non-resident deposits. The lower recourse to official aid was also attributed to other factors such as structural changes in global capital flows, lack of matching resources, delays involved in project appraisals and tender finalisation due to administrative bottlenecks, lack of cost related tariff structure for power and delays in land acquisition. Net inflows to India, as a result, fell sharply during the 1990s.

26.5.2 Adverse Repercussions and Limitations: Adverse repercussions of foreign aid are also noteworthy. Opponents believe that foreign aid is neither a necessary nor a sufficient condition for emerging from poverty. There is considerably more to development than just injections of aid. Economic achievement depends on people's own faculties, motivations, ways of life, institutions and the policies of their rulers.

Foreign aid also creates feeling of inferiority among the people of recipient country. Aid impairs the spirit of competitiveness among LDCs. If aid is in the form of loans, it adds to the burden of debt which is already massive in amount in the case of LDCs. Repayment of loans leads to foreign exchange outflows from LDCs, accentuating their balance of payment difficulties. Almost invariably, aid is available to LDCs with restrictions, particularly regarding its use. The tying of aid may take the following forms:

1. **Source-tying or Procurement-tying:** It specifies where the recipient can spend aid. The spending restrictions usually take the form of tying aid to purchases in the donor country. This reduces the real worth of aid because it prevents recipients from shopping around the world to find exactly the goods they want in the cheapest markets. The recipient country must buy imports in the donor country and they are to be transported in ships of donor country.
2. **Use-tying:** Aid is tied to specific projects which may not be in line with the development goals of LDCs.

3. **Double-tying:** More often than not, both restrictions operate together, leading to double tying. This has been extremely expensive for LDCs. The prices from tied sources are much higher than the international prices.

Aid-tying is justified by the donors as necessary for overcoming their balance of payment deficits. Source-tying is also governed by the desire of donors to support their industries with excess capacity or to get rid of their surplus stocks of commodities. Thus, aid with strings is less useful for LDCs than it may appear overtly. In fact, tied-aid creates more jobs and leads to the establishment and expansion of more industries in the donor than in the donee country.

Endnote

1. International Monetary Fund, *Balance of Payments Manual*, Washington, DC, 1977, p. 408.

27

Environment, Climate Change and Economic Development

Productivity of an economic system depends, to a large extent, on the supply and quality of its natural resources. In fact, natural and environmental resources are the basis of all economic activities. Soil, forests, mines, water, air and other natural resources are productive assets of an economy. Poor quality of water and air adversely affects the health of population, causing reduced labour productivity and premature mortality. Similarly, soil degradation and erosion leads to reduced and inferior quality of agricultural output.

27.1 Economic Development and Environment

Economic development often depends on the utilisation and conversion of natural resources into useful goods and services. This process of consumption and conversion uses energy, minerals and other natural resources such as air, water, land and biodiversity. It also produces wastes which are released into environment with adverse impacts. Economic activities, in turn, affect the quantity and quality of natural and environmental resources. Mining, lumbering, manufacturing, fishing and a host of other economic activities change the stock of natural resources which calls for appropriate trade-off between the needs of present and future generations.

Increase in economic activities—due to growing population and/or enhanced consumption levels—often impacts environment negatively. Degradation of natural resources and losses in environmental quality adversely affect people at large. As a consequence of high level of economic activities, emissions, effluents and waste discharges exceed the carrying capacity of different resources. Economic growth without environmental considerations can cause serious damage to the quality of life of the present and future generations. It is in this context that economists distinguish between economic growth and economic development. Economic growth means sustained increase in per capita real income. Economic development is a much wider term. It includes economic growth and at the same time encompasses questions regarding patterns of production, distribution of national income, consumption behaviour of the people and concern for environment.

Economic progress improves our standard of living and makes our life more comfortable. On the other hand, it is this very progress that can lead to degradation of the environment. Any increase in national income would arise only from increased production of goods and services involving greater consumption of resources such as land, forest, fuels etc. whose supply is, essentially, limited. While some of these resources may be renewable, others get depleted and, ultimately, exhausted with continuous use. Any attempt to preserve the non-renewable resources might require compromising on the growth rates.

The conflict between economic development and environment is, essentially, a conflict between short- and long-run priorities, between the interests of current and future generations. Large exploitation of natural resources today, while increasing the economic growth for the current generations, would lead to gradual exhaustion and degradation of these resources, thereby reducing their availability to our future generations and adversely affecting their output, income and living standards.

27.2 Environmental Pollution

Demographic expansion, over exploitation of natural resources, mega development projects—with least concern for sustainability and conservation—have greatly affected the environment. The magnitude and alterations that humanity can make to environment, threaten to undermine the basic natural process that sustains biosphere. The process of economic development necessarily entails exploitations of natural resources. However, when such exploitation becomes indiscriminate and is undertaken without adequate environmental safeguards, the consequences can be disastrous.

Pollution can be defined as an undesirable change in the physical, chemical, or biological characteristics of the air, water or land that can harmfully affect health, survival or activities of human beings or other living organisms. Pollution refers essentially to a process by which a resource is rendered unfit for some beneficial use. Of the various kinds of pollution (air, water, land, noise, radiation and odour) that affect the quality of life in India, water pollution is by far the most serious in its implications for the health and well-being of the people.

Environmental pollution is one of the major problems faced by the world community, especially in the cities of the developing countries which have experienced unbridled growth of population, urbanization and industrialization. Municipal services—such as water supply and sanitation, drainage of storm water, management of solid and hazardous wastes, supply of adequate and safe food and housing—are unable to keep pace with urban growth. The unplanned location of industries in and around urban areas and volume of traffic have caused serious pollution problems. All these factors have led to deteriorating environmental conditions, adversely impacting the health of the people.

Pollution has become a major threat to the very existence of mankind on this earth. Pollution of various resources has gone to such an extent that people are unable to breathe fresh air and drink fresh water. True, advancements in science and technology have added to human comforts by way of automobiles, electrical appliances, supersonic jets, modern medicines, communications and entertainment. However, these blessings have been diluted by serious problems posed by ecological imbalances and climate changes.

Environmental degradation not only affects us but also has repercussions for future generations. Globally, the need for sustainable development is being emphasized. Sustainable development attempts to strike a balance between the demands of economic development and the need for protection of our natural environment.

27.3 Environmental Economics

Environmental economics is a branch of economics which deals with the inter-relationships between environment and development. Environmental economics examines the interface between economic agents and environment. Economic activities of human beings have a profound impact on natural environment. Hence, use/abuse of natural resources has raised many moral, legal and practical questions for present and future generations. There has been a gradual shift in many developed countries from command and control type of policy approach to environmental policy goals. Presently, many governments require cost-benefit analysis of policy options with regard to changes in environmental legislations by resetting environmental standards and introducing new policy instruments for environmental protection. Environmental economics has also made significant contributions to valuation techniques and design of new policy instruments for pollution control and management.

It is often said that gross domestic product (GDP) is not the best way of measuring the true well-being of nations, because the pursuit of growth can be at the cost of the environment. Conventional ways of measuring GDP in terms of production do not take into account the environmental damage caused by production of goods and services. Only after GDP is adjusted for environmental costs, that growth of adjusted GDP can be called a measure of the increase in total production in the economy. There is obviously a two-way relationship between environment and economic growth. Natural resources and raw materials such as water, timber and minerals directly provide inputs for the production of goods and services.

Due to its cross-cutting nature, and wide local and global stakeholder base, environmental governance needs to be strategic. An ideal framework should be anticipative, technically oriented, cognizant of legal issues, geo-politically relevant and forward-looking, capable of maximising national interests and progressive enough to make a social impact. Most importantly, management of the environment should include progressively adapting/changing actions that rely on sound scientific, technological, human-cognitive and collaborative principles.

27.4 Green Growth

Green growth involves rethinking growth strategies with regard to their impact on environmental sustainability and the environmental resources available to poor and vulnerable groups. It is significant to note that many stimulus packages announced globally to combat recession incorporated a green component. International experience is that green growth promotes inclusivity. Further, the renewable energy sector is relatively labour-intensive, with the potential for generating more jobs than the oil and gas industries.

Environment must not be considered as just another sector of national development. It should form a crucial guiding dimension for plans and programmes in each sector. This becomes clear only if the concern for environmental protection is understood in its proper context. Ecological degradation compromises the quality of life in the long-run.

27.4.1 Requirements of Green Growth: Low-carbon green growth is a pattern of development that decouples economic growth from carbon emissions, pollution and resource use, and promotes growth through the creation of new environment-friendly products, industries and business models that also improve people's quality of life. Thus, low-carbon green growth entails the following:

1. Using less energy, improving the efficiency with which resources are used and moving to low-carbon energy sources.
2. Protecting and promoting the sustainable use of natural resources such as forests and peat lands.
3. Designing and disseminating low-carbon technologies and business models to reinvigorate local economies.
4. Implementing policies and incentives which discourage carbon intensive practices.

Green growth is not anti-growth. Rather, it represents a change in how we manage economies to reflect a broader conception of what constitutes effective and sustainable growth. Environmental assets—water, land, air, ecosystems and the services they provide—represent a significant share of a country's wealth. Just like physical and human capital, natural capital requires investment, maintenance, and good management if it is to be productive and fully contribute to prosperity.

Green growth requires policies that are on their own terms good for growth, as well as for the environment, such as reforming energy subsidies or trade barriers that protect pollution-intensive sectors. It entails politically difficult reforms in the patterns of pricing, regulation, and public investment, and it calls for complex changes in behaviours and social norms. Importantly, green growth requires knowing when to go for the politically expedient rather than the economically optimal.

27.4.2 Advantages of Green Growth: The amount of CO_2 a country emits into the atmosphere depends on a wide range of factors, including the size of its economy, the level of industrialization, and the efficiency of its energy use, as well as population, lifestyle choices and land use changes. As a consequence of rapid and carbon-intensive growth, the Asian region has been fast becoming a major source of greenhouse gas emissions. The transition to a low-carbon economy will benefit emerging Asia in the following ways:

1. Many low-carbon interventions have important co-benefits for Asia at different levels, including the enhanced energy security associated with energy efficiency (on both the supply and demand side) and renewable energy projects. Human health benefits from interventions that reduce air pollutants, such as those from transport; and the environmental benefits that can be achieved through forestry and agricultural management, waste reduction programmes and employment programmes.
2. Interventions, which have positive economic rates of return and short pay-back time and should be undertaken irrespective of climate change considerations, can contribute substantially to the economic development of emerging Asian countries.
3. Asian countries that pursue low-carbon development, including the transfer of financial resources through the carbon market and new public programmes that support the reduction of emissions are likely to reap strategic and competitive advantage at the regional and international levels.
4. Emerging countries of Asia are likely to suffer disproportionately from the impacts

of climate change (drought, increased severity of tropical storms, sea level rise, etc). Asia has a strong interest in becoming a leading participant in global efforts on both emissions reduction and adaptation.

5. Low-carbon green growth will become more important as countries seek to take a pro-poor, pro-employment economic development path based on innovation.
6. Emerging Asia will have real social gains in the low-carbon green growth process by involving local communities to promote equity and fairness, along with improved air quality and other eco-system services.
7. Emerging Asia will become a leader in key green technologies and business models, and an important destination for the commercialization of key low-carbon technologies, green products and services.
8. Emerging Asia will be able to sweep away the short-term developmental thinking that has plagued the past several decades and replace it with paths delivering development that flourishes within ecological limits.

Low-carbon green growth is a unique opportunity to invest in change. Many analysts believe that the sooner emerging Asian countries take advantage of low-carbon green growth, the better it will be for their long-term development prospects, economic restructuring and their quest to find new drivers of growth. Even though the transition to a low-carbon green growth paradigm is a long-term process, the following years are crucial for Asia to seize the economic, social and environmental opportunities, gain competitive advantage and show global leadership through regional cooperation.

27.4.3 Inclusive Green Growth: Sustainable development has three pillars: economic, environmental, and social sustainability. We cannot presume that green growth is inherently inclusive. Green growth policies must be carefully designed to maximize benefits for, and minimize costs to, the poor and most vulnerable, and policies and actions with irreversible negative impacts must be avoided.

Rapid growth is necessary to meet the urgent development needs of the world's poor. However, growth will be unsustainable in the long-run unless it is both socially inclusive and green—the latter by ensuring that the earth's natural assets are able to adequately provide the resources and environmental services on which humans depend. Inclusive green growth requires tackling political economy constraints, overcoming deeply entrenched behaviours and social norms, and developing innovative financing instruments to change incentives and promote innovation, and thus address the market, policy, and institutional failures that lead to the overuse of natural assets. Greener growth is necessary, efficient, and affordable. It should focus on what needs to happen in the next 20 to 30 years to avoid getting locked into unsustainable paths and causing irreversible environmental damage.

Economic and social sustainability, on the one hand, and social and environmental sustainability, on the other, have been found to be not only compatible, but also largely complementary. Not so with economic and environmental sustainability, as growth has come largely at the expense of the environment which is why green growth aims to ensure that economic and environmental sustainability are compatible.

27.5 Climate Change

Climate change is a serious global environmental concern, which is primarily caused by the building up of greenhouse gases in the atmosphere. Recent discourse on climate change has underscored the fact that climate change occupies a high priority on the environmental agenda of international community.

Global climate change due to rising levels of green house gases (GHGs) in the atmosphere is one of the most serious environmental concerns of present time. The accumulated scientific evidence clearly indicates that if the rate of GHG emissions is not reduced very significantly, there will be a damaging effect on the global climate.

Since global warming is caused by total accumulation of GHG and each country's emissions add to the stock, the cost of each country's emissions is borne by the entire global community. Similarly, the benefits of reduction in emission by any one country accrue not to the country itself but to the entire global community. This is classically a situation characterized by externalities in which individual countries will not have a sufficient incentive to undertake mitigation unless all countries co-operate in what is felt to be a collective effort with an equitable distribution of the burden of reducing emissions.

27.5.1 Consequences of Climate Change: Climate change can lead to the following:

1. Shrinkage of glaciers.
2. Thawing of permafrost.
3. Lengthening of mid-to-high latitude growing seasons.
4. Poleward and altitudinal shifts of plant and animal ranges.
5. Decline in population of some plants and animals.
6. Earlier flowering of trees.
7. Changes in emergence of insects, and egg-laying in birds.

Associations between changes in regional temperatures and the observed changes in physical and biological systems have been documented in many aquatic, terrestrial, and marine environments.

Changing environmental attributes are sure to affect the species spectrum and depending upon the pace of change, the profile and composition of forests is also likely to change. In arid or semi-arid areas, productivity is expected to decrease. Trends of drying up of wetlands and degradation of ecosystems have been observed.

The water cycle is totally dependent on the temperature regime. Increasing global temperature and resultant faster retreat of most glaciers is expected to affect the snow-fed perennial water regimes. Accordingly, the vegetation status of catchments, magnitude and frequency of floods, precipitation, run-off and groundwater recharge may be affected. It may substantially affect hydropower generation and increase in irrigation withdrawal, due to higher crop evaporative demand.

Changes in the frequencies of extreme heat and cold, the frequencies of floods and droughts, and the profile of local air pollution may result in changes in occurrence of infectious diseases, leading to impaired child development and various health consequences of population displacement and economic disruption.

Estimates of crop yield responses to climate change vary widely, depending upon species, cultivation practices, soil properties, and direct effects of carbon dioxide (CO_2) on plants. Even though increased CO_2 concentration can stimulate crop growth and yield that2 benefit may not always overcome the adverse effects of excessive heat and drought.

In countries with predominantly agrarian economies, increase in temperature and reduction in precipitation could—in the absence of adequate irrigation and related infrastructural interventions—dampen the economic growth by reducing agricultural productivity. These impacts can be moderated by efforts at adaptation but these are expected to be costly and will impose a burden on both producers and consumers.

Adaptive options like health-oriented management of the environment (including air and water quality, food safety, urban and housing design, and surface water management), and appropriate medical interventions are normally related to income levels. Therefore, poor income levels are more vulnerable. Human settlements are expected to be accordingly affected by changes in resource productivity or market demand for the goods and services causing structural and functional adaptations leading to migration, and resultant living conditions. Climate change would, therefore, result in increase in the absolute number of people at risk of hunger unless these outcomes can be countered through the development of cost effective technologies.

In short, the serious consequences of climate change lead naturally to the question of what should be the response. Two types of responses need to be considered. The first relates to adaptation, i.e. measures that have to be taken given the very high likelihood that climate change will occur and will have adverse effects. The second relates to mitigation, i.e. steps to be taken that might reduce the extent of climate change. The two are clearly interconnected. The more effective the mitigation strategy, the less society has to worry about adaptation. Likewise, if mitigation is not likely to be effective, or cannot be organised effectively, then adaptation acquires special urgency. Reducing emissions is feasible but it is costly and it is not easy to determine how the burden of emission reduction should be distributed.

28

Sustainable Economic Development

Economic growth and development have to be guided by the compulsion of sustainability, because no country can afford to ignore the economic as well as the environmental threat that a fast-deteriorating ecosystem poses to its economy. No country is immune to the reality of climate change, ecological degradation, depletion of the ozone layer and contamination of freshwater.

28.1 What is Sustainable Development?

The concept of sustainable development is inextricably linked with environment protection. It is a strategy for improving the quality of human life while living within the carrying capacity of supporting eco system. It is clear from the above definition that sustainable development entails commitment, protection and preservation.

Sustainable development is that which meets the needs of the present without compromising the ability of future generations. The heaviest burden in international economic adjustment has been carried by the world's poorest population. The consequence has been the considerable increase in human distress and over exploitation of land and water resources to ensure survival in the short term. Further, the desire to solve all social and human problems at one stroke has influenced the pace of development. Its reaction is visible in the atmosphere and in natural, physical and social environment. Awareness regarding the consequences of this event has developed into a consensus referred to as ecological concern.

Sustainable development advocates economic progress in an environmentally responsible manner. Sustainable development attempts to strike a balance between the requirements of economic development and the need for protection of the environment. It seeks to combine the elements of economic efficiency, inter-generational equity, social concerns and environmental protection. Although, the term sustainable development has many interpretations, it generally refers to non-declining human well-being over time.

Sustainable development is a pattern of social and structured economic transformations (i.e. development) which optimizes the economic and social benefits available at present, without jeopardizing the likely potential for similar benefits in the future. The primary goal of sustainable development is to achieve a reasonable and equitable distribution level of economic well being that can be perpetuated continually for the future human generations. Sustainability is about meeting the needs of the present without compromising the ability of future generations to meet their needs. It is about preserving the environment and biodiversity for future generations, and about being cautious with our natural resources and climate. But sustainability is also about guaranteeing human rights and a life in dignity, free from want and poverty for all people living today.

Developing countries have options other than to *grow dirty and clean up later*. Much that is useful can be done now. Clean air and water and solid waste management are basic needs, and many environmental policies enhance productivity and poverty alleviation. So while poor countries should focus on meeting basic needs and expanding opportunities for growth, they need not do so at the expense of unsustainable environmental degradation. Further, environmental performance does not automatically improve with income, so policy action is needed anyway. Finally, it may be impossible or prohibitively expensive to *clean up later*, either because of the irreversibility of environmental damages like the loss of biodiversity, or because *lock-in* will make subsequent shifts to more environmentally benign structures and processes extremely costly.

28.2 UN Sustainable Development Goals (SDGs)

On January 1, 2016, the 17 Sustainable Development Goals (SDGs) of the 2030 Agenda for Sustainable Development, adopted by world leaders in September 2015 at an historic UN Summit, officially came into force.

SDGs are the blueprint to achieve a better and more sustainable future for all. They address the global challenges, including those related to poverty, inequality, climate, environmental degradation, prosperity, and peace and justice. The Goals interconnect and in order to leave no one behind, it is important to achieve each Goal and target by 2030.

These new Goals that universally apply to all, countries will mobilize efforts to end all forms of poverty, fight inequalities and tackle climate change, while ensuring that no one is left behind.

SDGs build on the success of the Millennium Development Goals (MDGs) and aim to go further to end all forms of poverty. The new Goals are unique in that they call for action by all countries, poor, rich and middle-income to promote prosperity while protecting the planet. They recognize that ending poverty must go hand-in-hand with strategies that build economic growth and addresses a range of social needs including education, health, social protection, and job opportunities, while tackling climate change and environmental protection.

The seventeen goals are as under:

Goal 1: End poverty in all its forms.
Goal 2: Zero hunger.
Goal 3: Health.
Goal 4: Education.
Goal 5: Gender equality and women's empowerment.
Goal 6: Water and sanitation.
Goal 7: Energy.
Goal 8: Economic growth.
Goal 9: Infrastructure, industrialization.
Goal 10: Inequality.
Goal 11: Cities.
Goal 12: Sustainable consumption and production.

Goal 13: Climate Change.
Goal 14: Oceans.
Goal 15: Biodiversity, forests, desertification.
Goal 16: Peace, justice and strong institutions.
Goal 17: Partnerships.

28.3 Sustainable Development Framework for Mining Sector

Minerals are valuable natural resources being finite and non-renewable. They constitute the vital raw materials for many basic industries and are a major resource for development.

28.3.1 Mining Activities and Ecological Balance: The metallurgical and mineral industries constitute the core of the industrial sector as they provide the basic raw material for most of the industries. The metallurgical industries are highly capital-intensive. They are also energy-intensive and highly polluting, and make large demands on the infrastructural sector in terms of coal, power and railway transportation. The efficiency of use of various inputs in the metallurgical industries is, therefore, of paramount importance as it has a significant impact on the rate of growth of the economy. Due attention should be paid to adopting more effective measures for environmental protection and restoring ecological balance.

Sustainable development has become a global agenda. Like other development-related activities, mineral exploration and exploitation also adversely affect the environment. For sustainable development, the key issue is managing natural resources including minerals optimally without disturbing the ecological balance and containing natural hazards.

The role of earth scientists has, therefore, become important, especially since environment problems cannot be resolved in isolation through engineering solutions only or even through legal and administrative actions. In the domain of environment and earth system studies, one of the goals will have to be continued updating of the geo-scientific database.

28.3.2 Integrating Economic Activity with Environment Integrity: It is recognized that mining, unless properly regulated can have serious adverse environmental and social consequences. On the one hand, mining disturbs the soil, water and ecological regimes and on the other hand—unless accompanied by proactive measures to promote inclusiveness through social, education, health and other interventions—it can lead to alienation of the local population, and assume socially unacceptable dimensions. This has necessitated fresh thinking on policy approaches and systems that ensure that mining is done in a way that causes least damage to the natural resources such as air, water, soil, biomass, and also benefits local communities in the most appropriate way.

One of the greatest challenges facing the mining sector today is integrating economic activity with environment integrity, social concerns and effective governance systems. The goal of that integration can be seen as more sustainable development. This requires a robust framework based on an agreed set of broad principles, an understanding of the key challenges facing the sector at different levels and in different regions and the action needed to meet or overcome them. In other words, a process is needed for responding to these challenges for protecting the rights and interest of all involved, fixing a set of priorities, and ensuring that action is taken at appropriate levels. It calls for an integrated set of institutional and policy instruments to ensure minimum standards of compliance as well as responsible voluntary actions. It also requires variable measures to evaluate progress and enable consistent improvements.

Exploration, development, production, and disposal of minerals affect the environment and ecology of the mined area. Mining has to be done in a way that causes least damage to natural resources such as air, water, soil, and biomass.

An issue that poses a challenge to the mining industry is that of abandoned mines. Mines abandoned or closed without taking necessary measures can have serious environmental and social consequences.

28.3.3 Mining and Land Use Management: Mineral development is one of a number of competing land uses. Due to lack of planning and other frameworks to balance and manage possible uses there are problems and disagreements in the matter of control, use, and management of land. Exploration and mining pose significant challenges in terms of land access and management. The most appropriate use of land is best decided within an integrated land planning framework that balances competing interests such as between national and local levels or between mining and conservation. There are trade-offs that may be made in order to generate benefits in one domain, but decisions on these should not be taken without inclusion of and negotiation with all those likely to be directly affected. A broad consensus must be achieved on the management of protected areas (e.g. forests) and the trade-offs involved. The local stake in the success of protected areas and resources available to manage them, needs to be ensured.

The decision whether or not to mine a certain area should be undertaken through a democratic decision- making process and should be based on an integrated assessment of ecological, environmental, economic, and social impacts. The planning process will be more effective in the presence of equitable and inclusive rules of tenure, compensation schemes for those affected, and strong governance, including mechanisms for arbitration where necessary.

Mitigation of natural hazards, including landslides, is one area where geo-scientists can play an effective role. For this, gathering of base-line geological data and related information, its critical analysis and monitoring will be the key to understanding the basic physical processes which cause the phenomenon, its area of influence and the magnitude of impact.

28.3.4 Environmental Impact Assessments (EIA) and Environment Management Systems (EMS): Mining activities have a significant environmental impact. Managing this impact effectively requires dealing with issues such as handling of immense quantities of waste, acid drainage, effective mine closure planning, and restoration of the ecological balance. Modern practices in mining operations represent a great improvement over the past but these have not spread to all parts of the industry and the world. The objective of best practice is to ensure that critical natural capital is maintained, that eco-systems are enhanced where possible, and that mineral wealth contributes to net environmental continuity.

Mining produces very large quantities of waste and decisions about where and how to dispose of the waste are among the most important in the mineral cycle. In this context, the mining plan becomes vital in that it must not only enable optimal mining to prevent wastage of national resources but ensure that extraction processes do not damage the environment. The best way to obtain protection of the environment is to ensure the development of a mine closure plan at the outset of operations. This can guide individual decisions taken during mining itself to ensure that they are oriented towards this end.

EIA is perhaps the most widely used tool of environmental management in the mineral sector. EIA, as part of EMS, has to integrate environmental responsibilities into everyday management practices through changes in organisational structure, procedures, and processes. Loss of biodiversity is loss of natural capital and is irreversible. Convention on Biological Diversity)—adopted during the Earth Summit held in Rio de Janeiro in 1992—provides the mineral sector with a sound basis for taking appropriate steps for preserving and enhancing biodiversity in its areas of operation and engaging in constructive dialogue and partnership with the biodiversity community.

28.4 Economic Instruments for Promoting Sustainable Development

The role of economic instruments in financing and promoting sustainable development is well recognised. The following economic instruments can help achieve sustainable development through their influence on behavioural patterns leading to sustainable consumption and production in the economy:

28.4.1 Environmental Taxes: An environment or green tax is imposed on a product that damages the environment, in an attempt to reduce its production or consumption. Well-designed environmental taxes and other economic instruments can play an important role in ensuring that prices reflect environmental costs, in line with the *polluter pays principle*. Environmental taxes can be simple and efficient financial instruments for improving the productivity of natural resources. Environmental taxes on water and fossil fuels need not be part of the general revenues of the Government. Rather they should be directly ploughed back into environmentally sustainable action on these fronts. Coal cess is a good example of environment tax imposed by Government of India in recent times, whose proceeds are channelled to the National Clean Energy Fund. Some benefits of environment taxation are enumerated below:

1. They provide incentives for measures that protect the environment, and deter actions that lead to environmental damage.
2. Economic instruments such as taxes can enable environmental goals to be achieved at the lowest cost, and in the most efficient way.
3. By internalizing environmental costs into prices, they help signal the structural economic changes needed to move to a more sustainable economy.
4. They can encourage innovation and development of new technology.
5. The revenue raised by environmental taxes can be used to reduce the level of other taxes. This could help reduce distortions, while raising the efficiency with which resources are used in the economy.

28.4.2 Subsidies: There has been a growing recognition of fiscal and environmental implications of the subsidy policies in energy, water and agriculture sectors. Most of these subsidies pose a threat to the environment. For example, in India the subsidy on diesel has distorted the use of energy in transport and industrial sectors, and worsened the problem of hazardous air pollution. Similarly, excessive use of nitrogenous fertilizers and over-drawing of water, backed by subsidies at both Centre and State levels, is playing havoc with the sustainability of soil and water eco-system.

28.4.3 Non-monetary Incentives: Non-monetary incentives are policy instruments that typically do not have a monetary value, but definitely have a financial impact that promotes sustainability. These incentives can be used as a bargaining tool by the Government to encourage conservation of resources in an economy. Activities such as those encouraging judicious use of water, planting trees, car pooling and avoiding use of plastic bags can be rewarded so that it encourages the practice, and acts as an example for others. Through the initiation of innovative policies and awards, the Government can provide recognition, which will encourage sustainable development amongst the citizens and the firms.

28.4.4 Eco-Industrial Hubs: An eco-industrial park (EIP) or estate is a community of manufacturing and service businesses located together on a common property. Member businesses seek enhanced environmental, economic and social performance through collaboration in managing environmental and resource issues. By working together, the community of businesses seeks a collective benefit that is greater than the sum of individual benefits each company would realise by only optimizing its individual performance. The goal of an EIP is to improve the economic performance of the participating companies while minimizing their environmental impacts. Components of this approach include green design of the park infrastructure (new or retrofitted); cleaner production; prevention of pollution; energy efficiency and inter-company partnering. An EIP also seeks benefits for neighbouring communities to assure the net impact of its development is positive.

In short, there is unanimity on the imperative for maintaining the environment, restoring ecological balance, and preserving and adding to the forest wealth of the nation. Nevertheless, if the mineral wealth of the nation is to be exploited in the interest of overall development, then conservation has to be pursued consistently with the needs of development. Mining intervention should not only ensure the least damage to the environmental and ecological balance but also proactively add to the natural capital by such measures as regeneration of flora and fauna along with all other depleted resources such as water and soil in areas affected by the intervention.

Sustainable development is a difficult balancing act in countries with low incomes. Society has to simultaneously accomplish three things with trade-offs: improve economic well-being with social justice for the present generation, yet manage with more restrained use of land, air, forest, energy, and water resources, and protect future generations. The choices are more difficult in developing countries because they affect people's livelihoods. Such a *stewardship* to succeed therefore needs to respond to people's needs, share information on choices and costs, and ensure participation and ownership.

29

Globalization and Integration of World Economies

29.1 Globalization Defined

Globalization implies widening and deepening integration with the *globe*, i.e. with people and processes abroad. The 1990s witnessed a paradigm shift towards market-oriented economic policies and a careful dismantling of obstacles in its wake. Globalization has resulted in the creation of a new business framework. The trend towards the evolution of a global society is generally thought of in economic terms and in terms of the consequences of the revolution in communication technologies. There is undoubtedly much greater economic integration among the nations of the world today.

Finance has also globalized. One can invest in companies anywhere in the world and purchase financial instruments (stocks and bonds) from any company from almost anywhere in the world. Many pension funds are in fact invested abroad and a financial crisis in one financial centre quickly spreads across the world at the click of a mouse. We can exchange dollars for euros and most other currencies easily and quickly, but the rates at which we exchange our currency often change frequently and drastically. In short, tastes, production, competition, labour markets, and financial markets are rapidly globalizing, and this affects all of us deeply as consumers, workers, investors, and voters. In short we live in a global economy.

Globalization is widely seen as the most important factor that could influence economies of nations the world over in the new millennium. The rapid advancement in information technology and communications has made it not just possible but absolutely essential for economies of the world to adapt or fall by the wayside. More changes can be expected in the business scenario specifically in terms of openness, adaptiveness and responsiveness.

29.2 Impact of Globalization

29.2.1 Growth of Transnational Corporations: Globaiization has resulted in the growing concentration and monopolisation of economic resources and power by transnational corporations and by global financial firms and funds. This process has been termed transnationalisation, in which fewer and fewer transnational corporations are gaining a large and rapidly increasing proportion of world economic resources, production and market shares. Where a multinational company used to dominate the market of a single product, a big transnational company (TNC) now typically produces or trades in an increasing multitude of products, services and sectors. Through mergers and acquisitions, fewer and fewer of these TNCs now control a larger and larger share of the global market, whether in commodities, manufactures or services.

29.2.2 Globalization of National Policies: Globalization process has led to globalization of national policies and policy-making mechanism. National policies (including economic, social, cultural and technological) that until recently were determined by the States and people within a country have increasingly come under the influence of international agencies and processes or by big private corporations and economic/financial players. This has led to the narrowed ability of governments and people to make choices from options in economic, social and cultural policies.

Most developing countries have seen their independent policy-making mechanism capacity eroded, and have to adopt policies influenced by other entities, which may on balance be detrimental to the countries concerned. The developed countries, where the major economic players reside, and which also control the processes and policies of international economic agencies, are better able to maintain control over their own national policies as well as determine the policies and practices of international institutions and the global system. However, it is also true that the large corporations have taken over a large part of decision-making even in the developed countries, at the expense of the power of the state or political and social leaders.

29.2.3 Flexible Production Processes: Globalization of the economies across the world has changed the notions of manufacturing, productivity and competitiveness. Flexible production processes and structures are being increasingly put in place to compete in very dynamic markets where product life is very short and discerning customers with higher purchasing power and more differentiated and international tastes are demanding much more product variety, higher quality and greater value for money. The new production systems are increasingly moving to the network form of enterprises, each contributing to the production and distribution according to their respective core competencies. Therefore, competitiveness now requires the ability to constantly take the most advantageous position or niche in the rapidly changing market environment.

29.2.4 New Business Framework: Globalization has also resulted in the creation of a new business framework. More changes can be expected in the business scenario specifically in terms of openness, adaptiveness and responsiveness. The most important dimensions of economic globalization are as under:

1. Breaking down of national barriers.
2. International spread of trade, financial and production activities.
3. Growing power of transnational corporations and international financial institutions in these processes.

While economic globalization is a very uneven process, with increased trade and investment being focused in a few countries, almost all countries are greatly affected by it.

29.3 Globalization and Developing Countries

The issue that concerns developing countries is how they can ensure greater participation of the weaker economies in the global process and what needs to be done to ensure that the course of globalization benefits more people in more countries. The uneven and unequal nature of the present globalization is manifested in the fast growing gap between the rich and poor people of the world and between developed and developing countries; and by the large differences among nations in the distribution of gains and losses.

This imbalance leads to polarisation between countries and groups that gain, and the many countries and groups in society that lose out or are marginalised. Globalization, polarisation, wealth concentration and marginalisation are therefore linked through the same process. In this process, investment resources, growth and modern technology are focused on a few countries, mainly in North America, Europe, Japan and a few East Asian countries. A majority of developing countries are excluded from the process, or are participating in it in marginal ways.

Although the developed world is in a dominant position and has been prepared to use this to further their control of the global economy, the developing countries have not done well in organising themselves to co-ordinate on substantial policy and negotiating positions. The developed countries, on the other hand, are well-organised within their own countries, with well-staffed departments dealing with international trade and finance, and with university academics and private and quasi government think tanks helping to obtain information and map policies and strategies. They also have well-organised associations and lobbies associated with their corporations and financial institutions, which have great influence over the government departments.

On the positive side, globalization has compelled developing countries to improve overall economic management, and make their economies efficient. To get a share of global capital and technology, developing countries have to upgrade their social and economic institutions through administrative, legislative and legal reforms. The quality of governance has to improve to encourage productivity and efficiency. Political stability has to be established. In this context, following lessons can be drawn from East Asian countries:

1. Developing human capital is a basic pre-requisite. Successful globalization and the knowledge economy require educated, healthy and skilled people.
2. It is necessary to build up domestic savings and put them to productive use.
3. Sound economic management and macro-economic balances are necessary. Large fiscal deficit is a serious obstacle to globalization.
4. Good governance at the national and sub-national levels builds confidence among investors.
5. Transparency has to be established in the functioning of both government and business units.
6. Free and open market economies require effective regulatory authorities because role of government changes from control and regulation to governance and facilitation.
7. Modernised capital markets with effective regulatory authorities are necessary to impart confidence to investors by maintaining stability and regulating speculative forces.

Globalization has helped the smaller, emerging economies gain access to world markets, emergent technologies and collaborations. This has also given them a window to the developed world and helped them understand the significant role of globalization as an instrument, which could be utilised not just to achieve economic efficiency, but also eradicate poverty.

29.4 Globalization and Women

29.4.1 Adverse Effects of Globalization on Women: With the growing globalization and liberalization of the economy as well as increased privatization of services, women as a whole have been left behind and not been able to partake of the fruits of success. Mainstreaming of women into the new and emerging areas of growth is imperative. This will require training and skill upgradation in emerging trades, encouraging more women to take up vocational training and employment in the boom sectors. This will also require women to migrate to cities and metros for work. Provision of safe housing and other gender friendly facilities at work will need to be provided.

Another facet of globalization is related to the fact that many persons especially women will be severely affected with the advent of setting up of industrial parks, national highways, special economic zones (SEZs) etc. as huge tracts of farm land are likely to be acquired for this purpose. This would require massive resettlement of the displaced persons and their families. It is therefore essential that a viable resettlement policy and strategy is formulated and put in place immediately which clearly reflects the needs of women impacted by globalization/displacement.

With the removal of all quantitative restrictions on the import of various products, the self-employed women's groups, especially in the informal sector, have started facing competition from the low-priced imported consumer goods which are invading the Indian market. Although this has the imminent danger of displacing a large number of employed/self-employed women, but at the same time, the process of globalization has also opened up opportunities for women entrepreneurs for exporting their products to the markets all over the world. Globalization has thus opened up new challenges for the realization of the goal of women's empowerment. Hence, strategies should be designed to enhance the capacity of women and empower them to cope with the negative economic and social impacts of the globalization process.

Several studies have indicated that adverse consequences of globalization are disproportionately borne by women. Increased mechanization leading to displacement of female unskilled workers, increased migration of male workers in traditionally women-dominated areas, increase in female-headed household due to migration of males are some of the trends established in various studies.

Globalization has presented new challenges for the realization of the goal of women's equality, the gender impact of which has not been systematically evaluated fully. However, it is evident that there is a need for re-framing policies for access to employment and equality of employment. Benefits of the growing global economy have been unevenly distributed leading to wider economic disparities, the feminization of poverty, increased gender inequality through deteriorating working conditions and unsafe working environment especially in the informal economy and rural areas. Strategies need to be designed to enhance the capacity of women and empower them to meet the negative social and economic impacts, which may flow from the globalization process.

With upgradation of skills, opportunities for employment of women exist in several areas such as health services, food processing and crafts. Key areas of concern include women in small subsistence farming households, women workers in garment and textiles who will face increased competition after the phasing out of the Multi Fibre Agreement in 2005, and women displaced by new technologies in sectors such as construction, which have traditionally absorbed large numbers of women.

With the onset of trade liberalisation, women are linked to the global economy to a very significant extent, as producers, entrepreneurs, service providers, consumers and citizens. There is a need to identify capacity constraints and entry barriers that prevent women from securing gains from trade. Trade- elated awareness and capacity building of the women stakeholders need to be prioritised.

The globalization process has, in some countries, resulted in policy shifts in favour of more open trade and financial flows, privatization of state-owned enterprises and in many cases lower public spending particularly on social services. This change has transformed patterns of production and accelerated technological advances in information and communication and affected the lives of women, both as workers and consumers. In a large number of countries, particularly in developing and least developed countries, these changes have also adversely impacted on the lives of women and have increased inequality. The gender impact of these changes has not been systematically evaluated. Globalization has also affected cultural values, lifestyles and forms of communication.

In countries with economies in transition women are bearing most of the hardships induced by the economic restructuring and being the first to lose jobs in times of recession. They are being squeezed out from fast growth sectors. Loss of childcare facilities due to elimination or privatization of state work places, increased need for older care without the corresponding facilities, continuing inequality of access to training for finding re-employment and to productive assets for entering or expanding businesses are current challenges facing women in these countries.

29.4.2 Opportunities Offered by Globalization: Science and technology, as fundamental components of development, are transforming patterns of production, contributing to the creation of jobs and new job classifications, and ways of working, and contributing to the establishment of a knowledge-based society. Technological change can bring new opportunities for all women in all fields if they have equal access, and adequate training. Women should also be actively involved in the definition, design, development, implementation and gender impact evaluation of policies related to these changes. Many women world-wide are yet to effectively use these new communications technologies for networking, advocacy, exchange of information business, education, media consultation and e-commerce initiatives. For instance, millions of the world's poorest women and men still do not have access to and benefits from science and technologies and are currently excluded from this new field and the opportunities it presents.

The patterns of migratory flows of labour are changing. Women and girls are increasingly involved in internal, regional and international labour migration to pursue many occupations mainly in farm labour, domestic work and some forms of entertainment work. While this situation increases their earning opportunities and self-reliance, it also exposes them—particularly the poor, uneducated, unskilled and/or undocumented migrants—to inadequate working conditions, increased health risk, the risk of trafficking, economic and sexual exploitation, racism, racial discrimination and xenophobia, and other forms of abuse.

Further, globalization has dramatically changed the conditions under which the work for gender equality must be carried out, especially in high growth countries like India. While globalization has generated opportunities for local producers and entrepreneurs to reach international markets, it has at times intensified existing inequalities and insecurities for many poor women. Since the gains of globalization are often concentrated in the hands of those with higher education—those who own resources and have access to capital—poor women are usually the least able to seize the longer term opportunities offered.

This disadvantage has been exacerbated as in most of the countries, policies reflect a commitment to global norms of markets and social policy is increasingly determined by market dynamics. Market friendly policies generate high growth rates that fail to translate into improved standards of health, education and human security. Feminist scholars have highlighted the gendered impact of such policies, many of which increase women's job vulnerability, unpaid work burden, while reducing state level resources that might be used to provide a social safety net. Owing to dissent voiced by feminist scholars on the widespread assumption that gender inequality as a challenge can be overcome with effective and sustained advocacy as it is more about mindsets and less about policies, especially economic policies, there have been some attempts to integrate economic and social policies but gender concerns have not been accorded requisite attention. These disadvantages have led to a situation where gains in women's economic opportunities lag behind those in women's capabilities.

29.5 Future of Globalization

Globalization is an irreversible trend and developing economies are also inevitably involved in the process. Developed countries should, therefore, carefully consider how to restructure the world trading system to accommodate developing economies, by enabling them to benefit from globalization while minimising external shocks. The World Trade Organization (WTO) should work more effectively, through an enlargement of waiver clauses which recognise the weaker position of developing countries.

Despite distortions and aberrations, globalization is a reality. Developments in information and communication technologies are unifying markets and people, cutting across barriers of space and time. At the end of the day, one has to understand and accept that globalization is the stratagem for the new millennium. Every country, developed and developing, has to accept this and formulate their economies around it.

The socio-economically disadvantaged are yet to benefit from globalization. The challenge to overcome the scourge of poverty remains a daunting task. The support of the poor for reforms and their involvement in the development process can be achieved only if they start benefiting from government policies. It is necessary to ensure that the poor and the deprived have a greater stake in economic reforms than at present for mobilising their enthusiastic participation in the development process. Economic reforms must be guided by compassion and distributive justice. Improvement of living conditions of the poorest and the weakest sections of society should be high priority areas of welfare and development programmes/schemes of the government.

No major economy in the world today can be viewed in isolation from the rest of the world. Given the size and the growing magnitude of interaction—in terms of trade, services, and capital flows—and the greater openness to globalization, every country is in a different economic milieu today than it was some decades ago.

29.6 Integration of World Economies

Prior to the initiation of globalization process in the 1990s and the establishment of WTO in 1995, countries around the world, particularly emerging market economies, enjoyed considerable leverage to shape their own national policies and policy-making mechanisms. The decoupling hypothesis held that even if advanced economies went into a downturn, emerging economies will remain unscathed because of their substantial foreign exchange reserves, improved policy framework, robust corporate balance sheets and relatively healthy banking sector. In a rapidly globalizing world, the decoupling hypothesis was never totally persuasive.

With globalization and anti-protection rules of WTO, domestic economic policies of countries have increasingly come under the influence of international agencies and processes or by big private corporations and economic/financial players. This has led to the narrowed ability of governments and people to make choices from options in economic and even social policies.

Decoupling hypothesis stood completely invalidated after the sub-prime crisis that emerged in the US housing mortgage market in the second half of 2007, and snowballed into a global financial and economic crisis. What started off as a sub-prime crisis turned successively into a global banking crisis, global financial crisis and then a global economic crisis (recession). It was billed by experts as the worst since the Great Depression of late 1920s and early 1930s that originated in the advanced economies and rapidly engulfed the whole world.

In a rapidly globalising world, the decoupling theory has not stood the test of time. No country can be an island.

29.6.1 Global Economic Crises Are Contagious: Economic malaises are contagious. A crisis in developed countries is bound to have an impact around the world. Monetary policy developments in the leading economies not only affect developing countries domestically, but also have a profound impact on the rest of the world through changes in risk premia and search for yield, leading to significant switches in capital flows. Changes in the monetary policy in the US are dictated by internal compulsions—to maintain employment and price stability—but the consequent volatility in capital flows impinges on exchange rate movements and more generally on asset and commodity prices. The monetary policy dynamics of the advanced economies thus involve sharp adjustments for the developing countries.

Private capital flows to developing countries have grown rapidly since the 1980s, but with increased volatility over time. Large capital flows to the developing countries can be attributed to a variety of push and pull factors.

The major push factor is the stance of monetary policy in the advanced economies. Periods of loose monetary policy coupled with search for yield in the advanced economies encourages large capital inflows to developing countries and vice versa in periods of tighter monetary policy. Thus, swings in monetary policy in the advanced economies lead to cycles and volatility in capital flows to developing countries. Innovations in information technology have also contributed to the two-way movement in capital flows. In response to these factors, capital flows to developing countries since the early 1980s have grown over time, but with large volatility. Pull factors that have led to higher capital flows in these countries have included the following: (a) strong growth over the past decade, (b) reduction in inflation, (c) macroeconomic stability, (d) opening up of capital accounts, and (e) buoyant growth prospects.

The transmission of economic crises in the developed world to emerging economies takes place *via* both trade and financial channels. In short, modern day world economies sink and swim together:

29.6.2 Contagious Nature of Business Cycles: Forces of globalization have led to substantial increases in international trade as well as financial flows since early 1990s. An issue in this context is whether increased integration has led to a larger degree of synchronisation of business cycles across countries. A global shock—say, an increase in global crude oil prices—will affect all countries simultaneously. For countries quite open to external trade, economic developments in their partner countries can get transmitted through exports and imports and this is expected to increase the co-movement of output across countries. A diversified structure of export destinations tends to weaken the co-movement of business cycles.

Trade as well as financial integration allows countries to specialise in industries in which they have a comparative advantage. This can result in more vulnerability to industry- or country-specific shocks but reduce cross-country output movements.

29.6.3 World Economy is Inter-dependent: Inter-dependence in the world economy is reflected in the flow of goods, services, labour, and capital across national boundaries. Besides trade in goods and services, the international flow of people (migration) and capital across national boundaries is another measure or indicator of economic integration and globalization in the world economy. People migrate primarily for economic reasons (i.e., to improve their standard of living and provide more opportunities for their children), but some do so to escape political and religious oppression. Most developed nations impose restrictions on immigration to reduce the inflow of low-skilled people (while often encouraging the immigration of highly skilled and technical people). Migration is generally more restricted and regulated than the international flow of goods, services, and capital.

In general, capital flows more freely across national boundaries than people.

Financial or portfolio capital (bank loans and bonds) generally move to nations and markets where interest rates are higher, and foreign direct investments in plants and firms flows to nations where expected profits are higher. This leads to the more efficient use of capital and generally benefits both lenders and borrowers.

Although labour migration generally leads to the more efficient utilization of labour, it also leads to job losses and lower wages for less-skilled labour in advanced nations and harms (through brain drain) the countries of emigration. Similarly, financial globalization and unrestricted capital flows lead to the more efficient use of capital throughout the world, as well as provide opportunities for higher returns and risk diversification for individuals and corporations. But they also seem to lead to periodic international financial crises, such as the ones that started in Asia in 1997 and affected most other developing countries, and the sub-prime housing mortgage crisis that started in the US in 2007 and affected the entire world in 2008 and 2009.

To sum up, globalization is a revolution which in terms of scope and significance is comparable to the Industrial Revolution, but whereas the Industrial Revolution took place over a century, today's global revolution is taking place under our very eyes in a decade or two. The 2008-09 global financial and economic crisis, the deepest of the post-war period, only slowed down the march of globalization temporarily. As all revolutions, however, today's globalization brings many benefits and advantages but also has some disadvantages or harmful side effects. In fact, there is a great deal of disagreement as to the extent and type of advantages and disadvantages.

Globalization is being blamed for world poverty and child labour in poor countries, job losses and lower wages in rich countries, as well as environmental pollution and climate change throughout the world. Although there is some truth in these accusations, an in-depth economic analysis will show that often the primary cause of many of the serious problems facing the world today lies elsewhere. Globalization has many social, political, legal, and ethical aspects, and so economists need to work closely with other social and physical scientists, as well as with the entire civil society, to give globalization a more human face. Globalization is important because it increases efficiency in the production of material things. It is inevitable because we cannot hide or run away from it.

30

Current Challenges Facing the Global Economy

World Economic Outlook released by International Monetary Fund (IMF) on April 19, 2022 has predicted 3.6 percent global growth for the years 2022 and 2023. Beyond 2023, the growth rate is estimated to decline to 3.3 percent over the medium-term. Why is global economy doomed to current and predicted dismal rates of growth? After rattling the world for almost two years, Covid-19 started abating and countries around the world gradually lifted restrictions to restart their economies. As if all this was not enough, global economy faced another round of disruptions and dislocations when Russia invaded Ukraine on February 24, 2022. The continuing conflict has already caused Europe's largest refugee crisis since the Second World War. All countries are facing the same challenge of increasing and improving the quality of jobs. Unemployment remains a key concern even for people who still have jobs.

Prior to the financial crisis of 2008, the world economy experienced an extended phase of buoyancy characterized by output expansion, burgeoning world trade, favourable financial and economic conditions, liquidity overhang and low interest rates. Economists termed it as a period of *great moderation*. However, the *great moderation* soon turned into *great dismay* when global financial confusion—simmering since August 2007—began unleashing its full fury in September 2008 with a series of failures of major financial institutions. The crisis traversed from the financial to the real sector and it looked like that the recession—which was still keeping world governments on tenterhooks—would be deeper and the recovery longer than earlier anticipated. Financial turmoil which surfaced in August 2007 in the USA financial system—as a result of defaults of sub-prime mortgage loans—blew into an unprecedented financial crisis engulfing international money, credit, equity and foreign exchange markets.

30.1 Financial Crisis of 2008

Recovery in the global economy was proceeding albeit at a modest pace and often falling short of forecasts. A decade after the financial and economic crisis, the global output gap was still substantial, the markets continued to be shaky, and the future was overshadowed by severe political risks. Due to high uncertainties, public and private investments remained subdued in most parts of the world. The pace of recovery varied from one economic region to another. Some economies—such as USA and UK—were above their pre-crisis output levels, while others—such as the Euro zone and Japan—were not. Emerging economies remained the locomotive of global growth, though there were differences among them.

Although decelerating, growth was still robust in China, weak in Russia and Bra-
while it was strong in India, Indonesia, and South Africa. Oil-producing and

countries like Russia, Saudi Arabia, Nigeria, Iran and Venezuela were adversely affected by sliding crude prices. Conversely, the drop in global oil prices provided a substantial stimulus to the economies of net-oil-importing countries, viz. Japan, China, India, Turkey and South Korea.

One of the reasons making the recovery process ineffectual was that trade was weak by historical standards. The weak recovery of world economy was also attributable to rising protectionism. According to the WTO, there was a significant increase in restrictive trade measures introduced by G20 economies since 2008. Import tariffs had remained low but regulatory burdens and non-tariff barriers—including onerous environmental and safety standards—impeded international trade.

30.2 Covid-19 and the Global Economy

Pre-Covid, the global macroeconomic landscape was chartering a rough and uncertain terrain characterized by weak growth of world output. The global economy experienced an unprecedented crisis in the year 2020. The Covid-19 pandemic forced countries to resort to lockdown that had a sudden and intense impact on the economic activity, financial markets and survival of the vulnerable sections of the society.

Covid-19 virus was first identified in Wuhan, a major industrial hub of China, in December 2019. The World Health Organization (WHO) declared Covid-19 a 'Public Health Emergency of International Concern' (PHEIC) on January 30, 2020 and advised that all countries should be prepared for containment, including active surveillance, early detection, isolation and case management, contact tracing, and prevention of onward spread. The exponential rise in the number of daily cases compelled the WHO to title this outbreak a pandemic on March 11, 2020, within a period of three months of its emergence. Since its first outbreak in Wuhan, Covid-19 has infected almost all countries of the world. It reached Antarctica in December 2020.

On April 29, 2020, President Trump hinted at the possibility of US claiming damages from China for latter's mishandling of the coronavirus outbreak. It is claimed that the coronavirus originated in a laboratory in Wuhan and China failed to stop it at the source. The developed world, led by Australia, is demanding an international probe into the causes of the virus spread, which China is vehemently trying to stonewall.

In the wake of the pandemic, most countries of the world resorted to lockdowns, resulting in cessation of almost all industrial and transport activities.

Although many countries have gradually lifted restrictions to restart their economies, the situation is not likely to return to pre-Covid period soon due to following reasons:

1. Tariff barriers and tariff wars among nations, particularly between US and China.
2. Protectionist policies.
3. Turbulent financial markets.
4. Geo-political tensions, particularly between US and Iran, Turkish invasion of Syria, civil war in Yemen.

These conditions reflect extreme risk-aversion behaviour of global investors, thus putting many economies under considerable stress. The dynamics for a strong, sustainable, balanced and inclusive growth will probably remain weak in the foreseeable future.

30.2.1 Impact of Covid-19 on the Global Economy: In the wake of Covid-19, global economy suffered unprecedented disruptions and dislocations.

A. Economic Loss: There was tremendous loss of production, income and employment. The shock of the pandemic was extremely unconventional in terms of its size and uncertainty, with its impact dependent on unpredictable factors like intensity of lockdowns, extent of supply chain and financial market disruptions alongside societal response to the associated public health measures. The pandemic has been unique in its wide-ranging effects on almost every section of the economy and the society. The global health crisis prompted by pandemic, in addition to an enormous human toll, has engendered the largest economic shock since the Great Depression of 1930s. [1] The pandemic and associated lockdown measures led to a *de facto* shutdown of a significant portion of the global economy, thereby triggering a global recession.

The pandemic threatened all that was taken for granted, viz. mobility, safety, and a normal life itself. This, in turn, posed the most formidable economic challenge to India and to the world. In the absence of a cure or a vaccine, public health policy became central to tackling this all-pervasive crisis. The imperative of flattening the disease curve was entwined with the livelihood cost of an imminent recession, which emanated from the restrictions in economic activities from the lockdown required to contain the pandemic. This inherent trade-off led to the policy dilemma of *lives versus livelihoods*.

The pandemic induced border closures and supply disruptions interrupted the international provision of goods and services. Trade has, however, played a critical role in responding to the pandemic, allowing countries to secure access to vital food and medical supplies. Some sectors (such as airlines, hotels, energy, and financials) have been more affected by the lockdown and social distancing, whereas those that are less contact-intensive (information technology, communications) have fared better.

On June 8, 2020, World Bank released its report titled *Global Economic Prospects* and predicted that world economy would shrink by 5.2 percent in 2020. Advanced economies would experience growth falling by 7 percent while emerging economies (including India) as a group would see a growth decline of 2.5 percent. According to the report, Indian economy would shrink by 3.2 percent in the fiscal year 2020-21. The report, which contained an assessment of economic shocks from coronavirus pandemic shutdowns, noted that the pandemic has plunged the world into a severe recession, deepest since the Second World War. Covid-19 has devastated countries (including India) around the world in terms of human and economic loss.

B. Demand-side and Supply-side Shocks: The pandemic has been a unique economic shock that has triggered both demand and supply side shocks simultaneously across economies around the world. Demand declined due to the following reasons:

1. Loss of incomes.
2. Curtailment of spending options due to closure of all contact-sensitive activities.
3. Weak growth prospects.
4. Fear of contagion.

5. Triggering of precautionary savings.
6. Increased uncertainty and hence lower confidence.

The supply chain disruptions were caused by the following:

1. Closure of economic activity.
2. Restricted movement of labour, owing both to official restrictions and private decisions.
3. Fall in international trade and tourism.
4. Risk aversion among businesses.
5. Uncertainty regarding the post-pandemic economic prospects

30.2.2 Global Policy Response to Covid-19: The virus has posed an unprecedented challenge for policy-making, globally and nationally. It has tested the mettle of policy-makers to deal with uncertain, fluid, complex and dynamic situations having far-reaching socio-economic implications. It has also tested the frontiers of medical science, which rose to the challenge by developing an effective vaccine within a year.

Governments and central banks across the world deployed a range of policy tools to support their economies such as lowering key policy rates, quantitative easing measures, loan guarantees, cash transfers and fiscal stimulus measures.

Monetary authorities across the world have eased monetary conditions with broad-based cuts in short-term policy rates and reserve requirements to support activity and provided emergency liquidity support to stabilize financial markets. Several central banks around the world engaged in unconventional monetary policy interventions in the form of long-term asset purchase programmes, re-lending facilities, relaxation in asset provisioning requirements and supporting credit provision to a wide range of borrowers. The corresponding injections of reserve money into the banking system have been effective in stabilizing bond markets, reducing bond yields, boost equity prices without putting pressure on exchange rates.

The pandemic raised unprecedented health challenges on a global scale and posed unique policy dilemmas. To help mitigate the spread of the virus, many countries implemented necessary measures. These included school closures, restrictions on non-essential business activities, prohibitions of public gatherings, suspension of public transport, restrictions on movement, border closures, and travel bans.

These social distancing measures included public information campaigns, broad-based testing, and contact tracing of individuals who were potentially exposed to known cases. Lockdowns and travel restrictions imposed significant supply-side constraints on national economies, drastically reducing output and employment in sectors that are usually resistant to business cycle fluctuations, particularly non-traded services. The deep economic contractions across many countries and heightened uncertainties about the post pandemic global economic landscape, however, may set back long-term growth prospects. Similarly, there are indications that protectionist tendencies have increased around the world in anticipation of the growing possibilities of slower growth in advanced economies.

30.3 Current Challenges before the Global Economy

30.3.1 Slow Growth and High Unemployment: The most serious economic problem in the world today is the slow growth and high unemployment facing most of the countries. *World Economic Outlook* released by International Monetary Fund (IMF) on April 19, 2022 predicted 3.6 percent global growth for the years 2022 and 2023. All countries are facing the same challenge of increasing and improving the quality of jobs. Unemployment remains a key concern even for people who still have jobs. Youth unemployment is a bigger concern. Another concern in the labour markets is that labour force participation is not growing as rapidly as before and this puts a cap on potential growth.

30.3.2 Excessive Volatility of Exchange Rates: On the monetary side are the excessive volatility of exchange rates, i.e. the very large fluctuations in the international value of national currencies and their large and persistent misalignments. Periodic financial crises have also led to financial and economic instability and dampened growth in advanced and emerging markets alike as, for example the financial crisis that started in Southeast Asia in 1997 and in the USA in 2007. These can disrupt the pattern of international trade and specialization and can lead to unstable international financial conditions throughout the world. They have also led to renewed calls for reforms of the present international monetary system and for more international coordination of economic policies among the leading economies.

30.3.3 Rising Protectionism: On the trade side, the most serious problem is rising protectionism in advanced countries in the context of a rapidly globalizing world.

In the study of the pure theory of international trade, we see that the best policy for the world as a whole is free trade. With free trade, each nation will specialize in the production of the commodities that it can produce most efficiently and, by exporting some of them, obtain more of other commodities than it could produce at home. In the real world, however, most nations impose some restrictions on the free flow of trade. Although invariably justified on national welfare grounds, trade restrictions are usually advocated by and greatly benefit a small minority of producers in the nation at the expense of the mostly silent majority of consumers. The problem is now exacerbated by the increasing competitive challenge that advanced countries face from the leading emerging market economies, particularly China and India. Widespread fears of large job losses have led to calls for protection from foreign competition in advanced countries, especially the US. The challenge for advanced countries is how to remain competitive, avoid major job losses, share in the benefits of globalization, and avoid increased protectionism.

30.3.4 Poverty in Developing Countries: The deep poverty in many developing countries, resource scarcity, environmental degradation, climate change, and the danger they pose for continued growth and sustainable world development are other problems.

Even though many developing countries, especially China and India, have been growing very rapidly, some of the poorest developing nations, particularly those of sub-Saharan Africa, face deep poverty, unmanageable international debts, economic stagnation, and widening international inequalities in living standards.

Growth in rich countries and development in poor countries are now threatened by resource scarcity, environmental degradation, and climate change. In the face of rapidly growing demand, particularly by China and India, and supply rigidities in producing nations, the price of petroleum and other raw materials has risen sharply during the past few years, and so has the price of food. In many leading emerging market economies protection of the environment takes a backseat to the growth imperative. We are witnessing very dangerous climate changes that may have increasingly dramatic effects on life on earth.

30.3.5 Unfinished Doha Round of Trade Negotiations: The Doha Round of trade negotiations in the WTO which began in 2001 remains unfinished due to differences among members on various issues. The scope of Doha Round of negotiations included agriculture, market access for non-agricultural products, services trade, trade-related aspects of intellectual property rights (TRIPS), rules (covering anti-dumping and subsidies), trade facilitation and so on. The conduct, conclusion and entry into force of the outcome of the negotiations were parts of a single undertaking, that is *nothing is agreed until everything is agreed*.

The Doha Round had made very little progress after 2008. Throughout 2009 and 2010, discussions continued but no headway was made on any substantive issue in the negotiations. However, the subject featured on the agenda of almost every major international meeting and there were strong affirmations of political support for an early conclusion of the Doha Round. Discussions continued in Geneva during March and April 2011, in a variety of formats. Reports on each area of the negotiations were issued on April 21, 2011. These documents provided an overview of the status of negotiations in each area covered in the Doha Development Agenda. While they indicated significant progress in many areas, they also captured the wide gaps remaining on many issues.

Progress was very slow due to wide gaps in the expectations of the members. There were several attempts to bring the talks back on track and to build on the results already achieved in the negotiations. There were constant attempts in the WTO and in other forums like the G20 to resolve the impasse. During the Ministerial Conference of the WTO held in December 2011, members once again reaffirmed their belief in rule-based multilateral trade and their commitment to resolve the issues in a transparent way through consensus.

The prolonged hiatus in the Doha Round talks is a matter of concern. It is not for want of willingness on the part of developing countries to engage, but is the result of an apparent perception among some developed countries that they would not gain much from the Round. The neglect of the Doha Round is unfortunate and jeopardises an opportunity to strengthen multilateral trade rules.

30.3.6 Risk-aversion Behaviour of Global Investors: Besides economic and financial risks, the world faces elevated geo-political risks. The world is grappling with following issues and concerns:

1. Achieving high levels of nuclear safety.
2. Maintaining a rules-based maritime order and achieving maritime security.
3. Strengthening the system of multilateral treaties/arms trade treaty.
4. Fighting trafficking of migrants and tackling causes for refugee crises.
5. Protecting marine environment.

6. Ensuring food security.
7. Dealing with climate change.
8. Fighting terrorism and its financing.

These conditions reflected extreme risk-aversion behaviour of global investors, thus putting many, and in particular, commodities exporting economies, under considerable stress. Problems and challenges facing the world can only be adequately addressed by a major worldwide cooperative effort, and a change in world governance.

Endnote

1. US and other market economies of the world suffered a business depression of extraordinary severity in the early years of 1930s. The demand for goods fell sharply and so also the prices. Many business firms failed and million of workers were rendered unemployed. These events revealed that something was seriously wrong with the working of a capitalist system. Out of the turmoil of depression came a book that had a profound effect on the thinking of economists. It was titled *The General Theory of Employment, Interest and Money* (1936) authored by British economist John Maynard Keynes (1883-1946). This work was immediately recognized as a revolutionary landmark in the history of economic ideas.

Bibliography

Bibliography

Acemoglu, D. (2009), *Introduction to Modern Economic Growth*, Princeton University Press, Princeton.

Aghion, P. and Howitt, P. (2008), *Economics of Growth*, MIT Press, Cambridge, Massachusetts.

Aghion, P. and Durlauf, S. (eds.) (2005), *Handbook of Economic Growth*, Elsevier North-Holland, Amsterdam.

Banerjee, A.V. and Du o, E. (2011), *Poor Economies: Rethinking Poverty and the Ways to End it*, Random House, India.

Basu, Kaushik (1998), *Analytical Development Economics*, Oxford University Press.

Belmont, Williamson (2011), *Trade and Poverty: When the Third World Fell Behind*, MIT Press, Cambridge.

Cavalcanti, T., Mohaddes, K. and Raissi, M. (2012), *Commodity Price Volatility and the Sources of Growth*, IMF Working Paper 12/12, International Monetary Fund, Washington DC.

Chenery, H.B. and Srinivasan, T.N. (1989), *Handbook of Development Economics*, Volumes 1 and 2, North-Holland, Amsterdam.

Clummang, Robert A. (1979), Economic Growth and Economic Development: Counterparts or Competitors, *Economic Development and Cultural Change*, Volume 28, No. 1, October.

Cooper, R.N. (2002), *Growth and Inequality: The Role of Foreign Trade and Investment*, Annual World Bank Conference on Development Economics.

Croix, D. and Michel, P. (2002), *Theory of Economic Growth: Dynamics and Policy in Overlapping Generations*, Cambridge University Press, Cambridge.

Dalgaard, C.J. (2008), "Dual Economies and International Total Factor Productivity Differences: Channelling the Impact from Institutions, Trade, and Geography", *Economica*, 75 (300).

Duraton, G. (2014), *Growing through Cities in Developing Countries*, Policy Research Working Paper 6818, World Bank, Washington DC.

Easterly, W., Levine, R. and Roodman, D. (2004), "Aid, Policies, and Growth", *American Economic Review*, 94 (3).

Erickson, L. and Vollrath, D. (2004), *Dimensions of Land Inequality and Economic Development*, IMF Working Paper 158, International Monetary Fund, Washington DC.

Galor, O. (2005), "From Stagnation to Growth: Unified Growth Theory", in Aghion, P. and Durlauf, S. (eds.), *Handbook of Economic Growth*, North-Holland, Amsterdam.

Gollin, D., Parente, S. and Rogerson, R. (2002), "Role of Agriculture in Development", *American Economic Review*, 92 (2).

Haddard, M., Lim, J., Pancaro, C. and Saborowski, C. (2012), *Trade Openness and Growth Volatility*, Working Paper 1491, European Central Bank, Frankfurt.

Harris, J. and Todaro, M. (1970), "Migration, Unemployment and Development: A Two-Sector Analysis", *American Economic Review*, 60 (1).

Jha, R. (2007), *Fiscal Policy in Developing Countries: A Synoptic View*, Working Paper 2007/01, Australia South Asia Research Centre.

Lord, W. (2001), *Household Dynamics, Policies, and Economic Growth*, Oxford University Press, New York.

Meier, G. and Stiglitz, J. (eds.) (2001), *Frontiers of Development Economics*, Oxford University Press, New York.

Meier, G. (2000), *Leading Issues in Economic Development*, Oxford University Press, New York.

O'Rourke, K.H. (2002), *Globalization and Inequality: Historical Trends*, Annual World Bank Conference on Development Economics.

Organization for Economic Co-operation and Development (OECD) (1997), *Economic Globalization and the Environment*, OECD, Paris.

Perman, Roger , Ma, Yue, McGilvray, James and Common, Michael (2003), *Natural Resource and Environmental Economics*, Pearson Education/Addison Wesley.

Radelet, S., Clemens, M. and Bhavnani, R. (2006), *Aid and Growth: The Current Debate and Some New Evidence*, Working Paper 133, Centre for Global Development, Washington.

Ravallion, Martin (2016), *Economics of Poverty: History, Measurement and Policy,* Oxford University Press.

Ravindranath, N.H. and Sathaye, J. (2002), *Climate Change and Developing Countries*, Kluwer Academic Publishers, Netherlands.

Ray, Debraj (2009), *Development Economics*, Oxford University Press.

Scott, S.C. and Lawrence, R.Z. (2004), *Has Globalization Gone Far Enough?* Institute for International Economics, Washington, DC.

Singh, T. (2010), "Does International Trade Cause Economic Growth?", *The World Economy,* November.

Smith, D.M. (1981), *Industrial Location: An Economic and Geographical Analysis*, John Wiley, New York.

Srinivasan, T.N. (2001), "Trade, Development, and Growth", *Princeton Essays in International Economics*, Number 225, December.

Thirlwall, A.P. (2011), *Economics of Development*, Palgrave Macmillan.

Todaro, Michael and Smith, Stephen (2012), *Economic Development*, Dorling Kindersley India Private Limited.

World Bank, *World Development Report* (various years), World Bank, Washington, DC.

World Trade Organization (WTO) (1995), *Regionalism and the World Trading System*, WTO, Geneva.

Yamazawa, Ippei (2000), *Developing Economies in the Twenty-First Century: The Challenge of Globalisation*, Institute of Developing Economies, Japan.

Index

Index